Contents

© Caitlín Matthews 1995

First published in Great Britain in 1995 by
Element Books Limited
Shaftesbury, Dorset SP7 8BP

Published in the USA in 1995 by
Element Books, Inc.
PO Box 830, Rockport, MA 01966

Published in Australia in 1995 by
Element Books Limited for
Jacaranda Wiley Limited
33 Park Road, Milton, Brisbane 4064

Reprinted 1996

Cover and textual illustrations by Anthea Helliwell
Cover design by Max Fairbrother
Designed by Roger Lightfoot
Typeset by Footnote Graphics, Warminster, Wiltshire
Printed and bound in Great Britain by
J W Arrowsmith Limited, Bristol, Avon

British Library Cataloguing in Publication
data available

Library of Congress Cataloging in Publication
data available

ISBN 1–85230–616–5

EARTH QUEST

Singing the Soul
Back Home

Shamanism in Daily Life

Caitlín Matthews

ELEMENT

Shaftesbury, Dorset ● Rockport, Massachusetts
Brisbane, Queensland

Singing the Soul Back Home

Caitlín Matthews is the author of twenty books on Celtic, Goddess and mystical traditions. She has lived and worked in a shamanic way for twenty-eight years. With John Matthews, she teaches Celtic shamanism and an awareness of native British lore and traditions. She has a shamanic practice in Oxford.

For John Cutrer, a great soul

ACKNOWLEDGEMENTS

My greatest thanks go to the spirits who have accompanied me on my life journey: they are my teachers. To John Matthews, my husband, for lovingly maintaining the tree of tradition and to our son, Emrys, for all his insights and delights. To Felicity Wombwell and R. J. Stewart for the inspiration of their pathways. Special thanks go to Jonathan Horwitz, a shamanic teacher of great skill and wisdom, as well as to the Middle Oak Drumming Circle for their support. Thanks to all the Passionate Priestesses for healing laughter and deep soul-nurture. Finally great thanks to all my Celtic shamanism students and those clients who have shared their journeys with me for the purposes of this book: journey extracts are verbatim, but personal details have been changed.

NOTE TO THE READER

The techniques and exercises in this book can generate both temporary and permanent changes of consciousness within any individual or group. For balanced development you are advised to use them within the context of ideas and ethics outlined in the main text. As with all transformative techniques or traditions, responsibility for end results or effects rests solely with the user.

Foreword
Re-membering

WHEN I WAS A little girl, my mother made me a huge multi-coloured blanket out of squares of wool. This blanket quickly became my friend. It kept me warm on cold days and nights, and played with me in all my games. Most especially, it was my cave.

I would lie on the floor and put it over and round me, tucking in the edges, so that no chinks of light could penetrate. To an outside observer, I was just a child playing at being an unmoving rock. However, within were the stars, the mighty forests, the deep seas. In the darkness of my cave, I met many beings who came to play with me. Most of the time, they told me stories and informed me about the universe. I talked to them all the time, even in public places, to the mortification of my parents. Their embarrassment eventually became so great, that I was forced into ever more solitary places in order to pursue the dialogue. Who I was talking to was the question that preoccupied my parents. Instinctively, I knew that this question could not be answered to their satisfaction, since they did not share that world of mine.

What were these beings like? Some were animals, some were people and others were not like anything I then had a name for. These abstract and sometimes geometrical shapes burned behind my eyes in dancing colour. I called them 'the Shapers'. Platonists would recognize them as intelligences of the platonic realms, perhaps; qabalists would recognize them as the flashing colours of qabalistic vision.

The animals and humans spoke of a world I was preparing for, but the abstract beings hinted at wider worlds which were

outside my young experience. The animals showed me how to rejoice in my body, to enjoy speed, tracking, dancing, how to endure, be patient and accepting. The humans, whom I now know were the deep ancestors, talked to me about lives before birth and about human relationships: they helped me understand why I had such a young body and such a mature understanding. I am very grateful to them for this, for it was a terrible burden I could not share with a soul, this knowledge of mortality and reincarnation. Adults thought me broody and miserable, and I think that was a fair assessment of my childhood, with no human being with whom to share my experiences. But they did not see the moments of ecstasy which were as private as sexuality and perhaps not unconnected with that vital impulse. But the beings also taught me singing and encouraged me to use my voice to express the wonders of human life, as well as to sing sorrow into joy.

My lasting reservoir of wonder and delight was brought to me by the Shapers. Their form of communication was instantaneous and subtle, speaking directly to my soul. They showed me shape and pattern, interaction and connection, quantity and quality, rhythm and notation – the great philosophical principles of my childhood. These teachings, which were nonverbal, have been very useful to me in my daily life, as well as guiding me into the uncharted worlds of creative shamanism. I also see now that the rather dull, culturally-restrictive upbringing I had, was the ideal soil for the shamanic communication I was receiving. With no books and few toys, I was driven as surely to the spiritual teachings of my blanket-cave as any shamanic apprentice forced by their teacher to watch ice melt for days at a time is driven to hear and understand the voices of the spirits.

I now know that the images I saw before my eyes accord with what scientists call phosphenes – neurally induced light-patterns which are common to all human beings and cultures. Their prismatic brilliance and intricacy may have a scientific explanation, but all I know was that the patterns they made were my teachers. Some hallucinogens produce similar effects, but I received these impressions quite naturally.[1] They are commonly experienced by people when they first start shamanic work, as was the case with a friend of mine, an Estonian artist. By drawing the patterns observed in her first shamanic journeys,

she began to make sense of her experiences and to receive teachings by the spirits. I believe it is by tracing similar patterns in our lives that we can re-member the creative worlds we enjoyed in childhood and reconnect with the cosmic web whose filaments thread our universe.

Our childhood play is a time of discovering the universe. Play is about becoming and acting out, about discernment and understanding. In play, we discover our soul-food, our ability to recreate ourselves. Without this consolation and soul-food, we become 'dead', which is often what happens when we grow up. Anything which subsequently reconnects us with the source of creative play is accordingly held precious by us.

I discovered my own reconnection when I later began to research the ancient Celtic world. I came across descriptions of Gaelic poets in the Western Highlands of Scotland who, up until the seventeenth century and beyond, still practised the ancient Celtic shamanic method of incubating a poem. Poet-masters gave their pupils a subject for composition and then the pupils would retire to the 'houses of darkness', where they lay unseeing, without communication, often with a large stone on their stomachs to keep them wakeful. In this darkness, they would track their composition down the pathways of metaphor and poetic pattern.[2] I grew more and more excited as I read this, for I knew that this was closely akin to the method of shamanic communication I had myself developed (or been taught) as a child, when I lay curled up, unmoving for many hours under my woollen blanket.

When I grew up I trained to be an actress and began to encounter the spirits in different ways, through the techniques of body and voice; I began to look forward to an acting career. But the spirits had other plans for me. They arranged a series of consecutive ordeals which I endured, first quite stoically, then with increasing passivity, as I began to relinquish most of my power until I had no creative outlet left and was danger-ously ill. This crisis, which is sometimes grandiloquently termed 'the shamanic illness', is something that comes to many of us. Being brought low by the circumstances of life helps us to see clearly into the heart of multi-dimensional reality, so that we may focus more perfectly on the spirits' gift and learn to only trust that. My illness lasted eight years, during which time I was pronounced incurable by three specialists. My will to live

was seriously diminished by these prognostications, and I began to enter that half-world which is neither living nor dying.[3]

I now see that I could only remember my place in the universe by being temporarily railroaded to one side of it. In this state I drew near once again to my former companions of subtle reality, somehow realizing that they could assist me where medical practitioners could not. They woke me up to the fact that I had become inured to my illness and that I needed to ask for their help very urgently. Instead of dismissing my old companions as figments of my imagination, I actually began to turn to them as teachers who had healing wisdom. They told me to cease taking chemically based medication and to turn to the helping powers of homoeopathic medicines. I regained full health in six months. My recovery was also brought about by simple but necessary gifts: the supportive gift of love and the restorative gift of self-respect.

By rekindling the fires of my creative soul, my companions ensured my active return to the universe. This re-membering of myself constituted a major soul-restoration which changed my life. I made a promise then that I would offer my life to the rekindling of the creative soul-life in others by whatever means I could, to help 'sing the soul back home'.

One of these ways has been to explore, write and teach about the spiritual pathways of Britain and Ireland, helping people reconnect with their land and the rich traditions that imbue it. This has been a necessary re-membering for the fragmented soul-life of these islands.

Another part of my work has been the awakening awareness of the ancestral and spiritual presences of our heritage, especially a reappreciation of the divine feminine among those who have been orphaned of female spirit – whether men or women. As a 'midwife of the soul' I rekindle the creative fire of the soul's hearth so that the fragmented soul can be welcomed home.

I remain a walker between the worlds within my own native tradition in Britain, having learned from the land spirits, from ancestors and non-human spirits, as well as from the deep presences within my culture and Celtic ancestry. I have also trained in non-cultural, core-shamanism. I am at home wherever and however people inter-relate with the free passage of Spirit.

Now that you know what kind of person is talking to you in

these pages, I will retire and let you read on. This book gives the fruits of my experience and teaching in simple and practical ways, so that you may be reconnected with the cosmic web of the universe and walk between the worlds. It aims to put you into deep communion with the power and Spirit of the cosmic web, which is always available. As you practise these teachings you will learn to trust this process, and become animated by it; and as you become animated by it, you will be shown by your spirits how to sing your soul back home.

Caitlín Matthews

Introduction
Approaching the Threshold

MY INTENTIONS IN WRITING this book have been to communicate clearly methods of shamanic practice which can be implemented in everyday life: these have been taught to me by my spirits and teachers; they are not mined out of cultural contexts of which I have no understanding. There are no terrestrial or cultural boundaries in the otherworlds: the knowledge that you find there is universal in application.

Shamanism is found in traditional societies throughout the world. It is one of the ways in which our ancestors connected with the universe. But it is not only for far-off times and peoples: it is being experienced by many people today who are exiled from their traditional background. It is thus the heritage of all people, and there are many different people, groups and institutes teaching shamanism each with their own cultural, ethnic, methodological and anthropological ways of doing so.

This book will not enable you to become a shaman, although it will help you live *shamanically*. I want to show how you can use shamanism creatively, how you can be 'a walker between the worlds' – be skilled in moving between the worlds of physical and 'subtle' reality, and learn from, connect with and co-operate with the spirits who are also inhabitants of the universe.

Why should you wish to do such a thing? Shamanism reveals to us the unspoken subtext, the patterns which interweave our lives; it shows us connections which no other earthly means can. We learn to read and recognize the subtle messages encoded in or received by our soul. We learn how to do this by becoming aware, not just of physical reality – the world which

is apprehendable by our senses – but also of the subtle reality of the spiritual world which encompasses it.

This requires a great leap of understanding for many people today, since we have grown up in a society which neglects or ignores subtle reality in all its aspects: our society is impatient of artists, visionaries, mystics and all people who cross-reference their lives and actions with an unseen reality.

Not everyone finds shamanism to their taste. Its parameters may be too wide for some people, and they may be happier exploring the unseen worlds through a form of meditation or with the backing of a spiritual association.

Walking between the worlds brings us to a non-dual experience of the universe, aligning us with all that is, seen or unseen. This in turn will bring a spiritual dimension to our daily lives as well as a practical dimension to our spiritual lives. Rather than isolating us in a personal spiritual enclave, it will bring us into greater contact with what is happening around us.

This book is not intended to blast open otherworldly gates so that you are sucked inside; it is intended to help you find the doors and pathways already in your life, to explore what resonances you have upon the cosmic web so that you are enabled to sing the soul back into your life. To this end, the first three parts unfold quite slowly, so that you will gradually gather together the relevant instructions and begin to focus upon your own direction before you strike off into the otherworlds. I have concentrated upon the daily applications of this work and have purposely chosen examples and parallels from Western culture in order to help the reader identify with concepts proposed in this book.

It is not my intention to alienate any reader from her spiritual tradition. The practice of shamanism is compatible with the practice of any spirituality: it may provoke a more profound appreciation of your religion's mystical application or bring you to a wider understanding of certain religious strictures. Shamanism speaks of spirits; but every religion, even the most apparently monotheistic, contains spiritual beings – angels, faeries, ancestors, great teachers – all of whom communicate with and assist us in our lives. Where you may encounter difficulties with shamanism is if you adhere to a strongly dualistic faith in which everything is seen as either good or evil.

This book has many 'permissions': this is not because I am a bountiful being who holds authority for all things, but because the encouragement to be resourceful and creative is so rarely given in our everyday lives. Printed words in our society have all the weight of holy writ. In shamanism, however, speech and personal experience have a greater authority than what is written. Oral tradition no longer enjoys the primacy it has in traditional societies so the permissions which appear in these pages are to be taken as oral encouragements. Thus:

Permission to recreate yourself and to explore creatively what you experience from this book is here given.

HOW TO USE THIS BOOK

Before you read the main text, please read this. It will save you a lot of time and frustration.

1. Read this book through at least once and understand the shamanic concepts and principles *before* attempting any of the practical exercises.

2. There is a glossary of specialist words and expressions used in this book on page 231. Some terms used are particular to this book.

3. Since shamanism is, and always has been, practised by both women and men, female and male pronouns have been used in variation, both when talking of shamans and elsewhere.

4. This book will not qualify you as a shaman. If you wish to use shamanism to help others then seek out a personal teacher. (See Resources on page 239.) Ensure that you map the otherworlds from personal experience before you teach, help or counsel others.

5. Try skills the way they are set out here. If you can't work these after a series of good and sequential attempts, then adapt them intelligently and creatively, with recourse to your own spiritual allies and helpers.

6. When you have established a firm bond with your shamanic allies, trust their advice and help. If they give you different

instructions from those in the book, ask them how to implement and practise these. You retain your free will in this work. Steps for recognizing and confirming your allies are given on pages 101–102.

7. Shamanism is not a solitary but a social practice: the more you practise it to help the universe the better. However, it is certainly not a substitute for therapy of any kind.

8. Do not mix these practices with others you have learned in other non-shamanic disciplines. Do not treat them as psychological exercises.

9. Keep your sense of proportion by regularly, preferably daily, visiting the natural world.

10. Keep your sense of self-importance in check with humour and common sense.

Important Note

The practices in this book can be very powerful. Please do not attempt any of them if you are suffering from any mental instability or are taking consciousness-changing drugs or potent medications where driving is contra-indicated.

The use of these practices outside a strong personal ethical framework is inappropriate and sometimes dangerous. All writers and teachers have a responsibility to their readers and students – to guide them safely and surely, to present effective skills and methods which can be reproduced, to ensure that the writings/teachings are transmitted clearly and respectfully. In any book where the writer cannot personally supervise the reader's training, there is the danger that the reader's interest in dynamic techniques may outrun ethical foundation work. Shamanic training is usually undertaken in the context of a traditional society where the apprentice is rooted in ethical, familial and tribal lore. This is not so in modern society where people may learn techniques at workshops and yet lack any ethical framework.

Be aware that this work has a real effect. Do nothing if your intentions are vague or unfocused.

Permission to take responsibility for your experiences is here given.

Key

This book unfolds in a sequenced way which is keyed into your growing comprehension of the subject: this means that certain instructions relating to practical shamanic journeying appear before you are ready to undertake the practices. This key will help you go directly to the appropriate part of the book for the journey instructions you need.

No previous experience of shamanism? – Read the whole book first

Grounding procedures – Chapter 4/2 and Chapter 6/1

Journey procedures in general – Chapter 2

The sequence of a journey – Chapter 2/1 and Chapter 2/2

How to source – Chapter 2/1

How to journey – Chapter 2/2

Finding a guardian animal – Chapter 4/1

Finding a Middleworld teacher – Chapter 4/1

Finding an Underworld teacher – Chapter 5/1

Finding an Upperworld teacher – Chapter 6/1

Framing your question – Chapter 2/3

Acknowledging the seven directions – Chapter 4/2

Help with journey problems – Chapter 2/3 and 7/1

Interpreting your journey – Chapter 7/1

Improving journey skills – Chapter 7/1

Recognizing power-loss – Chapter 8/1

Recognizing soul-loss – Chapter 8/1

1.   The Shamanic Universe

He who desires the Soul, who plays with the Soul, who makes love with the Soul, who attains ecstasy in the Soul, becomes his own master and wanders at will through the worlds. But they who know otherwise are dependent. They dwell in perishable worlds and cannot wander at will.

Chandogya Upanishad

1. SHAMANS AND SHAMANISM

I searched in the darkness, I was silent in the great silence of the dark. That is how I became a *angaqoq*, through visions and dreams and meetings with flying spirits ... The ancient ones dedicated their lives to the work of keeping the world in balance; they dedicated it to great things, immeasurable enormous things.

Najagneq, Eskimo shaman

SHAMANISM HAS EXISTED since the beginning of time. A shaman is a person – man or woman – who can enter alternative states of consciousness at will to travel in spirit between this world and the otherworlds in order to find healing, knowledge, guidance and help for themselves and others. A shaman works with power and energy, calling upon the help of many spirits. She works closely with a full repertoire of spiritual helpers, who choose to help her. The shaman's continually expanding experience sets up pathways between herself and spiritual beings, facilitating a trust that links different realities.

She is able to mediate between the everyday world and the unseen realms, becoming a bridge of living Spirit.

Shamanism is distinct from other magical and visionary techniques in that part of the shaman's soul makes a spiritual journey, flight or voyage between the worlds. Methods of divination, mediumship or healing may have *shamanistic* elements, but they are not technically shamanism unless such a spirit journey takes place and the knowledge, healing or help brought back is implemented in our world. Shamanism is used by indigenous peoples the world over. Many retain ancient techniques, and others have adapted ancestral skills for new situations.

World Shamanism

Shamanism is now associated in most peoples' minds solely with North American nations or Siberian peoples. But it exists in many other places as well. Circumpolar peoples from China to Alaska continue to practise it, despite the overlay of Christianity or Marxism, while Central Asian shamanism from the Middle to the Far East continues underneath the teachings of Islam and Buddhism. Areas of India, Africa and South America retain many shamanic practices as part of their mainstream spirituality

Some of the following words, drawn from worldwide cultures, indicate the extent of shamanism around the globe:

bhopa – Hindu – shaman
hatali – Navajo – medicine person
awenydd – Welsh – inspired one
mudang – Korean – female shaman
noaide – Saami (Lapp) – shaman
gongsai/jinpo – Zhuang (Chinese) – male/female shaman
angaqoq – Inuit – shaman
sangoma – Zulu – shamanic healer
dhami – Nepalese – shaman
curandero/a – Central American – male/female shamanic healer
llapo – Tibetan – oracular shaman
bhitan – Pakistan – shaman

The ancestors of Western peoples also used shamanism; but the shaman's role became fragmented, subsequently devolving

upon a multitude of people: priests, storytellers, healers, judges, diviners. In most cases, the essential shamanic component was lost, although individuals and scattered families have retained intrinsic shamanic practices in their hereditary skills of healing, mediumship and divination. Some social pockets have also retained certain skills and still guard certain shamanic doorways in collective folk-customs. A close study of European folk-customs and archaic spiritual practices reveals that shamanism is well rooted in many European countries, although this evidence is frequently overlooked or discounted, and labelled a manifestation of atavistic superstition or witch-craft.[1]

World shamanic traditions developed according to the kind of societies in which they were found: nomadic, pastoral, hunting. The movement of animals or the behaviour of the elements were critical factors in existence and different needs affected the kinds of shamanism which developed. Environmental factors and ways of life shaped the spiritualities of early people.

Ake Hultkrantz believes that shamanism is 'one of the strongest powers behind the historical formation of religions',[2] but it is rarely manifest today as a religion in the Western sense. It most often appears as a healing practice within a religion. In parts of Central and South America today, for example, *curanderas* (shamanic healers) call upon both Catholic saints and indigenous gods in their practices. Similarly, in Tibetan Buddhism the ancient, pre-Buddhist deities are invoked for oracles and healing. In some places shamans provide certain ritual and healing functions for their society which are not met by the predominant spirituality of that people or region.

The Calling

Shamans are always chosen for their role by the spirits of the universe, for shamanism is not a self-elected vocation: so the one who determines to become a shaman as an ego-enhancing exercise will not succeed. Shamanism may run in the family. When someone is called to be a shaman, he may attempt to avoid the calling for the very good reason that shamanism is one of the most demanding of vocations, the shaman being

available simultaneously to the spirits as well as to future clien-
tele. This avoidance may also spring from a fear of dealing with
spirits and the otherworlds they inhabit. The avoidance of a
shamanic calling usually results in a massive loss of power
or soul, frequently leading to life-threatening illness. This
'shamanic illness' is generally cured by a full acceptance of the
spirit-dictated vocation.

Training

The training of shamans is usually undertaken by both spirits
and human teachers who are themselves shamans. The
apprentice learns by assisting the qualified shaman and so
integrates her own growing shamanic knowledge with practical implementations of techniques, and the reactions of clients
to specific treatments. The acceptance of trainee shamans by
their community is critical, for they cannot practise without
people.

Why Do People Consult Shamans?

People need shamans' help for health, work and relationship
problems and for making ritual sense of changes in life-patterns
from birth to death. In response to these needs, shamans seek
out solutions, cures, rituals and information from the spirits in
the otherworlds.

Contemporary manifestations of shamanism reflect the
changing needs of society. Our present needs are little different
from those of ancient and indigenous societies: health, work
and relationship problems and making sense of life-patterns.
But in addition to these common needs, we may add those of
urban Western life: the need to address the soul-loss which
manifests in feelings of incompleteness and meaninglessness,
alienation, addiction, self-mutilation, and lack of self-esteem
and vision. Modern medicine has found solutions to many
physical illnesses and modern psychiatry attempts to heal what
it sees as mental illness. Subtle illnesses and imbalances are
largely ignored or marginalized, nor are their needs addressed
by the major religions who do have the apparatus to discern

spiritual cause and effect. It is left to shamanism and a host of complementary therapeutic disciplines to address the soul.

Modern shamanism addresses contemporary problems and helps people reconnect with the earth through rituals and healing practices. The creation of rituals by shamanic means re-empowers people who have been disempowered by religious ceremonies which alienate rather than reconnect. The immediacy of walking between the worlds, of implementing what is discovered there re-authenticates each individual's spirituality.

Misconceptions About Shamanism

Shamanism is a primal spiritual practice that has somehow survived into our time. This survival has been ensured by the *usefulness* of shamanic skills. If ancient techniques are lost it is because they are no longer useful. People simply do not consult ineffective shamans: these soon have no clients, no income and no status in society. Chandra, a Nepalese *dhami* (shaman) speaks humbly about this:

> . . . a man can learn many things from his failures, but failures can create uncontrollable needs and weaken his soul. For that reason, a *dhami* must always bring satisfaction and success to the people around him, even small successes, for only then will the souls gain strength to take a next step.[3]

This philosophy of small, incremental successes is central to shamanism which, since it deals in spirit, is very much concerned with 'keeping the spirits up'. This leads us to a clarification of certain misconceptions about shamans. One of these concerns the alleged charlatanism of shamanism. All shamans work in the context of their society, wherein their practices are performed publicly. Like any showperson, the traditional shaman will accordingly 'play to the gallery', utilizing illusions and sleight of hand to enhance the healing or seance. Many people have assumed that the use of such tricks must significantly devalue whatever shamanic work is done, or mask a complete inability.

Some early anthropologists who studied shamanic cultures were of the opinion that shamans were epileptic, since they seemed to behave in hysterical and irrational ways, often

falling to the ground. This view has been abandoned by most academics, although it was still popular until recently among Soviet researchers to whom any truck with spirits was evidence of fraud or mental derangement.[4] In working with spirits, shamans frequently experience intense shaking and physical agitation and, since it is difficult, if not impossible, to remain upright once soul-flight has begun, shamans usually sit or lie down suddenly. I cannot discover any evidence for the allegation that shamans are hysteric, weak-minded or nervous individuals: on the contrary, living shamans demonstrate a balanced, well-integrated and creative personality.

Some people have acquired the notion that, because some shamans utilize cross-dressing in their spiritual work, they are homosexual or transvestite. Shamans can be of either sex and of heterosexual or homosexual orientation: sexual orientation does not determine the ability to shamanize. There are distinct shamanic traditions of a woman taking on a male spiritual persona, or a man taking on a female one and dressing accordingly: this is in accordance with the principles of non-duality, not sexuality.

Traditionally, many shamans are perceived as 'tricky' or 'mischievous'. While it is true that many people are fearful of those who wield or mediate otherworldly powers, it is also true that most shamans have a sense of responsibility towards their clients. The playful or trickster behaviour of the shaman is often an attempt to lighten the serious nature of much of the work, as well as to keep open the ways between the worlds. The entry of the clown, the *heyoka*, upturns the normal order of things, permitting authority to be mocked and breaking down the barriers between what is possible and what is not. In the midst of this licensed holiday from the normal is a sacred opening which allows healing and transformative experience to take place.

Shamanic teachings are entrusted to those who love the universe and wish to be in its service, but there is always the chance that some unscrupulous student will use it for herself. Unethical shamans exist, as do corrupt judges and mercenary doctors. Self-serving practitioners who offer public service are to be greatly feared, for they have no disinterested compassion to balance their skills. Most societies make distinction between shamans and sorcerers. A shaman *co-operates* with the spiri-

tual worlds and their inhabitants, beseeching their appropriate help; a sorcerer *manipulates* the spiritual worlds and seeks to command their inhabitants without their advice. This book is concerned with shamanism, not sorcery.

Shamanic practice always runs hand in hand with rituals of purification, as well as prayers for assistance and thankfulness to the spirits; these remind the shaman that he is not solely responsible for bringing about changes. Such rituals keep the shaman in a balanced enlightenment which sustains ethical practice. The 'habitual intuition' by which shamans live and work is developed by drawing upon the web of knowledge amassed by experience and perception; it is maintained by the daily practice of sacred tradition.

Shamanism Today

We now seem to stand near a perilous abyss where the sacred culture of many peoples currently practising shamanism may be forgotten or overwhelmed by a blanket Westernization. I say 'seem to stand' for shamanic knowledge is never utterly lost, since we need only make the soul-flight to recover information and methods. We are also aided by a movement which I believe is superintended by the otherworldly guardians of wisdom. Before any massive crisis which destroys ancestral networks of remembrance and understanding, there is usually a movement to record and remember what is threatened by loss. Like the second-century traveller, Pausanius, who toured the sacred centres of Greece prior to the institution of Christianity as the state religion of the ancient world, recording indigenous spiritual practices, or antiquaries like John Leland (c. 1503–32) who recorded the ancient sites of Britain prior to the destruction wrought by the Reformation and industrialization, so too many anthropologists have explored and recorded shamanic cultures in the twentieth century.

During this present century, an anthropologist's visit to a primal culture has often heralded the demise of that culture. But with more sensitive approaches and methodology, modern anthropology has redressed the balance and brought us knowledge of many unknown practices so that the precious heritage of sacred shamanic knowledge has been recognized and re-

corded. Shamanic knowledge has not been codifiable in the same way as the humanities or philosophies before this century, but it may well find greater cogency in the coming century.

Shamanism is an experiential practice; knowledge of spirits and otherworlds stems from shamans who journey thither: it cannot be fully comprehended or annotated by theoretical anthropologists, only by those who experience this for themselves. Fortunately, many anthropologists now approach shamanic traditions as students, often becoming apprenticed to living shamans. Foremost among these practical anthropologists is Michael Harner, who was a student of the Amazonian Jivaro Indians. He has utilized knowledge of this culture and of worldwide shamanic traditions to form the Foundation for Shamanic Studies, which teaches core or non-cultural shamanism worldwide. Such centres have reintroduced shamanic ideas and practices to Western culture. We might view such developments as third wave shamanism: the first wave belonging to primal peoples and discrete cultures, and the second wave to the admixture of shamanism with other spiritual traditions. We do not yet clearly know how this shamanic third wave will affect the West, but its techniques are already rippling out faster than the ethics and social context of shamanism can be understood and integrated.

Shamanism is rapidly becoming the most overused and misappropriated word of the late twentieth century. Too many people read a book, attend a workshop and become 'instant shamans', or else rejig their therapeutic training and add the word 'shamanic', in the hope that this will align their work with the current fashion. Shamanism is in danger of becoming warped. Imperfect understanding, cultural reclamation and exposure to unrelated 'new age' techniques often devalue what is a worldwide tradition with local specialities.

Shamanism isn't a therapy, although it may have a therapeutic effect. Psychotherapists of many kinds may wish to append the role of shaman to their list of skills but, although analysts may study client's dreams and visions, they do not act as shamans, since they do not accompany clients on journeys or journey on their behalf.

Especially dangerous is the teaching of shamanic techniques

without a firm grounding in any ethical or personal spiritual practice. The learning of shamanism cannot be compared with learning to draw or speak a foreign language: shamanic knowledge comes with a set of responsibilities towards the universe. Working with any form of power requires a long training and a broad practical experience.

Apprenticeship to a shaman is not easy in Western culture since, to learn from a living shamanic tradition, the student must assimilate an alien cultural tradition. After training, the student's task is then to see how the teachings can be applied to her own culture, without disrespecting the teaching or bewildering clients or students.

The reasons why Western people are seeking shamanic wisdom and traditional knowledge are not difficult to understand. Urban living has eroded the ties of land and clan, and distanced us from our sacred heritage. The overwhelming response among white, spiritual seekers to indigenous cultures, especially the North American kind, comes from a deep need to belong to a tribal family where sacred wisdom is revered rather than traduced.

When we first encounter the attitudes of indigenous people, our Western viewpoints are turned upside down, for among them money is irrelevant to status, the oral teachings have a stronger validity than the written word, and the messages of the otherworlds are received with respect. Where Western science attempts to manipulate the physical universe, 'native science is a way of bringing people to a higher knowledge . . . to the *still, quiet place*'.[5]

Often, in an attempt to reach this kind of holy simplicity, Westerners have striven to become like indigenous peoples, to live like them and imitate their customs. Though this emulation usually derives from people's heart-felt urge to change their life, there can also be a kind of spiritual dishonesty about such imitation. Those without a spiritual tradition often warm themselves at other fires before they understand how the fire is kindled, but ultimately they must return to their own hearth and make fire there. Such is the challenge of this book: to kindle the sacred fire and feed it until it warms your whole life. Spirit is catching and it alone will show you how to respond if you are sensitive to the way it blows.

How to Start

How, then, can anyone who lives outside a traditional culture receive a shamanic training?

Each culture has its own roots, songs, stories and traditional wisdom in which sacred heritage lies encoded. The effect of the shamanic path is to place our footsteps in those of our ancestors, to reconnect with the universe, to become purposeful once more. Each person has ancestral guardians and spiritual teachers who stand ready to guide them: it is these who will help you if you decide that this is your path. While this book will not make you a shaman, it will set your footsteps on the shamanic pathway and help you become a walker between the worlds. When we accept the reality of other worlds and have travelled between them, our attitudes to daily life will change. As we become aware of the inter-relatedness of all that we do, think, are, we will no longer be able to disregard the subtle urgings of Spirit and power within us.

Practice 1: Grounding

In ancient times, few people actively sought out a shamanic vocation; their innate caution taught them to keep both feet on the ground, not to spin off dancing with the spirits. Today shamanism is new and exciting, and many people positively desire to propel themselves into the otherworlds and 'get high'. Shamans may visit otherworlds to gain information, healing or advice in order to help people, but to do so they *need to come home again*. Finding out where home is is essential, which is why you should regard this practice as basic. (See also Chapter 4.) Perform grounding after all shamanic work, so that you return gently to yourself.

The following things will earth or ground you:

breathing evenly
bringing to mind mundane purposes
bringing your awareness back to your body, mind and
    emotions
eating or drinking
gentle humour

being outdoors and becoming aware of your surroundings
recording your experiences

Create your own grounding sequence, based on your own
needs and reactions. After any shamanic work, ensure that you
are ready to perform ordinary tasks, especially driving, in a
safe way.

Practice 2: Recording Practices

Essential knowledge and personal shamanic experience can
dissipate like dreams unless it is recorded. After the practices
in this book, permit yourself assimilation time. Sit and write
down your experiences, however vestigial or wacky they may
seem. Enter into the experience with all your faculties; how did
it make you feel? what was the most salient feature of the
practice? Do not worry if you cannot understand the experience right away; fragmentary information is often referenced
again in subsequent practices. Some experiences make no
sense for months or even years, and so your record becomes a
very special way of assimilating understanding. In your notebook record journeys, dreams and thoughts. If you are more
of a pictorial person, you might prefer to draw pictures of your
experiences, or if verbal to record them on tape.

**Permission to enjoy and learn from your experiences is here
given.**

2. THE SPIRIT OF THE UNIVERSE

All things are full of Gods and Powers.

Epictetus

The threefold gifts or dimensions of shamanic work are Spirit,
power and ecstasy. In shamanism we become the filaments of
Spirit, using the bridges of power and ecstasy to mediate between one world and another.

Spirit is like a subtle aroma which permeates all things but
which is not detectable to our physical senses. In the practice

of shamanism, as in our everyday mystical interface, we are continually reminded that Spirit is everywhere. The daily wonders of weather, seasons, gifts, synchronicities and patterns encompass our lives in an ever-changing yet connective dance. We instinctively know that these things are not random occurrences, yet we feel that neither are they ultimately dictated as fixed and immovable: a creative chaos threads the complexity and simplicity of the universe. If we acknowledge Spirit, we also acknowledge the existence of an unseen reality, which we shall call 'subtle reality', which exists alongside the physical reality of our tangible existence.

The acceptance of another reality is the most radical challenge of shamanism for the modern person. There is no easy way to come to this acceptance, as any instruction that anything exists beyond our physical senses is contrary to contemporary society. The walker between the worlds may find that a provisional acceptance of subtle reality 'as if' it existed is a bridge to the work.

Monotheism and Animism

Shamanism is often defined as 'animism': a world-view in which everything is understood to have its own spirit or 'anima'. This is vastly different from the currently received monotheistic basis of Western belief which sees one god, the architect of creation. Can only one approved story of Spirit explain what we know of the worlds, both seen and unseen? It would seem unlikely.

Indigenous shamanic responses to Spirit are and have been various; some have resulted in the formation of major religions focusing on a single deity, while others have remained pragmatically animistic. Shamans were the first people to communicate images of Spirit, the first to mediate between the unseen worlds and our world. The many forms of Spirit underlie the deities venerated through the world, although monotheism does not strictly recognize any fragmentation of Spirit. Each major religion has its own mystics who keep open the lines of communication between the worlds, but these are little spoken of and are reserved for 'professionals', not the laity for whom the subtle reality of the unseen has been sub-

sumed in a welter of ritual practices which veil the glory of Spirit.

Subtle Reality

The experience of mystic and shaman are comparable, if we regard mystical experience as communication with other-worlds. The similarity of shamanic techniques worldwide, without traceable connections or transmissions, begins to make sense if we realize that every shaman born has travelled in and learned from the otherworlds and their inhabitant spirits. However, the result of the scientific world's dismissal of subtle reality and the churches' insistence that only their versions of subtle reality are authentic is twofold: some say that there is no subtle reality at all and others that subtle reality is more diverse and accommodating than religions have indicated.

Some people have explored the latter proposition themselves and proved it to their own satisfaction, but what of those who believe there is no subtle reality? These are a strange tribe, the first of their kind in the history of world anthropology. We live in extraordinary times when people disbelieve in spiritual worlds and beings. This total disregard for subtle reality makes it very hard for the mystics and visionaries who perceive it to live in our society. I am not speaking of people of extraordinary gifts, but of everyone who experiences mystical insights and knowings on a daily basis. The common, mundane nature of mystical experience is one of the best-kept secrets; its neglect and cover-up has given us a society in which we have no framework for speaking about our mystical perceptions – be it a sudden impulse or synchronicity, the urge to write a poem or song, or a vision of immense beauty.

Spirit

Shamanism is better understood, not as a religion, but as a way of life. While it acknowledges that Spirit is in all things, its manifestations are not generally worshipped in some formal religious way, although there are indeed many ceremonies to revere Spirit. Shamanism doesn't require us to give up our religion. When Margaret Umlazi, a Christian Zulu now work-

ing as a *sangoma* (shamanic healer), first received the call to shamanize she asked a wise *sangoma* about this very matter. Her response was: 'You do not have to give up Jesus to be a *sangoma*; the more sources of power you have at your disposal, the better.' Accordingly, one of the images on Margaret's wall is a picture of Christ.[6]

When Spirit calls us, it totally changes our lives. In past eras, many people have received the help of a shaman but few have wished to become one. When the call to shamanize arises, it is often severely resisted; eventually, the candidate submits since resistance becomes life threatening. This seemingly coercive spiritual call should be regarded in the same light as that of an artist who says, 'I must create or die!' Spiritual conversion works along the same lines. We can look at the example of St Paul who converted from a Christian-hating Jew to the primary missionary of early Christianity. He heard the voice of God on the Damascus road, was stricken blind and lay immobile for three days; he could only be healed when he acknowledged the will of God (Acts 9). In exchange for his healing he had to dedicate his whole life to Spirit.

If we ignore Spirit, we immediately become imbalanced and lose touch with reality. We fall into disease, separation and disharmony. To reconnect with reality, wholeness and harmony we must acknowledge the Spirit in all things. This does not mean becoming a strict religious believer, necessarily, although it might do, but involves a recognition that *Spirit is reality* and the willingness to inhabit that reality.

This is in direct contradiction to Western understanding: modern Western belief comprehends 'reality' as 'that which we can see and touch, that which is genuinely existent and true'. The gradual erosion of the totality of reality has left many suspicious and distrustful of Spirit. This is especially so since the authority of Western religion has begun to decline. Having dictated how and what people should believe for thousands of years, orthodox religions are now being rejected as authoritarian and manipulative. In truth, Western society has ignored for many centuries the validity of Spirit.

Another reason that shamanism is so popular at this time is because people are seeking to restore their own spiritual authority. Rather than believing in just one story about Spirit and making that their personal myth or 'story to live by', they

seek their own spiritual connection. The re-empowerment of our spirituality is essential, but not at the expense of suffering or manipulation. Human beings hunger for absolutes and ultimate definitions of all kinds: they seem to want to create a cosy certainty. This is why fundamentalist religion is so attractive: it has no moral ambiguities, only straight, clear lines of action. People of real Spirit, of all disciplines, are often the first against the wall, among others, when an outbreak of fundamentalism seeks to overwhelm individual and creative expressions of Spirit, witness the Cultural Revolution of China, the purging of artists in Cambodia, the slaughter of educators, artists and people of Spirit in former Yugoslavia, the persecution of actors and others under the McCarthy regime in the USA.

Spirits

Shamans work with Spirit, yet they each have their own helping spirits. Just as a mirror may be shattered yet each shard still give a perfect reflection, so must we understand the spirits of the universe as refractions of Spirit. The refractions of Spirit are discernible even in what we consider to be the monotheistic religions: the ninety-nine holy names of Allah and the Islamic angels, the qabalistic aspects of Yahweh in Judaism, the trinitarian aspects of God and the myriad saints in Christianity. But they may also appear in a human, tree, animal, stone, star, place; even objects such as musical instruments, toys, masks, pictures have their indwelling Spirit. (You can read about the different forms of Spirit in Chapter 3.)

Spirits are not usually apprehendable by the physical senses; they have their own volition or power; they do not have to be believed in to be experienced. When shamans co-operate with spirits, they do so to help reveal or restore the harmony between all things.

We are unique in the history of the world in that we have ceased to believe in the indwelling *numen* or Spirit of all things. It is only our children who recognize this spirit and honour it in their play. The Greeks called the indwelling inspirational Spirit the 'muse' or 'daimon'; the latter name (pronounced daymone) has been banished from our language and its true meaning is not reflected by the associated word, demon.

However, we still dedicate new-born children with the spirits of saints, by giving them their names, hoping that the virtue of the saint will protect and inculcate the child. The names and spirits of heroic and philanthropic people are associated with hospitals, sports associations and welfare foundations in the same manner.

You are full of spirits: many special magics, secret skills and creative gifts. These make you uniquely yourself. Spirits visit us: some stay with us, others are just passing through. It depends on whether you are a willing host/ess and are interested in playing with your guests. Co-operating with the spirits is very important. Many people spend lives of misery denying the gifting powers they were born with. Spirits are the teachers and helpers of the shaman and no shamanic work can be done without them.

Suppression of our Creative Spirits

To acknowledge our spirits is not the dire business that the movie world and fundamentalism have warned us against. Consider the spirits that assist a master cellist. This instrumentalist has probably been born with the spirit of music in her. She has cultivated her gifting spirit by going to classes as a child, and delighted in the power of her cello to voice the inspiring spirits of composers whose bodies are now dust. She may have gone to the ends of the earth to seek out supreme technicians of the cello, courting their help and advice and apprenticing herself to their skills. At last, she emerges as a virtuoso in her own right. No one hearing her on the concert platform doubts that this accomplished instrumentalist has full trust in her spirits to help her fingers over the finger-board and to sustain her bowing hand. No one would wish those spirits to go away.

And yet, we are often supremely frightened of our creative spirits; we neglect them and cause them to migrate. We lose our power when we lose our creative spirits. Many of us are bludgeoned out of our creativity by life's circumstances, some of us actively avoid our creative spirits because of the unsettling feeling of a roller-coaster that they set up in our lives. We instinctively realize, perhaps, that if our spirits are to abide

in and work with us, we are going to have to do something active about this.

We have grown up in a culture which permits only the existence of its own authorized spirits – we call them saints, God, the Virgin. Some religions, especially Christianity, have blackened ancient cultures so relentlessly that indigenous wisdom and beliefs have come to be seen as sorcery, and their gods and spirits as devils.

In Brazil, this process has been creatively reversed. The *orixas* or powers of *candomblé*, a syncretic fusion of Yoruba (West African) religion with Catholicism which flourishes in and around Bahia, are daily presences and inspirations. A woman may feel close to both the strong warrior goddess, Iansi, and St Barbara, matron of lightning; a man may feel the indwelling presence of both the god Xango and his associate St Jeremiah. In *candomblé*, each 'son or daughter of the saint' learns to become one with their indwelling *orixa* in ecstatic dancing, drumming and singing. *Candomblé* has successfully restored its native spirits to centre stage, while retaining the Catholic personas of these spirits.[7]

Finding our Guardian Spirits

When we first go seeking our own guardian spirits we start in familiar territory, seeking purposefully for helpful spirits of benign intent. These helping spirits, who are disposed to be our allies and with whom we probably have connection, already know and see our search for them; they wait only to be invited or approached.

Many people associate subtle reality with illusion and have no trust in it or its denizens. You may wish to 'test the spirits to see if they are from God' (I John 4, 1), but the only way you can do that is first to meet them. The surest way to proceed is to use all the common sense you would show if meeting any new acquaintance. Trust takes time to be established. Consider any long-term friendship which you have and you will understand this. When we first journey into subtle reality, we steer blindly unless we can trust at least one spirit friend.

Meeting the spirits may not be easy. A radical deprocessing of Western attitudes and expectations is often required before

we can journey in soul-flight or gain the help of spirits. The workshop-tourist's demand for quick results is not always gratified: after all, why should his guardian spirit appear on demand this particular weekend, if he's ignored subtle reality all his life? Shamanism is not quickly learned.

If we go looking for our helping spirits with fear and suspicion then we make our journey more arduous. The nature of Spirit is neither good nor evil; the refractions of Spirit are distillations of energy, like electricity, wind or fire. A shower may bless the garden but a flood may destroy it. The gradations of power in spirits are all expressions of Spirit. The major part of a shaman's duty is to deal with spirits on their own terms, acting as a mediator and sometimes director of spiritual energy. It is usually a matter of inappropriate rather than 'evil' spirits: of clearing out or extracting unwanted accumulations of Spirit from one place or person where they are causing blockage or illness, rather then of exorcism and banishing.

For example, we call wandering human souls ghosts. These are not evil, usually just lost. A shaman's job is to help these souls pass to their appropriate place in the otherworlds. Some spirits of place can be rather like errant children, both mischievous and disruptive. A shaman would seek to discover why they were behaving this way, possibly as a result of human disrespect to the site in question, and to calm the disruption. Many of life's problems result from spirits colonizing each other's space. The etiquette of co-existence with spirits is something which we learn through walking between the worlds.

Permission to listen to your creative spirits is here given.

3. THE POWER OF THE UNIVERSE

In a society which is rapidly losing touch with the strictly codified subtle realities of state religions, many people are drawn to shamanism so as to explore those realities for themselves. And one of the most attractive features of accessing subtle reality is power. Unfortunately rather more people are drawn to the power of shamanic techniques, than to the power of Spirit itself.

Use and Misuse of Power

Shamans believe and work with the power of Spirit, which sustains, changes and flows through all things. This power of Spirit is the vital energy of the universe, it is life. Shamans bring life by reconnecting the broken links of power.

Like Spirit, the word 'power' has problematic associations in our language. It bears the connotation of 'authority', usually of the dictatorial or censorious kind. I am talking about the power of life, the vital energy of Spirit which runs through all. At no point am I talking about power as a mode of violence or tyranny.

In the Amazonian culture of the Desana Indians it is believed that the quantity of energy or power is fixed and that 'man must remove what he needs only under certain conditions and must convert this particle of 'borrowed' energy in a form that can be reincorporated into the circuit'.[8] By manipulating power, our society has lost its spiritual authenticity and we have cut ourselves off from the reciprocal circuit of Spirit and power. It is no wonder we are spiritually gasping for breath.

Power flows through all of us. It does not 'belong' to us, but is a vitality common to all. It comes into us, passes through our being and moves on again. It is always entering and leaving us, like our breath. To speak of 'possessing power' is as ridiculous as 'owning the air in our lungs'. By all means, try to keep 'your own air' in your own lungs, if you can: you will only succeed until your next exhalation! When the pathways of the Spirit are blocked, then power cannot flow. Those who have kept the pathways open are often feared by those who have not: the latter consequently often harbour jealousy of any creative skill.

The cosmic web which connects all life is like an electrical grid: each part of it hums with power. Wherever disconnections and blockages occur, the power cannot flow. No single being distributes this power: all beings are responsible for keeping it flowing. We each share in it in the same way that everyone swimming in the sea shares in the water: some bodies displace more water than others. It is not apportioned equally, but is available to all.

Those who are spiritually aware are generally perceived to be 'powerful' in the sense of being livelier, more integrated and less unbalanced than others; they may achieve more in a shorter

time, be more open to ideas and therefore more resourceful. Being a 'powerful person' does not make you stronger, healthier or more successful than others, necessarily. The more pathways we walk through the worlds, the more power-cables connect us. But to whom more is given, more is required.

Our power, our vitality, derives from many sources: from light, from food, from a secure environment, from supportive and loving relationships, from culture, from spiritual engagement with the universe. When any of these channels of vitality is fractured, we begin to lose power. We may neglect areas or have unclear motivation, or we may give away our power to others – for example, when we unhealthily abrogate our self and our needs. Sometimes, we unwillingly relinquish our share of power to someone who is coercive or dominating, who has discovered how to play with our emotions. We can lose power by being threatened, cajoled, invaded, overwhelmed, whether by people, accident or trauma. In all instances, the natural power-cables connecting us with the cosmic web are fractured and power begins to leak away. The resulting power-loss may lead to illness, soul-fragmentation or sometimes death. A person lacking power will be dispirited, tired, frustrated, and generally disengaged from daily life. Only by re-sourcing the power of the universe can she build up her resistance.

Among the many songs that are sung in esoteric groups is a circle song which tells us that 'where there's fear, there is power'. The poet Rainer Maria Rilke wrote that our deepest fears are like dragons guarding our deepest treasure. Dealing with fear requires courage. Many people feel it is easier to live with the self-imposed controls of fear than to experience the liberation of the power that lies beneath the fear. Shamanism cracks through such restraint and puts us in touch with our power-treasury. (Ways of restoring power and vitality are dealt with in Chapter 8.)

There is much talk of 'empowerment' and 're-empowerment' in esoteric training circles, as though this were the end product of such training. Similarly, many people are drawn to shamanism because it seems to offer them instant empowerment. By walking between the worlds we may indeed enhance our vitality and power, but we do well to remember that this is only an incidental effect, that shamanism is not a therapy, that a deeper commitment and responsibility are required. A true appreci-

ation of how we receive and give out power in accordance with the laws of the universe only comes when we live in alignment with those laws. The realization that neither we personally, nor our species, is the mainspring of the universe will keep our practice ethical.

Like Spirit, power is non-dual: it is itself, but it can be misplaced. The shaman's duty is to reconnect and restore broken power-lines, as well as to remove and re-circuit inappropriate accumulations of power. Such work is not done indiscriminately nor without recourse to the cosmic web of power which connects all things; the circumstances surrounding any shamanic action are first investigated in both physical and subtle reality to discover whether a course of action is appropriate.

It is only by consulting the whole universe through the networks of Spirit and power that healing connections can be re-established. Wherever one part of the cosmic web is healed, power is restored to the whole web, benefiting all.

Permission to draw upon and share the power of the universe is here given.

4. THE DANCE OF ECSTASY

The experience of shamanism leads to a sense of non-duality where the contraries of life are dissolved and replaced by a primeval, paradisal wholeness; where memory is restored to the forgetful, unity is given to the separate, transmutation comes to the stagnant spirit. The soul, having partaken of the otherworlds, experiences total freedom and bliss. This sense of non-duality is called ecstasy.

Ecstasy sounds dangerous, chaotic, uncontrolled. Our society encourages us to be in such rigid control that very few people now experience ecstasy as an everyday thing. The abandonment of dance, the joy of sex, the freedom to enjoy life to the full is the common heritage of all, yet perhaps only a few young adults enjoy these to any degree. But we must distinguish between this and the shaman's experience of ecstasy which is purposeful, not recreational; he journeys forth for the benefit of others, not for the personal thrill of the ride. For him, ecstasy is the result of sharing in the non-duality of the cosmic web.

Most mature adults have lost the key to subtle reality, except in dreams; they are imprisoned in a cage of physical reality, doomed to walk the mundane round of existence without sparkle or soul. The prisoners of physical reality are often controllers, who have difficulty going to sleep easily, who find it difficult to delegate duties and may have problems in learning to swim or in situations where deep trust is required. These people are not closed to Spirit by any means; they often yearn for some tangible token that Spirit flows through their lives. The problem is, they just can't let go of physical reality long enough.

Soul-journeys are fuelled by rhythm, sound and movement. The shaman's soul is propelled into subtle reality. To do this the shaman must relinquish control, as we do to swim or sleep successfully. Anyone who has learned to float knows exactly what I mean here. The way to float is to let go and trust the water to support you: try and take control of the water and it is easy to get into a panic. Those who learn to trust water become skilful and successful swimmers, able to go where they please, using a variety of strokes. Shamans are similarly able to journey because they learn to trust and enjoy the sensations of journeying.

Shamanic ecstasy is fuel which propels the soul to other-worlds, but this does not mean that the shaman abrogates his will or self-discipline. The combination of discipline and ecstasy is the alchemy of shamanism. For the shaman is an alchemist, facilitating changes to substances, lives, emotions and souls through the realignment of power and Spirit.

Ecstasy helps free us from our earth-bound reality and opens doors and windows which society usually bars shut. It liberates us from seemingly insuperable problems, enabling us to see resourceful and spiritual ways of working things out. Our culture has associated Spirit with stricture and rigidity; consequently, it neglects Spirit, is ignorant of how power flows and fails to understand how ecstasy can be more than recreational.

If we are alive to the Spirit and power within us, then the non-duality of ecstasy can be the vehicle of our lives.

Practice 3: Mapping your Spiritual Journey

Look over your life so far and map the course of your spiritual journey. Where has Spirit inspired you and touched your life?

Your journey might include mystical experiences where you were touched by Spirit, visits to places of beauty and power, books, music, inspiring people, insights and thoughts. These events, influences or experiences may not be specifically religious or conventionally mystical: if Mickey Mouse has changed your life, if watching a tree cut down has altered your spiritual perceptions, then include it. Review your spiritual itinerary: what patterns, significant factors, and connections do you see? Which features are continually repeated?

Practice 4: Sources of Power

You are a living terminal of the universal power-house. Many power-currents and cables flow through your life. Review your present life-style and assess the sources of power that you consciously and unconsciously draw upon. These might include the kinds of foods you eat, the emotional relationships you have, the cultural influences you draw upon, the spiritual sources which you access. Take a large sheet of paper and draw a flow-chart, with yourself at the centre, of these lines of power leading into and out of you. Now follow one of these lines back as far as you can go. Example: if you have written down 'fruit' as a source of physical nourishment, explore the source of fruit: tree, earth, rain, sun. If you take back all the power-lines to their source, you will make an interesting discovery about the nature of power and Spirit.

Practice 5: Unzipping your Passion

Our lives are wound with prescriptions – don't, can't, mustn't. The restrictions which bind us have often arrived unannounced or may have been the result of circumscribed periods in our lives when such rules were a necessary survival mechanism; whichever is the case, we are often unable to enjoy life at all. Allowance and permission are the first gift we can give ourselves to help restore the flow of universal power into our lives. Sometime this week, do something you really want to do for the love of it: swimming, walking, reading a novel, eating chocolates, buying a nice thing you want but don't need. Give

yourself permission to enjoy this, take time to appreciate it. Don't sanction something just because it incidentally gives pleasure to someone else – expedience and self-effacement are not what this practice is about.

Although it may seem frivolous and unnecessary, this practice is a valuable way to bring the zest and freshness back into your life, especially after a period of denial. You may also need to re-inforce this practice by finding a book, a piece of music, a place or friend who encourages you to reach into the originality of your soul and do something unusual, uncharacteristic and fun.

Permission to recreate yourself is here given.

5. THE COSMIC WEB

Without any doubt there is something which links material energy and spiritual energy together and makes them a continuity. In the last resort there must somehow be but one single energy active in the world.

Hymn to the Universe
Teilhard de Chardin

This book invites you to become a walker between the worlds. To do this, you need to know just where the thresholds of those worlds lie and how to cross them. They are not difficult to find. The doorways and pathways lie all about us. As children, we knew them intimately in our secret play; like Alice in Wonderland, we explored the multi-dimensional complexity of the cosmic web, which was inhabited by the spirits with whom we played. The tragedy of our growing up is that we are seduced into giving up any contact with the web, to join the adult world where people are largely disconnected from it. When Dylan Thomas wrote 'Rage, rage against the dying of the light', it was this creative illumination, our connection with the web, that he meant, I believe. As adults, we lose our easy access to subtle reality, except through dreams or through meditation and other spiritual practices.

The all-pervasive nature of Spirit connects all things in a cosmic web of relationship. When we become aware of it, we feel the flow of power and ecstasy within us; when we separate

ourselves from it, we feel depressed and uneasy. When we say, 'things just flowed along that day', or 'it was just one thing going wrong after the other', we are expressing our connection to or disconnection from the cosmic web.

This feeling of unity and connection is so sought-after, that many people have dedicated their lives to its pursuit. In an ashram, monastery or retreat, it is easy to feel our connection. But shamanism is not about acquiring a self-absorbed sense of well-being for our personal nirvana, it is about reconnecting our individual physical world with the rest of the web, then, with the help of our spirits, mediating between the physical and subtle realities, and helping realign whatever and whoever has become separate from the cosmic web. This involves an exploration of the otherworlds, where they are, what they contain and how their inhabitants relate to us, so that we can then make whatever personal changes are necessary to work in this way.

Soul-fragmentation

Western society allows us to be aware in our body and in our mind; it sometimes permits us to be aware in our psyche, but it gives no importance to our soul, parts of which have become homeless. The West has become increasingly soulless, driven by economic survival and seeking satisfaction in fatuous and hollow pursuits, avoiding spiritual challenges and promoting quick-fix political solutions.

Throughout the world, shamanism recognizes that human beings have a multiple soul consisting of several parts. The number of parts varies: some cultures recognize two or three parts, others several more. In traditional societies, soul-parts are held to reside in different parts of the body – in the blood, hair or breath for instance – and to be able to travel forth at will, as in dreams.

In this book we will be talking about the way these composite soul-parts can become involuntarily ejected, stolen or lost. We each have multiple soul-parts which usually function in complex and efficient ways: they enable us to live ordinary lives and we are not usually aware of them. But if a soul-part becomes ejected due to the shock of an accident, or through

trauma such as divorce, burglary, rape, bereavement, we suddenly become aware of having mislaid something. An inability
to heal or recover or function as we once did is the signal of
soul-loss, or more accurately, soul-fragmentation.

Each part of our soul needs to be with us, to enable us to pay
proper attention to the different dimensions of our lives: to be
emotionally aware, to give love, to appreciate what is true and
beautiful, to respect the boundaries of others and ourselves, to
discern danger. If one or more soul-part is missing, we begin
to find some of these things difficult or impossible.

Soul-fragmentation can happen to societies and groups as
well as to individuals. The signs are clear to read in the West,
in meaningless violence, addictions and self-mutilations. In
many ways our society resembles a long-caged animal lacking
self-respect or purpose, declining at the end of its chain. Our
society is a prisoner of one reality.

The shamanic task is to restore self-respect and purpose to
both individual and group by retrieving the lost soul-parts.

Reconnection

By seeking reconnection with the cosmic web, and exploring it
we are not seeking to escape the confines of our physical world;
by walking the ancient pathways, we are not striving to enter
the past. Shamanism wants only to sing the soul back home,
so that the primal harmony of the cosmos may be re-experienced
by all. When shamanic students first encounter some part of
the cosmic web and behold its unity, beauty and harmony,
they weep tears both of joy and recognition and of regret for
wasted time and opportunity. Nothing can prepare us for the
flood of remembrance which flows into our being when we
perceive the worlds of the web and realize that we too are
connected.

It is for this reason that shamans journey, that artists paint
and sculpt, that musicians play, that poets sing: each practitioner upholds his art, her skill to the death in order to keep
those doors of perception open, that others may be led upon
the pathways of power, ecstasy and life to behold the web and
to become a part of it. It is for this reason that we must uphold

the imagination as a faculty of the soul, and keep our own imaginations brightly polished to refract the luminous and all-pervading beauty of the cosmic web. If we resonate with the web, we will immediately be able to perceive what brings nurture and inspiration and be able to reject whatever is artificial, spurious and self-seeking.

Our background and education are still very much rooted in the Age of Reason, which forswore religion and otherworldly realities as pretence and superstition. During the last thirty years, since the 1960s, the tide has turned and we are beginning to understand and reaccept the validity of subtle reality.

Scientists, physicists and cosmographers have sought to express the interconnective nature of matter with time, space and dimension in a variety of ways: from the parallel universe theories of Brian D. Josephson, through the divine milieu expounded by Teilhard de Chardin, to the cosmic wormholes of John Archibald Wheeler. Such theories of universal interconnection parallel shamanism. Furthermore, both scientists and shamans agree that specific techniques of consciousness can make us more aware of such relations. A growing understanding of cause and effect, both physical and subtle, is being expounded by the new science, and this echoes the shamanic experience of reciprocity. Not only do we receive power and benefit from connection with the web, we also give back thanks and power in return. Refusal to share in this manner usually results in separation from Spirit.

I believe that we are ready to comprehend the cosmic web once again. New technology and communication networks have interlinked our physical reality in the last fifty years. Now the work of restoring the network of our subtle reality must begin. We have begun to listen to shamans and indigenous peoples who respect the cosmic web and already interact with it. One of our major drawbacks as 'civilized' and literate people is our very urbanity and literality; we need the wisdom of the web-keepers. We have lost our sensitivity and perception of subtle reality, we easily throw off any understanding of it, gravitating towards the familiar ground of mundane reality. We have been conditioned to be separate, disconnected and proud of our independence.

The Three Worlds

Our disconnection from the web is increased by the absence of any subtle reality cosmology. Indigenous peoples see the inter-relationships of the cosmic web as complex and various. In contrast, our perception of otherworlds and states is supremely unsophisticated: *up* for heaven, *down* for hell! Throughout shamanic traditions, the subtle worlds are portrayed as zones of activity and function. Each people and land has its own perceptions of these zones, but the most common model is three tiered, as shown in Figure 1a.

This diagram is a model, not a representational map. The upper, middle and lower worlds are experienced as real and complex, not flat and two dimensional. They are interpenetrated by a central axis, sometimes called the pole, pillar or ladder of the heavens, or the *axis mundi*, or, as here, by the great tree. The image of the central tree is a universally compelling one, for its roots draw upon the depths of all that has been, its trunk rises up in strength in the present moment and its fruits soar into the heights of potent futurity. It is the major highway along which shamans travel.

The three worlds are encompassed by the cosmic web which must be imagined as interpenetrating it, multi-dimensionally, from all angles. The two-dimensional image in Figure 1b cannot begin to convey the true sense of dimensionality and the vigour with which the cosmic web can be accessed from all points within this cosmological totality. Like a safety-net, the web surrounds and connects all that is, whether in physical or subtle reality.

As we walk between the worlds, the intersecting filaments of the web are close at hand. Even if we travel at speed in soul-flight, our allies and helpers are there to remind us and help us reorient ourselves. As we explore the otherworlds more thoroughly, we will find more connecting ways between the worlds; we may also discover further worlds within worlds. Some cultures envisage three further worlds in each zone, making a total of nine; others recognize seventeen or thirty-three or ninety-nine. We will not be making so complex an exploration in this book, but will pay close attention to the three world model (which is expounded fully in Chapters 4, 5 and 6.)

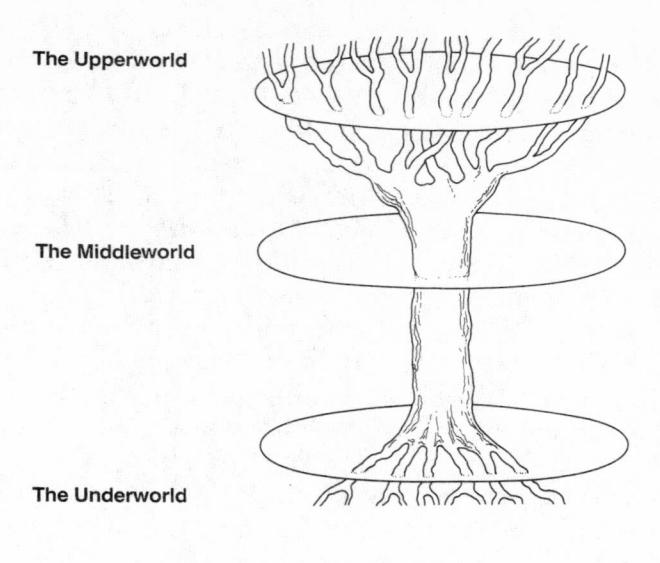

The Upperworld

The Middleworld

The Underworld

Figure 1a. The three worlds

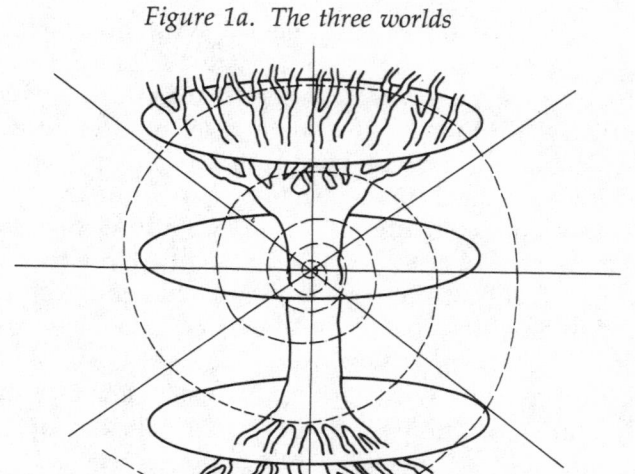

Figure 1b. The cosmic web encompassing the three worlds

The three worlds are part of all cultures worldwide, even in Christian European culture. We see it reflected in Dante's *The Divine Comedy*, where Dante is accompanied by the classical poet Virgil on a tour of a lowerworld, defined as hell, and of a Middleworld, defined as purgatory; while he is led by Beatrice and other female allies into an Upperworld, defined as para-

dise. Each of Dante's worlds has nine levels; but we should remember that it is not precisely analogous to the shamanic three world model. Rather, it is a dualistic and Christianized diminishment of the ancient tradition of the three worlds.

Walking between the worlds, we begin to understand the original dynamics of inner space for ourselves, without the overlay of restrictive theology. We are already aware of the physical reality of the Middleworld, which lies about us in everyday life; some of us may also be familiar with the subtle reality of the Middleworld. We are using the rich and sustaining power of the Underworld when we reach into our memories, when we use our deep instincts, when we access primal foundations. We come into contact with the bright illumination and mercurial flow of the Upperworld whenever we access connective patterns and ideas, when we evoke sources of universal wisdom, whenever we seek out new ways of working.

Most people experience connection with the three worlds and access the cosmic web in some way, although few do this consciously or with repeatable skill. For them, only the physical part of the Middleworld is real: they may experience the sudden closeness of a far-distant friend or pick up a sense that they should not travel on a particular road, but these feelings are put down to coincidence or imagination, not to subtle reality. Similarly, people who sense a dead relative guiding them or who feel that they are being instructed by an eminent teacher, don't realize that they have had contact with spirits from the under or upper worlds.

One of the reasons why early anthropologists assumed that many shamans and indigenous peoples were schizophrenic or mentally unstable was because they could conceive of physical and subtle realities simultaneously – a skill which the anthropologists themselves no longer utilized. We ourselves are in no doubt when we are thinking, imagining, recalling or dreaming: we can switch perceptual modes skilfully. But with our growing dependency upon the visual media and our neglect of subtle perceptual modes, our skills can decline. If we add to this a complete dearth of words to describe mystical or otherworldly states and take away any social framework in which such states can be aired, it is no wonder that subtle reality and its inhabitants have been expelled from our culture. Yet, when

they are first exposed to it, many people are amazed at how easily and speedily shamanism works.

Any attempt to codify or understand the immensity and connectedness of the universe can really only be an approach. Some approaches have gone further and defined the universe so completely that these definitions – religions, philosophies and political trends – have become binding and obligatory, so that to disbelieve in them has been a criminal or heretical act. Shamanism has no desire to impose a rigid definition of reality upon anyone: it is happy to accept a loosely associated framework of regionally various experiences which have resonance, harmony and connection.

On the Threshold

As you stand on the threshold of reconnection with the web, you may be wondering about the advisability of shamanic work. It is common to fear stepping through the veil between the worlds: what terrors will you experience? What dangers will you meet? Be assured that your innate common sense, instinct and perception will not abandon you as you walk between the worlds: please take them with you. The unknown is not evil, it is just unfamiliar. When you travel to a foreign country, you have guides who know the country and speak its language to help you. This book is also preparing your way, helping you gradually to become familiar with the landscape and features of the three worlds.

Those who travel fearfully, always suspicious of those they meet, always expecting problems, usually encounter them. Those who travel with purposeful intention, who keep alert and treat those they meet with respect, usually become good travellers. Healthy caution should always be tempered by a trusting heart. Fear in shamanic work usually arises from a lack of trust, in ourselves or in our spiritual allies. Absence of self-confidence stems from loss of power and self-esteem which are endemic in our dependent and passive culture. But if we start with familiar landmarks and become acquainted with our helping spirits, we will walk between the worlds safely and in growing wisdom.

A Bushman trance dancer described his journey through the cosmic web like this:

> I enter the earth. I go in at a place like a place where people drink water. I travel a long way, very far. When I emerge, I am already climbing threads. I climb one and leave it, then I climb another one . . . You come in small to God's place. You do what you have to do there . . . Then you enter the earth, and you return to enter the skin of your body.[9]

That is all that is required of you: to go forth, to listen and communicate and to return. In the next chapter we will explore the practicalities and dynamics of how you do this.

Practice 6: The Cosmic Web

Sit in any area where you can be private and uninterrupted. Consider the physical reality networks currently operative in your life and circumstances: the people, places, work, activities, group memberships. Draw an interconnective chart of these influences upon yourself.

In another session, consider the subtle reality networks operative in your life. This is more difficult, requiring you to go deeper into yourself. You might include the unspoken or unacknowledged connections between yourself and others, the connections between your and others' beliefs, the links you have with other animal species, with those who are dead, the effects of your activities upon those not yet born. Draw an interconnective chart of these influences upon yourself. Superimpose one chart upon another – where are the significant connections?

In a follow-up session, sit outdoors, once during the day, once during the night: both times, consider how *you* impinge upon the cosmic web. Compare your findings. What have you learned?

Practice 7: Wishing True

Review any wishes you've made in the past; for example your childhood yearning for a rocking-horse, your adolescent desire to meet a pop-idol, your adult wish, uttered in anger, that

someone might drop dead. Discard them if they are no longer desired: these wishes are taking up space in you and in the cosmic web. To do so, just reverse them aloud; for example, 'I no longer wish for a straighter nose'. If you wish to cancel forgotten wishes you might now regret, say so out loud.

You may wish to make a new wish, or to reinforce an old one. Before you do this, consider how it would change your life, what repercussions it would have on any living creature now alive or yet to come, how it would shake the web. This is not an exercise in cosmic manipulation nor in selfish desires, but in attuning to the power which runs through the cosmic web and learning to trust and respect it. If your wish, and it doesn't have to be a personal one, stands up to scrutiny, now describe it and make it exciting to yourself, with all your senses. Send your wish out into the universe on free wings, without reserve. Without trying to manipulate the manifestation of your wish, bring it to mind regularly, but let it be free to manifest if it wants to, remembering that things don't always come to a satisfactory conclusion on our terms.

Permission to experience the cosmic web is here given.

2.   The Shamanic Journey

People must believe what they can, and those who believe more must not be hard upon those who believe less. I doubt if you would have believed it all yourself if you hadn't seen some of it.

The Princess and the Goblin
George MacDonald

1. OTHER DIMENSIONS

Through the simplest alterations of consciousness, we can enter a world of living interaction and unity.

Shamans, Healers and Medicine Men
Holger Kalweit

THE FEATURE WHICH TYPIFIES SHAMANISM and sets it apart from mediumship, channelling or other forms of spirit-communication is the shamanic journey. Shamans actively seek out the help of spirits, visiting and communing with them in the three worlds, by means of the soul-flight.

The idea of the shaman travelling in other realities is outrageous to many people – a fantastic illusion at best, an imaginary fraud at worst. Yet throughout history and in all cultures, we hear of examples. The Italian Franciscan ecstatic, St Joseph of Cupertino (1603–63) was often seen in two places at once; the Hasidic *tzaddikim*, the spiritual masters of qabala, were able to make the *kfitzas haderech* or miracle journey, appearing to people in need many miles distant. Even people with no training or aptitude send out a soul-part when a loved one is in

need, actually seen or felt in many cases by the receiver. These are all instances of Middleworld journeying.

To understand the shamanic journey, we have to comprehend the soul. Westerners generally perceive the psyche or soul as the individual unit of personality, while the Spirit is seen as the immortal unit which continues after death. In qabala, the human soul is threefold: the *nefesh* or 'animal soul' which bears the vitality of life, the *neshemah* or 'the breath of God' and the *ruach ha kodesh* or 'spirit of enlightenment' which acts as a bridge between the two.[1] For the Kogi Indians of Columbia, *aluna* or the 'generative intelligence' of memory forms a bridge between the human spirit and the universe.[2]

The shaman skilfully uses different soul-parts to divine the universe. When she journeys, the soul-part/s governing the body's involuntary maintenance-system (circulatory and respiratory systems, for example) are left behind to guard the body, while the soul-part/s go forth into the otherworlds. This method of soul-travelling can never be forgotten and is frequently used involuntarily by those whose lives are in danger or who are suffering from shock. When the anaesthetized patient on the operating table perceives himself lying there, this is called 'a near-death experience'. The soul of such a patient may travel further and experience entering paradise or meeting dead relatives. In the Western Mystery tradition, when a magician seeks to travel across countless miles to learn something, it is called 'astral travel'.

Shamanic journeying is distinct from the near-death experience or from other traumatic soul-ejection since the shaman always enters the otherworlds voluntarily and purposefully by specific routes, travelling through already-mapped terrain and encountering familiar spirits. Although these journeys may unfold in various ways, they are not undertaken in a random fashion.

Shamans journey to the otherworlds in a different state of consciousness from that which we experience every day. Human beings live by varying their modes of awareness quite dramatically, according to their needs. Major forms of awareness include the following:

Total absorption (no sense of separation between self and other, as in mystic rapture)

Intense concentration (playing a musical instrument)
Vigilant awareness (when driving or searching for some-
thing)
Day-dreaming (voluntary fantasy)
Ordinary awareness (walking along, performing simple
tasks)
Drifting consciousness (involuntary when ill or sleepy)
Sleep (of varying densities of consciousness)
Unconsciousness (coma, only involuntary life-functions
operative)
Death (cessation of consciousness from a physical viewpoint)

Drugs can either enhance consciousness or diminish it to varying
degrees. The use of trance-inducing plants among traditional
shamans causes the suppression of body awareness but a
heightening of soul awareness.

The consciousness of a shaman while shamanizing has often
been described as 'trance' or 'ecstasy', which may be very
misleading, since 'trance' implies reduced consciousness and
'ecstasy' an exalted, rapturous awareness. These expressions
have been coined by non-shamans since they are descriptions
of how shamanism *appears* to the observer: the shaman dances
and sings loudly (ecstasy); the shaman falls to the ground and
lies motionless (trance). Neither expression is really accurate. We
have already mentioned the ecstasy which may arise, but this is
not always a feature of the shamanic session: fear, expectation,
joy, wonder, uncertainty and trust are experienced as well.

Sourcing

To describe the condition by which shamans enter into soul-
flight through the three worlds, Michael Harner[3] has suggested
'shamanic state of consciousness' or SSC, which is a better term
than 'trance' or 'ecstasy', but I will use a simpler word: 'sourcing'.
This unconventional verbal use of a noun is the nearest I can
get to the experience by which we enter the otherworlds. A
source is an original fount, usually where water or primal
wisdom arises; when we enter the otherworlds to access spiritual wisdom, we are returning to the source of Spirit, power
and ecstatic non-duality.

During sourcing, the shaman actively and purposefully seeks out and returns to his source – in one of the worlds – remaining totally aware of the experience he is having and trusting that all his body functions will operate automatically until he returns. During sourcing, the shaman may be unaware of things happening in the room, but not so unaware that he could not return to ordinary consciousness at need if, say, fire broke out. Certainly, some traditional shamans may reach so deeply into their source that they remain journeying for many hours: this is a rare occurrence, a condition which we can confidently define as trance.

Shamans source at will when need arises, for at the source help is to be found. Sourcing is like plugging into an electrical socket: it fills the shaman with an energy and illumination which, though it is all about us, is seldom experienced in normal life. It is a way of rerooting ourselves in our centre. When we have lost our awareness of that centre and seek to return to it, we are 'rerooting' or finding our spiritual centre again.

During sourcing, a shaman's consciousness expands to comprehend not only the everyday world but all its spiritual forms too; it moves freely and journeys into otherworlds. Sourcing utilizes that part of the soul's awareness which is frequently dormant or 'unconscious' in everyday life.

Sourcing is a form of intentional consciousness, wherein delight, intense concentration and involuntary receptivity are simultaneously experienced. For, although the shaman may decide to visit one of the worlds to seek out a helper, she does not direct the journey. Her helpers will take her to different parts of the otherworlds, show her things of which she is previously unaware. While at the source, she may speak in languages unknown to her and access many forms of knowledge not in her personal database.

The Sequence of a Shamanic Session

At this point it is probably useful for you to have some sense of the sequence of a typical shamanic session.

1. *A need or purpose* underlies all shamanic work. No shaman sets off randomly into the otherworlds without a good intention or an issue to resolve. The issue may be framed as

a question: 'How can love be restored between me and the friend with whom I have quarrelled?' or as a request for advice: 'Please show me what steps I can take next in this matter.'

2. *Preparing the place* where the shamanizing is going to happen comes next. This is usually indoors, or under shelter in a very remote place, if outdoors. The sacred dimension of the place and what is to take place within it is ritually realized by cleansing and intentioned preparation. External intrusions and interruptions are insured against.

3. *Inviting the spirits*. The shaman asks her spirits to come and help her, usually by song or speech, maybe also with dancing or ritual offerings of sacred smoke or grain.

4. *Sourcing*. Consciousness is retuned to the cosmic web by shamanic singing, dancing, rattling, drumming. This can be performed by the shaman herself or by an assistant. When the shaman is ready to journey she sits or lies down. Thanks to modern technology, it is now possible to journey quite deeply with the aid of a drumming tape and headset. The repetitive rhythms, cadences or movements all help the shaman reach her source.

5. *The journey* or soul-flight begins when sourcing has been successful and the shaman becomes overwhelmingly aware of the pathways which lead to her intended source. Her soul follows her usual routes to reach one of the worlds where her spirit helpers are. Solutions to problems are found with their help. The sequence of this journey is various and lasts on average from ten to forty minutes; its length may be governed by the length of a sound-source tape. Examples of typical journeys are given below in Section 3.

6. *The return* from sourcing is just as important. If an assistant has been providing a continuous sound-source, he will take his cue from the shaman's hand signals, body language or breathing to change the rhythm to sound the soul's coming home. If a drumming tape has been used, then after twenty to thirty minutes of drumming, the call-back signal will sound, calling the shaman's soul home. There is a brief period of readjustment to ordinary consciousness when the shaman assesses the information or advice gained.

7. *Thanking spirits and helpers* is never omitted, since it is by their help alone that solutions have been found. Again, offerings, songs or dances are often performed.

8. *Imparting or implementing* the advice gained on the journey is the final act, manifesting otherworldly help in a practical way.

This schema gives only a broad outline of one possible approach to the shamanic journey; shamanic sessions which involve working with clients or larger groups unfold in different ways.

Engagement

Shamanism requires a balance of relaxed awareness and concentrated perception; it is not a passive activity. The will is operative so that the shaman can choose to return at any time, exercise his usual commonsense judgements or make decisions during the journey. The experience of such journeys inevitably changes the character of the walker between the worlds: interfacing with the cosmic web brings spiritual and emotional stability as well as a physical and mental steadfastness which totally refute the notion that shamanism renders the practitioner fey or otherworldly. If, on the other hand, the walker between the worlds goes as a mere otherworldly tourist, without engagement, the same cannot be said.

Folk-wisdom represents this in the story of two daughters sent out to find a treasure. The younger daughter relates with compassion to the beings she meets on the way, so that they aid her quest and she returns successfully – with the additional gift of speaking gold and silver. But the elder daughter, desirous of similar success, tramps relentlessly over and through all beings she meets, receives no help from them and returns without achieving her aim, and with the consequent gift of speaking worms and spiders.

We take who we are and what we have accumulated with us into the three worlds. Of course it is possible to travel thither as a mere observer, as some kind of theoretical exercise, but this is not the shaman's way. It is like studying the art of painting and buying brushes, paint and canvas but never creating

your own picture. Unless we engage with the otherworlds through which we travel and become involved with their inhabitants, we cannot walk the web with any compassion or understanding.

We turn now to the dynamics and techniques of sourcing.

```
┌─────────────────────────────────────────────────────────┐
│           Practice 8: Modes of Awareness                 │
└─────────────────────────────────────────────────────────┘
```

One day this week, make a note of where your consciousness is focused from the time you rise until you go to bed. Be relaxed and not over-analytical in this, making a sample collection of random moments of the day.

Example: 8.45am intense concentration in rush-hour; 11.35am day-dreaming about me and Andrea on holiday; 2.40pm strong empathy with Roger who collapsed at his desk with heart trouble; 6.30pm mystical oneness with blackbird's song in twilight garden; 11.10pm drifted off to sleep worrying about tomorrow's presentation, which spiralled through my dreams all night.

Note what was happening during these moments, how easy it was to move from one mode into another, what was happening to your body, mind and emotions during this time.

2. RIDING THE SPIRIT WIND

> When I practised drumming and chanting . . . an unusual merging of mind and feeling took place, drawing me downward to a beginning of something. As I trusted its vertical pull, it took me to the fundamental elements of life.
>
> *Crossings: A Transpersonal Approach*
> Carl Levett

Carl Levett, an American psychologist who studied with an Indian shaman, is describing above the beginning of sourcing. In this section we explore the various means of sourcing.

Sourcing can be accompanied by irresistible waves of power such as are experienced in childbirth, a dissolution of all save the rhythm, brightness and vision of power. In sourcing we

become everything, we enter everything, and everything becomes and enters us simultaneously, in the same way that a
labouring mother and the baby coming forth from her womb
are also one in the cosmic birth struggle. I have purposely used
the image of childbirth because our first entry into the otherworlds is a real birth, where we are recreated and introduced
to our forgotten spiritual home or source. The awe, terror and
wonder of that birth are never to be forgotten.

While working on this book, I had a long, lucid dream in
which the spirits told me how any person can access inner
space, whatever their cultural or educational background. Four
factors are necessary:

1. The stillness
2. The container
3. The companion
4. The story.

These were explained to me as follows:

1. The primal *stillness* of our alert but relaxed attention must
   underlie all travel in inner space. This is usually attained by
   the simple process of stilling the body's tension, the mind's
   activity and the heart's desires and by focusing the soul's
   attention. This stillness is discovered through sound and/or
   through physical motions like martial arts, certain dance-
   forms, music-making and so on.

2. The *container* refers to the place from whence we start to
   journey as well as to our destination. This includes the interaction of time and space, as well as of knowledge of the
   pathways which lead us into the cosmic web. Our container
   can be as simple as an undisturbed room. In all instances,
   we focus upon our physical location, our connection with
   the earth on which we live, and upon the season. These are
   the gateways for our journey.

3. The *companion* is the spirit or ally who accompanies us. The
   companion is our guide upon our journey and we travel
   nowhere without one. To gain a companion, we must make
   an initial contact in special circumstances. This is described
   in the next chapter.

4. The *story* refers to the impulse for our journey, the reason
   we are travelling, and the answer which is mirrored in inner

space. No journey can begin without a good purpose: in-definite purpose creates meandering journeying where the story is fragmented or meaningless. (We will explore the ways we arrive at our story in the next section and will discover how to understand it more deeply in Chapter 7.)

There are many means of sourcing available to us. Traditional shamans attain passage to the worlds by the following means:

1. Rhythmic or percussive instruments (drum or rattle), re-sonant and sustained sounds (bowed and stringed instru-ments, voice).
2. Motion: dance, shaking, swaying.
3. Consciousness-altering plant medicines that are inhaled or swallowed.
4. A mixture of all or some of these.

These methods involve the engagement of the senses of sound, touch, taste and smell to bring about sourcing. Physical sight is normally obscured by mask, blindfold or by closing the eyes, thus enabling 'the inner sight' to be fully operative. During sourcing and the journey itself, the subtle senses are awakened and fully employed: intense tastes, smells, sounds and feelings are also experienced along with extraordinary visions.

This book does not deal with hallucinogens as a means of sourcing for a simple reason: these should not be used in

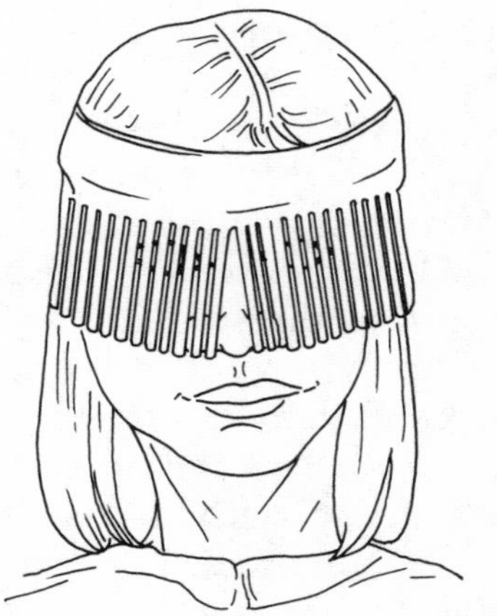

Figure 2. An eye-fringe

shamanism without the presence and guidance of a teacher who knows their potency and effect, and who is personally experienced in engaging with the spirits of and in travelling the pathways which lead from such plants. In a society such as ours which regards drug-use as recreational rather than sacred, the walker between the worlds is better off using simpler and equally effective methods which have no side-effects.

Eye-covering

The first aid to sourcing is an eye-covering: a simple scarf which doesn't impede your breathing will do. Dim light or darkness is best for this work and, while it is possible to journey in bright light, it is very difficult to begin sourcing without an eye-covering. If you are going to shamanize by movement or dancing, then an eye-fringe is helpful.

The Rattle

The common instruments of the shaman are percussive ones like the drum or rattle which produce repetitive sounds. The shaking of the rattle represents the life-spark itself. It is the first toy given to babies in many cultures; instinctively we understand the importance of the 'voice' of the rattle which 'speaks' in the hands of the infant. It can be equally effective in the hands of a shaman.

Even though you may intend to use a tape for shamanic journeying you should acquire at least a rattle since it can be used even when a drum is inappropriate. The rattle is used in a variety of ways: to evoke power, to accompany power-songs and dancing, to speak to the spirits of a sick person by being shaken over them, to divine and seek out information. It is a primary aid to sourcing. Its body represents the immensity of inner space, the vast womb of the universe, while the handle represents our connection with it. As the seeds, stones or fragments within the body are agitated, their motion, velocity and sound reconstellate the networks of the cosmic web within our remembrance and perception.

Among the Desana Indians of the Amazon, the cosmic symbolism of the rattle is even more dramatically obvious: the

gourd represents the womb, and the handle represents the phallus, while the tiny pieces of quartz crystal within the gourd represent the energy of the universe; when it is shaken in darkness, the crystals spark against each other and through slits illuminate the darkness like stars.[4]

Rattles are used throughout the Americas, while shakers, clappers and noise-makers of different kinds have been used all over the world. The ancient Egyptians and modern Copts use metal *sistra* (rattles), while ancient Irish vision-seers used branches from which bells were hung. Sometimes a rattling sound-source is part of the shaman's costume, with metallic bells, jingles and ornaments sewn on to the robe or belt.

It is quite easy to fashion your own rattle. But if you are unable to do so, then there are many kinds available from music supply shops and ethnic stores. Choose one with a handle. Listen to its voice: it should be pleasing to your ears, with a sharp, bright sound which is capable of many subtle changes, depending on how it is shaken. Avoid those big fat gourds which sound as though they are full of waterlogged cigarette butts. My husband was recently given a pre-Columbian clay rattle which had been broken and mended so many times it had no voice left. We filled it with tomato-seeds and resealed the top with clay and now, though very delicate and used only for planting ceremonies, it has a strong voice for our own times.

Drumming

Drums are used worldwide for ceremonial purposes, but the shaman's frame-drum, played with a beater, is the most useful kind of drum for sourcing. This is constructed of a wooden frame over which an animal skin is pegged, tied or tacked. The frame may be taken to represent the universe and all that is, while the skin can symbolize the energy, power and spirit of the cosmic web; the beater may represent ourselves, while the different rhythms of the hands or drum-stick represent the many pathways between the worlds which we set up by our interaction with them.

The frame-drum is played all over the world, in the Middle East, North Africa, Europe and the circumpolar regions, as well

as in the Americas. Drum symbolisms and usage vary considerably across the world, but some of the most interesting are found in Lapland among the Saami people where the drumskins are decorated with complex designs depicting the landscape of the otherworlds, and symbols of the shaman's spirits, pathways and helpers.[5] These drums were also used for divination.

The drum is one of the most powerful instruments of sourcing. It compels attention as its steady beat and body-moving rhythm build into a sustained, resonant song. It is no wonder Siberian shamans call their drum their 'horse'. As the drum gallops, so sourcing begins and the soul is carried away upon its quest.

Drumming 'allows shamans to align their brain-waves with the pulse of the earth'.[6] Surveys relating brain-wave patterns and drum-beat frequencies have been made, suggesting that theta waves of four to eight cycles per second relate to shamanic sourcing, as well as to dreaming and sudden insights.[7] Theta waves are actually accessed not only by the rate of the drum-beat, but also by the harmonies of the notes produced by the beater against the drum-head. This subtle web of harmonics is appreciable in any instrument, whether it be percussive, wind or stringed.

When listening to a drum, the journeyer listens not to the tap-tap of the drum-stick but to the resonance of the drum-skin and the music that it makes. Concentrating solely upon the drum-beat often *impedes* sourcing. Around the rim of your drum a galaxy of sound is waiting to be revealed. The rainbow harmonics which a drum-skin can emit, hollow out our ears in many different ways: I have known a single drum sound like a symphony orchestra, birdsong, a choir, a speaking voice, fireworks and even siege cannons, on one notable occasion! The true harmonics of any drum cannot be appreciated until the skin is 'drummed in' and warmed up. In ancient Sumeria as well as in modern Haiti, drums were given names at special dedication ceremonies, because they receive their souls at this time. This also happens in modern Haitian Voudun practices.[8]

If you decide to buy a drum, do not buy the cheapest. Bear in mind the following: most animal-skin drums go flaccid in damp weather and need heating; a very heavy drum is impossible to hold up for long without damping the resonance by

resting it upon your body or the ground; a single-beaded frame-drum is most portable and useful for this work. Animal-skin drums have the best and most responsive voices; vegetarian shamans can use synthetic-skin drums – these are widely available.

Other sound-sources may be readily used to the same effect: it is reported that a Saami shaman, temporarily without his drum, picked up a firkin lid and beat it with his knife.[9] Natural sounds, such as water flowing or dripping, bird calls, the wind in the trees, the clattering of reeds or wind-chimes, or attuning to the heart-beat can and have been used. Natural sound-sources are better than synthesized sounds. While it is possible to journey without sound, attuning to the rhythms of breath or by swaying, the sourcing is generally not so deep. Using such natural sounds or silences for sourcing is best attempted when you have first learned how to source using rattle, drum or voice.

I have used a variety of different things for sourcing, especially singing and stringed instruments of many kinds; at need and without any shamanic equipment, I have even used the sustained motor-noise of expel-air fans and cars, and even a pencil on the back of notebook!

All sound has vibration. Remember that all live sourcing-sounds are likely to be overheard by others; drumming is especially pervasive. Use of a drumming or rattling tape with headphones is a good compromise in urban situations, but do not become too dependent on canned sounds; give yourself a good live sound journey at least once a month. If you use a sourcing tape, ensure that it has a good clear call-back signal that you can recognize. A list of good sourcing tapes is given in the Resources.

Dancing and Singing

Rattles and drums are often accompanied by singing, dancing or both. These are often regarded as auxiliary aids, yet they are also primary ways of sourcing. Dance has always been a means of accessing the otherworlds, especially whirling or spinning. We are more familiar with the social aspects of dancing, but many of these have their roots in communal ceremonies which

reconnect people to their cosmological origins. (We shall be speaking more about the shamanic nature of dance in Chapters 4, 5, and 6.)

Our voice expresses our soul, and its tone, timbre and mood mirror our being to the universe. The burdens, sorrows or repressions of people can be heard in the restrictive and un-released nature of their voices.[10] Most people are aware of this and are consequently self-conscious about their own voices because they are so revealing. The burdens of world-sorrow may cling to the human voice yet, when we sing to the rattle or drum, when we seek to commune with our spirits and give them a voice, something quite miraculous occurs. A massive vocal release can be registered by the listener as the voice drops its cares and enters into the chorus of the universal song. We have few social frameworks in which we can sing and, unless there is some alcoholic lubrication to encourage them, most people prefer not to sing, so:

Permission to use your free singing voice is here given.

Rattles and drums may be wonderful ways of sourcing, but your own voice travels everywhere with you; it is your own free gift and a major means of sourcing.

The human voice seems to have become ashamed of itself since the substitution of the written for the oral tradition. Once, all laws, myths, customs and histories were stored in memory and recited aloud. Among indigenous peoples, the oral tra-dition still has primacy. For them, the utterance of the strict truth is a tribal necessity, since the sacred teachings are im-parted by the memory-keepers by word of mouth or in long incantations which are nothing less than a formal recreation of the world. These teachings, garnered from the otherworlds by a succession of walkers between the worlds, are commonly recited as an act of healing. Among the Navajo Indians of North America, such chants are immensely long, often lasting many nights; they must be performed with exactitude or the chant becomes invalidated.

The use of chanting, where the voice is often mid-way be-tween speech and singing, is common to shamanism. Specific chants are taught to shamans by their spirits; these chants are regarded as sacred regalia, to be held in trust by the shaman

and her successors inalienably. Chants of healing, of welcoming the spirits or of calling upon the powers of the universe soon become part of the personal sacred regalia of any walker between the worlds. These are the songs by which you will restore the human voice to its rightful task and sing the wandering soul back home.

Shamanic Assistants

This book has been written for use by a lone person, but shamanism has always been practised in a social context and the shaman invariably has a companion or assistant. For example, the Saami *noaidi* was often accompanied on his journeys by a women's choir which maintained the sound-source during his spirit-flight. One or more of them would watch over his body as he sourced, while the others guided his soul.[11]

If you do practise with a friend, ensure that he is as fully instructed as yourself. If you are going to make a journey and send forth part of your soul to the otherworlds, then you want to be confident that your physical and spiritual well-being are in good hands. Your companion must be able to sustain the sound-source competently and continuously, because he is responsible for the depth of your sourcing. If you're not sure how long you need to journey, then prearrange a hand signal to indicate to your companion that you've concluded. Make sure that the call-back signal is clearly distinct from the regular sound-source rhythm, so that you are called home safely.

Remember that all instruments used for sacred purposes should be treated with respect; they are the voices of the spirits and the vehicles of your sourcing. They shouldn't be used for mundane or frivolous purposes. When you have chosen a drum or rattle and have introduced yourself to your instrument as described in Practice 9, you may wish to dedicate it to shamanic work in a simple ceremony.

Sourcing enables us to ride the spirit wind, to fly free upon the cosmic web and walk between the worlds. It is a powerful way of working which should be treated with respect and used at appropriate times and in appropriate circumstances. The transfer of consciousness from the mundane to the otherworldly

is often sudden and shocking. One minute here you are drumming, rattling or singing; the next, you are away, intensely aware of other worlds and beings. This is why it is so important to have a clear grasp of your purpose and a full knowledge of where you intend to travel before you start. Ensure that you fully understand this before proceeding with the following practices.

Practice 9: Rattling

Take a rattle with a handle and experiment with it. Try shaking it at first, using only a small wrist action. Try shaking it two or three times a second for full effect: this is a rough estimate which you will adjust for yourself. Stand with eyes closed or covered, letting the rattle speak. Try it loudly and softly; shake it deliberately in straight strokes, shake it spirally with circulating strokes – note the sound changes. Now stop and formulate your purpose, which is – to meet and acknowledge the spirit of your rattle. Rattle for at least ten minutes and go with the sound, letting whatever impressions strike you unfold like a story or an imaged landscape. If you have a strong desire to move or sing with the rattle, do so. You may encounter the spirits of the plants, trees or minerals from which your rattle is made. Thank and praise them. Write down what you experienced.

Practice 10: Drumming

Take a drum and beater and explore the drum-skin: which parts of the skin have the best dynamics and resonances? You will find that the areas near the frame's edge are more musical than the middle. How hard or soft do you need to beat? Experiment with tempo, using slow deliberate strokes of one beat per two seconds, moderate strokes of one beat a second, faster strokes of two to three beats a second. When you know your drum a little better and the skin has been warmed up from use, cover your eyes and stand with drum and beater in a safe space. (It is important that any delicate or dangerous objects are clear of your space.) Stop and consider your purpose,

which is to meet and acknowledge the spirit of your drum. Drumming is a very strong way of sourcing which may take you very deep, very quickly, but keep your purpose in mind and follow the unfolding of any images, patterns, impressions or sounds without dissecting them. If yours is an animal-skin drum, you may encounter that animal's spirit. Thank it for giving its skin for this purpose, listen to its voice, acknowledge its help and wisdom. You may wish to move, dance, sing or call as you drum; allow this happen.

Practice 11: Singing

You may already have sung or chanted in the practices above, in combination with rattle or drum. This time, you will chant without any other aid but darkness. Stand upright, cover your eyes and put a finger in each ear. Now take a deep breath and sing or chant a lovely open O in the middle and comfortable region of your voice. Let the breath come easily through the hole of the O, letting your lips vibrate gently as you do so. The sound is centred deep within you. Breathe in again and repeat, this time taking one finger out of your ear. Get used to the free vibration of your own voice until you can chant without covering your ears.

Now bring to mind the cosmic web which permeates the universe. With eyes covered, gradually allow your voice to describe the cosmic web in sound – if words or syllables also come then let them – but let your voice express the cosmic web in whatever way it wishes to do so. Focus entirely upon the cosmic web and how you sense it, not upon your voice. If the results do not seem coherently song-like, don't worry: this is not a voice competition. Maintain this for at least five minutes. You may find that your own 'chant of the cosmic web' arises from this, a power-song which will help remind and reconnect you with the web at times when you are feeling less connected. Record this as best you can, on tape or by simple notation.

3. THE MIRRORED MESSAGE

I see everything all at once, without the delays of succession, and each detail is equal and equally lucid . . . Yet even as I look, as

if to remember forever this pristine world, already the forms become modulated into meanings, cease to be forms.

The Voodoo Gods
Maya Deren

This account by a white initiate of the Haitian shamanic tradition exactly expresses the experience of shamanic perception, which is subtly different from mundane perception. It is with the heightened perception of an artist or poet that the shaman experiences the otherworlds. This includes the simultaneous transmission of a great knot of imagery or material as well as the sense of being part of an enormous collage whose details are distinct yet inter-related. This inside/outside vision is common to all seers.

In Gaelic tradition, the second sight is called *do shealladh* or 'two seeings' and the Hawaiians call it *papalua*, 'double vision' or 'double knowledge'. The physical and subtle realities are seen at the same time. Fortunately, most of us do not possess this ability in ordinary life, for the involuntary stimulation of the second sight is a terrible affliction as well as a great gift. In shamanism, during sourcing, it is possible to have specific and voluntary sight of the subtle reality which surrounds a subject, whether it be the cause of an illness, or the hidden motivations surrounding any project in which we might be involved. It is to obtain such knowledge that shamans seek to enter the otherworlds; for though shamans may also be seers, most are not able to achieve the 'two seeings' without the aid of sourcing.

We access the otherworlds in order to discover knowledge, healing or help. All knowledge is discoverable in the cosmic web of the worlds: earliest human comprehension of the universe was brought about by the work of shamans accessing the cosmic web. Whatever is unknown may be found within the web.

But before sourcing begins, the shaman must assess the needs and possibilities, for the results of the journey are dependent upon the purpose which underlies it. One of the earliest of purposes for journeying may have been hunting, the locating of herds of animals by shamanic means. This is still done among the Inuit in the ice-locked Arctic regions, where the shaman will journey to the goddess of the sea in times of

hunger, requesting that she unlock the game penned in her house that the people may eat.[12]

In times and places where there are no books, no prior bodies of knowledge concerning the world, the shaman is the major means of discovering the unknown. It has been suggested that the vastly separated islands of the Polynesian triangle may have been colonized as a result of the *ariki* or shaman-chiefs shamanically journeying. By imbibing the narcotic *kava* (*Piper methysticum*) they discovered in subtle reality navigational courses which were then followed in actuality, across wide, unknown seas.[13] How many of the ancient world's staggering achievements have been suggested by the spirits through shamanic journey? The precise cosmological alignments of British megalithic monuments such as Stonehenge, Callanish and Avebury, and their technically arduous construction, have been much discussed, with explanations ranging from giant builders to alien construction companies from outer space, posited to detract attention from the real issue: that human beings somehow conceived the idea and physically achieved it with the help of the spirits.

Governments rarely invest their country's resources and talents in the exploration of something which, because it is not physically apprehended, is presumed to be non-existent. It is for such reasons that we have highly sophisticated technological and scientific knowledge and an almost total ignorance of subtle-reality technology. Our society now lacks the simple, daily structures by which our world and the otherworlds are bridged. We are curious about subtle reality, but few people are accomplished enough to find out.

We are used to thinking of knowledge as an empirical thing, which should be gained for its own sake, as a theoretical adjunct to our cultural achievement. Subtle reality may be studied by para-psychologists in a purely scientific way, but it does not yield its secrets to theorists, any more than the heart of music can reveal itself to musical mathematicians, who quantify notes and measure vibratory ratios. Subtle reality reveals itself to shamans because they journey into it with real needs. This enables them to become true technicians of subtle reality. Shamanic technology is often derided by theorists for its imprecise and subjective nature. The writer, Alan Ereira[14] re-

counts the story of an Amazonian shaman who had heard an alarming radio report of a then current world situation and was very worried by it. The way he interpreted what he heard was that apparently two men called USA and USSR were fighting over a prostitute called Israel who was giving birth to bombs which would destroy the world. With his shamanic peers, the shaman worked hard to lock the bombs inside a spirit ice-mountain where they could cool down. Although the shaman's interpretation of events is simplistic and symbolic in our eyes, nevertheless his shamanic action was successful because he had understood the nature of the world's need.

Framing your Question

The motivation of our journeys is of paramount importance. If our intentions are clear, then our sourcing will be apposite: we will be patched into the cosmic web in ways which help heal and reconnect. If we decide to make a journey just because we haven't done so for a while, without a purpose, our sourcing will be aimless and the journey without cohesion. It is as point-less as setting out in your car without any clear destination.

While shamanism can and does provide solutions to every-day problems, it is particularly helpful in issues which seem-ingly have no mundane solutions. If you have a headache, then you can take some aspirin; but if you keep rerunning a trau-matic incident over and over in your head, then you need a different form of help. Similarly, you can meet with someone with whom you've had a misunderstanding, but if that person died last week, you have no mundane means of effecting rec-onciliation. The analgesic of psychotherapy may be able to help you cope with such difficulties, but it is rarely able to communicate actively the powerful and effective answers of Spirit.

The ways in which we frame our purpose are important. Regard each quest or question as a key to one of the doors which leads between the worlds. Does your key fit the key-hole? You will be asking or seeking advice of your companion spirits, so the purpose must be a clear one. The following guidelines are offered to help you frame your purpose.

1. What is at issue? For example 'organizing my time'.

2. What kind of help are you requesting? For example 'How can my free time be organized more effectively?'

3. If it involves others, frame your purpose so that benefit accrues to them, not only to yourself. For example 'How can the free time which Felix and I have be organized in mutually beneficial ways?' Ensure that your purpose is not manipulative as in 'How can I get Felix out of the house so that I can enjoy myself?'

4. Is your question simple enough? If your issue has many correlatives, frame your question to include them all, or journey on each in turn: 'In what ways can I learn swimming, French and cycling in my limited free time?' It is wise to stick to one issue at a time rather than tacking on peripheral issues to the main agenda. If your issue is complex and the phraseology would be too unwieldy, you can frame it like this: 'Please advise me on organizing my time'.

5. Is your issue open to spiritual help? If you frame your question '*How can I* create more time in my crowded schedule?' you have closed the issue by asking only how *you yourself* can make changes. A better way of putting this issue would be, 'In what ways *can time be made* in my crowded life?'

The shamanic journey gives us a new slant on intractable old problems, proffering solutions which may afterwards seem obvious. Below (Practice 12), you are invited to create your own journey checklist.

What is Journeying Like?

We do not journey alone. During sourcing, we call upon our spirit companions to aid us and we always travel with at least one ally wherever we go. Our trust in our shamanic allies is our lifeline, ensuring that we do not become lost or confused; they help us to make firm decisions and encourage our good judgement.

Journeying is not unlike lucid dreaming wherein the dreamer is enabled to become interactive with the dream, rather than a mere passive observer of events. In journeys, different scenarios

or sequences often appear distinct as the acts of a play, with different locations and characters, but purposeful just like mundane journeys.

Our abilities during journeying become subtle: we can fly through the air, swim undersea, change shape or size, travel at superspeeds, experience timelessness or the superimposition of different times and places. All the dimensions familiar to you from folk and faery story are here borne out in personal experience.

Trusting the journey that you take is sometimes hard, because we have been brought up to believe in only one reality. Common fears are: 'Am I making this up?' 'Did I put that jaguar in the tree?' 'I must have an overactive imagination to see that!' People who are alive to archetypal symbolism are often disbelievingly astounded by their own archetypal experiences.

Shamanic journeys are not to be confused with journeys using guided imagery, where a scripted scenario or inner landscape is recited by a leader and meditatively travelled through by listeners. Most often, these non-traditional scenarios are invented ones. In traditional training of shamans on the other hand and in hermetic and religious schools actual journeys of shamans and mystics are used as models or examples. The pathways of the qabalistic tree of life, are one example, as are those of the Tibetan after death state, *bardo*, which teaches the ways between life and death. In my own Celtic tradition, I sometimes use 'soul-leadings', traditional scenarios and stories, to help lead students to specific locations and teachers. Such work is helpful for showing the way but it is not intended to be slavishly reproduced and followed to the exclusion of personal experience.

The shamanic journey unfolds in its own ways, without script. But that doesn't mean to say that you as the walker between the worlds are without any map. In Chapters 4, 5 and 6 we will familiarize ourselves with the three worlds, and the waymarks, doorways and pathways which take us thither.

Some students begin to enjoy shamanic journeying for its own sake, becoming virtual journey-junkies who zip between realities like otherworld tourists, trying to lap up all the sights and experiences, especially at the start of their shamanic work. Regulate your own practice by keeping your journeying to a minimum of four to six journeys a month; this way, you will

be better able to understand and assimilate your experiences. Your spirits will indeed help you, but if you are always appearing to ask their advice yet not allowing any time to implement it in your life, then you are hardly accepting or validating such help.

The shaman must be able to bring information, healing and power into our world in ways that actually inform, heal and empower. Unless this happens, all shamanizing is a waste of time. The implementation of advice is very dependent upon your understanding and interpretation of your journey.

Shamanism is not a one-way street. Journeying is not a form of escapism. If you journey merely to avoid your problems and to enjoy a little otherworldly sightseeing, you will surely encounter your mundane responsibilities in their subtle forms. Indeed, your spirits may place these encounters in your way, in order to help you deal with them. This also happens if you have failed to properly implement your allies' advice and go to make another journey: they may overturn your new issue in order to encourage you to deal with the last one.

Paradox, riddle and cosmic humour thread the shamanic experience with sparks of light. Many students of shamanism are thrown by its random humour and sharp paradoxes. In direct opposition to the physical reality norm where we work seriously and play playfully, shamans learn to play seriously, and to work playfully.

When the spirits appear as divine clowns they do so in order to make us vulnerable. Excessive self-awareness or a bloated ego preclude sourcing; we have to learn to forget ourselves, to empathize deeply with our spirits, letting our separate self-hood sink down like an ebbing tide.

When we source, we draw upon the imagination. Our society has taught us to distrust the imagination. In shamanism we must understand that imagination is a faculty of the soul, just as our sense of touch is a faculty of our body.

When our ordinary modes of thought and comprehension are turned on their heads, we are able to access 'lateral thought' and universal understanding. These impart rich gifts and ingenious solutions.

Some Examples of Journeys

Here are some sample journeys, drawn from the experience of myself and clients, to give you a flavour of their variety, wisdom and humour.

This first journey is one I took in order to ask how the spiritual and the everyday worlds can be practically combined.

> I arrived in the Middleworld and found myself a little up my tree where my teachers and animals sat on the platform of a tree-house. I asked my question and was shown a garden through a tall hedge. Within were the four tall, strong faery women of statuesque beauty and dignity. I was told that they came to protect us from soul-loss. They said we were not to let anyone take the power of Spirit from everyday life, for we were all guardians of Spirit. We were to defend the indwelling Spirit of all beings. Then I was shown the stars and the zone of Sophia, the atmosphere which shrouds our earth. The faery women instructed me to tell people that we must send up our deepest aspirations for the universe nightly to this boundary of the earth's soul that all beings might imbibe, dream and be nourished by the common pool of loving thoughts gathered there. We must bless the elements, and be aware of the messages of our bodies daily. We must dance to help keep our sense of connection between the worlds. If we maintained these things then all beings would learn to see these connections. The blessings of the elements were repeated to me in this vision:
>
> Blessed be the precious and preserving air, by which we are given life.
> Blessed be the precious and preserving fire, by which we are warmed.
> Blessed be the precious and preserving water, by which we are cleansed.
> Blessed be the precious and preserving earth, by which we are sustained.
> Blessed be the precious and preserving Spirit that is within and around me.

In accordance with instructions, I subsequently published this journey in our quarterly newsletter and shared it with students as a spiritual invitation for all to participate in the work of the faery people.

The second journey was taken by Malcolm, an independent

film maker, whose urgent question was 'in what ways can I next earn money?' He had been unemployed for a few months and was getting desperate.

A very confused journey to the Upperworld where I encountered water buffalo grazing at the tops of trees near a Disney castle. I asked my teacher my question and he rode with me on Cloud Horse (Malcolm's guardian animal) to the cave of the sun where I was bathed in liquid gold. This was very consoling as we had ridden through bewildering images of violence and birth. Afterwards we came to the most perfect house on a hill. Here lay the salamander or dragon which I'd seen in my morning's dream. It seemed to guard remembrance of my earthly home's security and enchantment.

Cloud Horse then took me to the Middleworld where I entered a world of wacky cartoon thirties gangsters. I asked who they were and they declared themselves 'the media mafia'. I had to fight them. In the ensuing chase, I went up a spiral staircase where I saw a beautiful woman looking out across a skyline for something. Time slowed completely. I followed her gaze which was like a lighthouse's beam only solid. Cloud Horse and I trotted across it and found a clock with animals, rather than numbers on it. It was at 4 o'clock, represented by a camel. I asked my question again and the camel said I would be working next in animation, but that I wouldn't be contracted again until next April. I went crazy then and demanded to know how I would live. For answer a seagull flew from the clock-face and started scavenging. My teacher appeared on the skyline and bade me go back.

Malcolm found this difficult to interpret. Subsequently, he realized that he was indeed scavenging just like a seagull, doing odd bits of freelance work for different companies, including preparing storyboards for a stop-frame animation short. He signed his next firm contract the following April, which was a long nine months after this journey. He got through this time by trusting his allies and continuing to journey for strength and help. The journey had been helpful in providing timeless and continuous support when he was confused, and suggesting that he not be over-proud at accepting whatever crumbs of work came his way.

The third journey is also work related. Janet took up her shamanic studies with great enthusiasm and received strong instructions on her journeys that she should pursue her studies

even further. She was also contemplating a return to work and had been offered a long-desired post at her *alma mater* university, however she was worried it would interfere with her shamanic work. Her question was 'should I take up this position?'

> My journey took me to Egypt, along with my animal. Most significantly, I met with one of my inner guides, the goddess Sekhmet. As I looked at her I was taken by complete surprise as the snake which sat prominently upon her sun-crown came alive and grew in seconds to fill my entire field of vision. He mangled and then devoured first my face and then my entire head. I recovered quickly only to find myself transformed into a sleek and beautiful lioness with two heads.
>
> One head was ravenous and hungry, and tried to pull my entire body backward in a search to fill her hunger. The other head, quiet and serene, ignored the agitated movement and kept her eyes focused on the blinding light before her, beyond the temple. It is her movement that quietly, without effort, brought the lioness to merge with the light.

Janet interprets her journey as follows. 'I take this to be a re-enforcement of my commitment to study shamanism. I have been turned into various animals on journeys but this particular lioness with two heads seems very significant. The one head looking back to my former position, and the other looking forward to a new, though as yet unmanifested, career. That the goddess should have to mangle and devour me in order that finally I see clearly what my uncertainty is about is very much in line with my training. Sekhmet gave me very clear understanding of my real insecurity about moving ahead into the unknown. The hungry head seeks the security of a known situation, hence its seduction.' It is also worth mentioning that Sekhmet is a lion-headed goddess, and that being transformed or having one's body altered is a common shamanic theme. Janet subsequently turned down the offered post and is continuing to explore many different aspects of shamanism.

You may be surprised at the amount of trust and credence placed by these walkers between the worlds in their journeys. We are so used to validating advice only if it is given by experts, that such seeming self-reliance seems shocking or impertinent. We are not obliged to follow the advice of our allies, but our journeys do inculcate a deeper sense of authority for our actions if we try to follow that advice. As you will see from

these journeys, trust in our spiritual allies and knowledge of the three worlds are intrinsically required before we set out walking the worlds.

Some Journey Problems

Before continuing, I would like to offer some help for those who experience a failure to journey. Some people find journeying very difficult and unproductive. The causes are most often over-expectation and an inability to let go of conscious control. If you are a person who is used to a very structured life-style or if you live in your head more than in your body, journeying is no doubt quite hard. A very few people cannot journey at all but that does not stop them from living a life that is connected with the universe.

Others often fail to read the signposts and identify them as such; such people believe they have not journeyed when in fact they have. Misleading expectations are often the trouble here, for journeying is not necessarily terribly exotic and usually unfolds so organically that the margin between journeying and dream or mind-wandering is difficult to establish. In such cases, *treat everything you experience during the period of your journey as information*. If you spend the whole twenty minutes touring your garden or being shown a plant, then ask how this experience related to the journey's purpose.

Here is a quick checklist of possible problems and solutions.

1. *Nothing is happening.* What's happening in the nothing-ness? Record your experiences, however vestigial. Maybe only one bit makes sense. Relate *any* feelings or impressions to your issue.

2. *I experience things episodically or erratically, not staying in one place for very long.* Are all your journeys like this? When you learn to let go and trust the experience, the 'story' will begin to join up.

3. *I become easily distracted and end up thinking instead of journeying.* Check physical comfort and minimize sound-sources likely to distract. (For example take the telephone off the hook, ask children to play elsewhere or more quietly.) When you feel yourself drifting, check in with your guardian animal.

4. *I fall asleep when I journey.* Check that your chosen time is a good one – for example not at end of day or when emotionally fraught. Normally if you sleep during a journey, the call-back signal will bring you awake; if your sourcing is very deep, you may pass from journeying into a deep sleep from which you will awake.

5. *I keep getting the same experience.* Have you dealt with the agenda of previous journey/s? How is the experience related to your journey's purpose?

6. *My experiences are so interesting that I don't get any further.* Don't analyse things during your journey, just observe, inter-relate or act and pass on.

7. *I have difficulty coming back.* Check that you can recognize the call-back signal and practise grounding methods (see page 10) on a regular basis before journeying again, or get a friend to call you back. In extreme cases, set up a muffled alarm clock in the same room, but not right next to you.

8. *My spirit helpers don't talk to me.* Check whether they are showing you things, using body-language or speaking directly to you without words.

9. *I can't go down my Underworld opening* (see Chapter 5). You may find that Underworld journeys are too difficult; choose an ordinary reality location as your chosen start-point and journey outwards from there, taking a Middleworld journey. People with claustrophobia, unhealed birth-trauma or deep-seated anxieties may find Underworld journeying impossible and should revert to Middleworld ones.

10. *I'm sure I'm making all this up.* The ease with which most people journey disconcerts them; surely it should be more complicated that this? Most people are able to slip straight into journeying but find difficulty accepting what they experience. Accept this ease with the unconditional gladness with which you greet a fine day, as a great gift.

11. *My experiences seem very two dimensional or colourless.* Many people with good mental control find it hard to let go enough. Allowing sourcing to happen is often unconsciously resisted. Try changing your method of journeying from a passive to an active one – dancing and singing rather than lying down with a tape-recorder.

12. *My head is full of babble*. Distractions happen to us all. The trick is to forget yourself, and indulge your willing suspension of disbelief: we are all used to forgetting ourselves when we watch a film or a play, becoming identified with the experience of the characters before us, so you are already able to do this. Concentrate on the harmonic vibration of your sound-source. Bring your purpose to mind and watch for the next part of the journey. Become more aware of what you are physically experiencing in your journey location.

13. *My 'book of dreams/symbols' says that dreaming/seeing teeth means 'great loss'*. Correlate your findings closely with *your own experience* and the intention of your journey. Don't worry about what Big Walking Bear says, or what Jung wrote, or what your therapist told you – *your* experience is the final arbiter!

14. *I lost/forgot my animal as I journeyed*. Losing or forgetting an animal is usually a sign of ungroundedness. Read Chapter 4. Always travel with one ally and keep checking for their whereabouts.

Finally, if nothing seems to be happening, check whether you are not trying too hard. Rest, do something else and try again another time. Remember, there are no correct ways of sourcing or journeying, only many ways. The procedures outlined in this book are guidelines or handholds only. Whatever you experience when you source will be unique to you; no one can direct what you experience on a journey, it will unfold in its own way. Any attempt by you to direct events will usually be immediately apparent: the energy, verve and organic nature of sourcing will go and it will become two dimensional and vague. How we understand the results of our journey will be explored in more detail.

Permission to experience and welcome the unexpected is here given.

Practice 12: Journey Checklist

As you have been reading, you have probably thought of many issues which are currently thronging your life on which you

need advice, help or healing. Make a list of some current personal concerns; these may include some of the following:

Work, relationships, spiritual vocation or direction, health.
Mysterious occurrences: 'Why do I always faint on planes?
  How can this be prevented in future?'
A lack of power or Spirit.
Inappropriate or unbalanced power.

You will have opportunities for journeying on these and other issues as you proceed.

Practice 13: Relaxation

Journeying requires good relaxation combined with clear and alert attention. If you suffer from problems with sourcing or journeying you have probably omitted to relax first. Relaxation is something we all theoretically recognize but seldom personally implement. Lie down on a firm surface, with your head and knees supported by cushions. If your space is limited, lie on the floor on your back with your shins and feet resting on a chair or settee. Be physically comfortable. Breathe in deeply and allow your body to fill with power-giving air. Breathe out deeply, allowing tiredness, tension and worry to pass out into the universe to be recycled as new energy. Feel the universe breathing you in and out. Breathe into all parts of your body, until you feel a warm looseness in your limbs. Feel the love and power of Spirit permeate your being. Let your focus go from yourself and experience the filaments of the cosmic web holding you up.

3.   Spirit Helpers

There are two things a person must do for himself or herself: find a teacher and choose a friend.

The Talmud

1.   KEEPERS OF MEMORY

It is absurd for men to vaunt their superiority over the animals when, in matters of great importance, it is they who are our teachers: the spider for weaving and mending; the swallow for architecture; the swan and nightingale for singing.

Democritus

WHEN WE BEGIN TO JOURNEY into the three worlds, our first task is to find and be befriended by otherworldly allies, spirits or helpers. These will be our guides and travelling companions for all future journeys that we take.

Many spirit helpers already stand by you, waiting to be called and recognized. With some you may work for years, others may pay only fleeting visits. If you look through your own address book, you'll see different kinds of people listed there: close friends, acquaintances, family, experts, companies, contact-people. Your various connections with spirit helpers will vary as much as does your contact with the people around you. There will always be the very special friend, the circle of close friends who always support you, as well as a wider network of companions upon whom you call at need. You will

need and find very many kinds of allies in your experience: mineral, plant, animal, human and non-human.

The Animal-Human Relationship

Animals connect us to the ladder of life-forms which leads back through time. They are the guardians of pre-human memory, inheritors of wisdom and teachers in their own right. Western philosophy often regards animals as 'just' the bridge between other life-forms and human beings, with humans at the head of the evolutionary pyramid and the food-chain.

The animal world is dependent upon both the mineral and plant realms for its existence. Animals and humans inherit the cellular and genetic treasury of both mineral and plant realms but they have complex brains and behaviour. Animals have mobility, which most plants and minerals lack; they form family relationships. Animals and humans are very close in kinship, as the Koran (Surah VI) reminds us: 'There is not an animal that lives on the earth, nor a being that flies on its wings, but forms part of communities like you.'

Our attitudes to animals are very revealing. Sentimental-ization and exploitation of animals are forms of animal abuse which purposely diminish their innate power and increase our own. The Malaysian Chewong people have a sacred law forbid-ding humans to tease or laugh at animals:[1] one wonders what they would make of Disneyland, performing circus animals or genetic manipulation.

Many domesticated species live with us as pets: where the individual spirit of the animal is respected, we can learn much from each other. The captivity and servitude imposed upon wild animals is less easy to tolerate or excuse. The word 'animal' derives from the Latin *anima* or soul, as if to remind us that human beings too are also animals who have souls. Animals are infinitely patient of our human clumsiness, our inability to read clear sensory signals and to comprehend the simplest soul-communication. It was the great naturalist, Konrad Lorenz, who wrote that it was 'animal politeness' never to stare another animal in the eyes; he himself always gazed at his animal friends with soft, unfocused eyes that encompassed their whole being.

Many people find using any part of an animal for nourishment or clothing repugnant. Vegetarians and vegans are rightly repulsed by the lack of true reciprocity between ourselves and animals, whom we regard as a commodity rather than as living beings. Factory farming and inhumane slaughter reflect the desacralization of our society and our separation from the cosmic web. People frequently ask whether meat-eating and shamanism are compatible. There is no one right answer to this; it depends on many factors. Our teeth proclaim us to be an omnivorous species, whose ancestors have eaten many food-stuffs in order to stay alive. Our attitude to our food is what counts. If you eat meat, you should acknowledge the animal's sacrifice; if you eat vegetables, it follows that you should do the same. If you live in the polar regions, like the Inuit or the Saami, then you are totally dependent upon animals for food and clothing since no vegetation grows for the best part of the year. The vegetarian option is not open to people living in these regions.

In his expedition to the Iglulik Eskimos in 1921–24, Knud Rasmussen reported one hunter as saying that, 'The greatest peril of life lies in the fact that human food consists entirely of souls. All the creatures we have to kill and eat, all those we have to strike down and destroy to make clothes for ourselves, have souls, as we have.'[2] Indigenous peoples who live by hunting or fishing, cope by employing rituals of respect and gratitude; they use every part of an animal, they do not kill breeding animals or those with young, they do not kill more than they need.

In our own time, animals are acting as important teachers, patiently enduring and revealing the truths which humankind is ignoring: that each life-form has its purpose in the universe, that certain wise memories are in danger of being lost from physical reality if we continue to eradicate certain species, that human beings are also animals, dependent upon and part of the food-chain.

We regard our human species as a totally different order of beings; however, we are merely more developed forms of the animal world. Animals have formed the basic template of human existence in both shape and behaviour, but humans have further developed these: our mobility has turned us from quadrupeds into bipeds, and we have learned the ability to

combine not just in family groups but in other social relationships. Humans have developed brains which not only reason,
but which can communicate and influence their environment.
But we still have to learn how to interact with other species in
a responsible way.

Within humankind we can see traces of many life-forms: our
bones have the density of the mineral world; our internal
organs have the liquidity and cell-structure of the plant world;
our outer physical shell betrays traces of earlier animal species
in our scale-like skins, in our nails and hair. Our brains have
the mineral realm's ability to create crystalline order, the plant
realm's ability to intuit and broadcast meaning in our sphere
of influence, the animal realm's ability to hunt and to desire.
We could not have acquired these traits and abilities without
the prior forms of life.

Some naturalists have begun to approach animals as kindred
rather than as objects of study, so that the cycle of ancient
relationship is being re-established. The spiritual relationship
between animals and humans has been an enduring feature
down the ages. Most tribal groups associate themselves with a
particular animal who is viewed as a progenitor or guardian.
During the rites of passage of many indigenous peoples, including North America and Africa, young people are enabled
to discover their particular guardian animal, and to learn its
lessons.

Animals as Helpers

Shamans work with animal spirits in a variety of ways. Each
has a primary guardian animal, often called a power-animal,
because it guards our power and resonates to our own distinct
nature or energy vibration. A guardian animal is our guide
between the worlds and the companion who helps us on
journeys, supporting our quest. Just as human beings are not
alone in physical reality, neither are shamans alone when they
travel to the otherworlds. No shamanic work is undertaken
unless the shaman can raise the help of at least one spirit; she
may work with more, but she will never pass into the three
worlds without a helper.

Many of us already feel a strong resonance with a particular

animal, and it is possible that it will be encountered when we go to find a guardian animal for shamanic work, but this does not necessarily follow. The kinds of animals which people acquire as allies are various. There is a good deal of confusion about this. Some people assume that they can shop around for the animal of their choice: when you go to meet your guardian animal, you will find that it is the other way about – the animal chooses you, not you the animal! Some people expect an imposing or 'noble' animal to turn up and are very disappointed when, instead of an eagle, they find themselves companioned by a rodent. All animals are equal in the cosmic web: none is better or worse than another, only possessed of different powers and skills. You may require the senses of a bat in your shamanic work rather more than you need the grace and strength of a tiger.

In seeking a guardian animal, there are some species which are less suitable as primary helpers. It is not usually desirable to have an insect or reptile as a guardian animal; this is not because of any negative quality in reptiles or insects, but because a guardian animal is usually one that is nearer in kind to our human condition. The chain of evolutionary life shows that our nearest cousins are mammalian and it is these who most often appear and offer themselves. Those with mammalian helpers are usually well grounded and integrated.

Having said this, there are exceptions: some people do have bird, fish and reptilian guardian animals because of certain special skills which they are able to mediate in their shamanizing. Such individuals are often less easy to be with: not because they have any negative intentions, but because the primary nature of their power-current feels less human, less mammalian to other people. Bird-people are often visionary, fish-people often explore hidden or submerged principles, snake-people often facilitate transformations, insect-people often work in organizational and networking ways. Such people often become specialists in their shamanic field, but they also need to work upon their mammalian and human relationships in order to manifest what they mediate. Bird, fish, reptilian and insect helpers usually come along when the shaman is more experienced, or is being taught specific techniques.

There are many books and divinatory systems available which define the qualities of guardian animals in human terms;

these are often supportive to our understanding, but remember that your personal experience of your animal is more important than the definitions of others.[3]

Practice 14: Seeking Permission

Human beings usually take the physical parts of living beings without asking permission. Thoughtless use of living beings creates blockages and imbalances, and merely compounds the current notion of the world as a convenient packaged place. Before using any part of a living being for shamanic work, be present in spirit to that being. Ask and listen before taking, seek permission and offer thanks for that being's sacrifice. It is the habit of some indigenous peoples to offer saliva or a hair from their heads, a song or some other offering as a token of exchange before plucking a herb or lopping a tree.

This practice may also be used when seeking to use some part of a being which is no longer living in physical reality, such as the feathers, pelt or horns of a road-killed animal. Before utilizing any parts of a dead animal, it is good to make a journey to its spirit and seek permission, since its spirit would be part of any shamanic equipment that you make. Similarly, if you are going to make use of the subtle essences, the very spirit of plants, for sacred or healing purposes, this permission is essential.

Asking permission should not become a pretentious practice which highlights your enlightened spirit to others; it is a private act of politeness which becomes habitual and creates a reciprocity between all beings on the cosmic web. Permission is more often granted than denied, if our need and intention are expressed; if you experience a massive 'no' to your request, go back and examine your true needs.

Permission to join the living network of the cosmic web as a soul is here given.

2. THE GREEN WORLD

When you can see each leaf as a separate thing, you can see the tree; when you can see the tree, you can see the spirit of the tree; when you can see the spirit of the tree, you can talk to it and maybe begin to learn something.

Storytelling: Imagination and Faith
William J. Bausch

Several thousand species of grasses, trees, herbs and other plants clothe our earth: we take their spectacular variety for granted, using them to provide us with food, medicine, shelter and clothing, and responding to the beauty of their flowers and scents.

The Abuse of Plants

The life of plants is still mysterious to most of us; we fail to understand that plants are also alive, that they have spirits. Scientific research has proved that plants have their magnetic force-fields, that they are sensitive to their surroundings and to the treatment they receive.[4] These findings have been greeted with derision among those who do not acknowledge their relationship to the green world, so that 'talking to plants' has become a byword in lunacy. Yet the amazing results of human communication with plants is a fact in both Findhorn, Scotland, and Perelandra, Virginia, where plant-life flourishes contrary to all the laws of physics.[5]

Elsewhere, a terrible expediency governs the way in which we regard plants. The widespread use of chemical pesticides to control plant growth and deter parasitic insects is achieved at a cost, for it tampers with the food-chain, poisons the soil, kills off micro-organisms and causes degeneration in the immune systems of all life-forms. Dr Jerome Weisner, science counsellor to President John F. Kennedy reported that 'Use of pesticides is more dangerous than atomic fall-out'.[6] The effect of such abuse upon the spirits of plants is incalculable. The eating of organically grown food-stuffs is not a luxury or a fad, it is a necessity for healthy living.

Ecologists, in order to convince governments to save unique habitats like the Amazonian rainforests, have argued the medicinal value to humankind of the many plants which grow there. However, the green world has its own dignity and status; it deserves to be respected for itself.[7]

Psychotropic Plants

Many traditional and some modern societies use psychotropic plants in order to enter mild ecstatic states in a recreational way, and the fermented and alcoholic derivatives of plants and their fruits are used socially all over the world (except in Muslim countries where they are forbidden). But shamans never employ such plants without good preparation and strong intention.

Throughout time, the strong spirits of ergots of barley and rye, hallucinogenic mushrooms, narcotic poppies and vines have been used to source the otherworld. Sacred traditions speak of the properties of plant soma, of the Holy Grail with its sacred drink which inspires and initiates. However, few people in the West have even been instructed in the use of psychotropic substances as a means of shamanic journeying; we do not have elders who can teach us the pathways, dangers and benefits. It is for this reason, and because our own society has a recreational attitude to drug-taking, that I have never advocated drug-use in combination with shamanism. It simply is not necessary, since other journeying methods are readily available. Traditional shamans may know how to journey by these means, able to adjust dosage to individuals and to help rescue souls from bad experiences, but in contemporary society, we have no such traditional knowledge, and the dangers of using substances whose effects and powers we have not been called to learn is immense. The recreational use of hard drugs is a form of self-abuse which, combined with an ignorance of otherworldly realities, can lead to extreme soul-loss and death. The dangers of being lost out in otherworlds are immense during drug-use. The disorientation of the seasoned drug-user is a fair indication of the soul-erosion that goes on; unhealthy dependencies on substances lead to irresponsible and criminal acts which injure the delicate web of life.

Plants for Food and Healing

How did our ancestors first discover the properties of each plant? The only method seems to have been physical experimentation, since there were no books to consult. But we may conceive of another way: that shamans sought communication with the spirits of the green world and received knowledge through journeying. My respect for our ancestors, who were taught the uses of powerful and poisonous plants by the spirits, is immense. This traditional wisdom was handed down to us, so that the core healing remedies are still derived from this ancestral knowledge. Myths speak of the mighty spirits of the green world who come to instruct humans in agriculture, in harvesting food and inspiration from plants. These myths are particularly strong in the Americas, which have retained memory of these spirit-contacts. The abundant plants of the Americas now appear on tables worldwide: tomatoes, potatoes, maize, squash and of course chocolate. (We should remember though, that the primal use of tobacco was and is for sacred, not recreational, purposes.)

The distillation of plant and mineral essences to form an alchemical tincture is the process by which the true 'elixir of immortality' is obtained, for they reconnect us with the cosmic web. The use of gentle essences, like the Bach Flower Remedies distilled in the county of Oxfordshire where I live, are invaluable ways of learning to work with plant spirits. These essences are now made all over the world, including California and Australia: check your local health shop. Such plant and flower essences are non-addictive and can help us slow down the accelerating pace of life and appreciate the spiritual wisdom of that plant.

Trees

Trees are the giants of the green world. Their wisdom is recorded in all societies, which look to trees as teachers who store and disseminate knowledge. Some of the earliest means of recording knowledge was by using the language of trees. The names for the letters of the Irish alphabet derive from trees, and the ancient Irish *filidh*, the vision-poets, preserved secret

teachings by means of inscribed staves of wood, known as *ogham*. Many methods of divining employed trees. The association of trees with language continues in our own time, with the use of wood-pulp to make paper; without trees, we would not be able to read books or newspapers. Quoting ecologist Eugene Odum, Gary Snyder writes:

> ... living matter is stored information in the cells and in the genes ... there is more information of a higher order of sophistication and complexity stored in a few square yards of forest than there is in all the libraries of mankind. Obviously, that is a different order of information ... It is the information that has been flowing for millions of years. In this total information context, man may not be necessarily the highest or most interesting product.[8]

The clearcutting of forests for timber and wood-pulp and the damage to trees by 'acid rain' affects all life-forms in a serious way. Vegetation exists by photosynthesis, where carbon dioxide is combined with water using energy taken in from sunlight to produce oxygen as well as the plant's food; animals breathe in oxygen and breathe out carbon dioxide. Thus plants and animals are interdependent. In addition, forests maintain the planetary environment: by evapotranspiration they pump water back into the air which causes clouds to form and these clouds reflect back the sunlight which would otherwise heat and dry up the regions beneath.[9] Plants are therefore a bridge between mineral and animal life-forms. We are discovering that we cannot tinker with the green world without detriment to the earth.

Practice 15: Harvesting Seed

One small seed is a storehouse and memory bank and can become the progenitor of many plants. The potential seeding capacity of any plant or tree is enormous. In wild places plants grow unchecked but around inhabited places human beings have encouraged flowering species and the plants which supply their table or pharmacy but have eradicated others as weeds. Discover which indigenous plant species are threatened with extinction in your land and acquire some seed which will flourish in your soil-type, climate and habitat. It is important that

you use seed which is indigenous to your region and not imported. Also ensure that, if the plant is not self-pollinating, you have both male and female varieties of seed to plant in the same place. Rare plant seeds are available from specialist suppliers, which are usually listed in gardening journals and herbal supply chains. Check that your local soil conditions are appropriate.

Holding the seeds in one hand, shake your rattle over them with the other, closing your eyes and allowing the rattle's voice to speak with the seeds. Sense the way in which these seeds are connected to the cosmic web and listen to their voices; communicate always with the spirits of the seeds. You may receive a power-song from the seeds which you can use when planting.

When the weather and season are correct for planting, prepare the earth carefully, quietly singing or chanting a song of preparation. Make a bed for the seeds with the care you would use putting a child to bed. Rattle over the earth; include rain, wind and sun in your song. Plant the seeds sparingly and tend them as they grow, protecting them against insects or birds which find them tasty, using natural and organic methods. Watch them grow and flower as the year unfolds. Be ready to harvest some of the seed-heads when they are ripe but leave some seed-heads on the plant to disperse naturally. Store the seed in a special pot; offer it to friends to plant in their gardens.

This method can be used for any plant, and whether in a garden or a window-box.

Practice 16: Plant and Tree Wisdom

The nineteenth-century Rabbi Nachman of Breslov said, 'How wonderful it would be if one could only be worthy of hearing the song of the grass'.[10] Using shamanism we can, for it is not just humans who talk to plants, but plants who talk to us. Contacting the spirits of plants can be done in both physical and subtle realities. Choose your plant or tree and study it carefully in its own habitat, always working with a healthy, living specimen. Be present to it in spirit and, without deep sourcing, ask it to share its wisdom with you. You will find that plants live at a much slower rate than animals. Thank the plant,

then record your impressions, cross-checking these with a book or someone who knows the properties of that plant.

When you have become proficient in journeying, you can extend this practice to journey to the plant (through your middle-world entrance – see Practice 23) in order to meet its spiritual form in a much more powerful way. Again, go with the intention of asking for wisdom or knowledge, and how it should be applied. Always listen carefully to what the spirits tell you.

If appropriate, ask questions about usage: which parts of the plant are to be used – root, leaves, flowers, stem? What is the purpose of plant? How is the plant to be prepared and administered – internally or externally? I always keep a regiment of herbals and plant-identification books on my shelves in order to cross-check everything I'm told by the plant-spirits themselves but these have never led me astray. However, the golden rule with all identification is: if you can't identify it or it looks remarkably like a poisonous species – *do not use it*. Never prescribe for someone else, unless you are a medically qualified practitioner.

Repeat these practices with different species of tree and plant. Some will become close allies in your work; keep parts of these plants in your shamanic bag (see Practice 61).

Insects

The human attitude to insects is often one of revulsion and insects are accordingly regarded as evil. To human eyes, they seem to have little usefulness. Universal shamanic healing practice reveals that spiritual intrusions in a sick body often appear to subtle reality vision as insect in form. I believe that they appear in these guises in the sick human body in the same way that insects often eat up what is diseased or wasted in plants. Insects may be tiny, creeping things, but they are also very powerful. Their functions vary tremendously. The winged pollinators are the long-range messengers of the insect world, while beetles and other burrowing creatures transform the soil. Insects and plants had a co-evolution: plants evolved into new forms as a result of insect pollination.[11]

The insect plant-helper has a close association with one or many plants. An insect helper lends its highly developed senses

to the shaman, helping her home in on specific plant-usages and the correlations between the plant qualities and a healthy ecological balance in all beings. Shamans will sometimes journey in the shape of their insect helper in order to seek out the best plant or herb for a specific illness.

If you are drawn to plant medicine the following practice will help you find an insect-plant alliance. If you want to work extensively with plants as a healer or herbalist, you will need to contact an insect helper to teach you plant wisdom, since insects are a bridge between plant and animal life. This is advanced work which appears here by virtue of its subject matter: do not attempt this practice until you are very proficient in otherworld journeying and have acquired and extensively worked with guardian animals and teachers *in all three worlds*.

Practice 17: Insect Plant-helpers

---

1. With your guardian animal, journey to a plant you've already visited. Commune with the plant's spirit and, together, call out for an insect helper to assist you in plant work.

2. Ask any insect if it is your helper. Follow the instructions for accepting or refusing it as given in Chapter 4.

3. The way you accept your insect is different, however: to cement your alliance, both of you eat a small portion of the plant, *in subtle reality*. Thank plant and insect.

4. Do not bring your insect helper back into your world. If you require its help in everyday situations, call it up through gentle sourcing.

3. THE STONE PEOPLE

I can see with the eyes of a stone, and think with its thoughts, and feel with its layers and strata.

Earthfasts
William Mayne

A few years back I met with a Cree medicine woman who was a stone companion: most of her spirit allies were stones. Her

greatest desire was to be worthy to become of one of the stone people herself, a wish which would baffle most people today who consider stones to be dead. Yet vegetable gums and other substances harden to become minerals like coal and amber and animals can become fossilized. Life-forms evolve, die and return to the earth, retaining memory: they take on other life.

Our ancestors have accorded special qualities to different forms of stone throughout time. We have valued precious stones and used them for their healing and prophylactic properties, for example the medieval use of precious stones to enhance personal characteristics and to effect healing is paralleled by the modern use of crystals and minerals. We have reverenced sky-falling stones – meteors – as gods: Moslems pray facing Mecca where lies the Qa'aba, a meteor once venerated as a Goddess. We have set up monoliths and stone circles – places of meeting, worship and dancing which endure across millennia. In Britain we hang up stones with holes in them called 'hag-stones', to bring health and luck, to ward off the evil eye.

Myths reveal strong belief in the spiritual virtue of stones. In the Germanic versions of the Grail legend, the Grail itself is a green stone which falls from Lucifer's crown. In Hindu scripture, Vishnu, the preserver, wears the jewel, Treasure of the Ocean, upon his chest which manifests itself in all that shines: the sun, moon, fire and speech. In Gnostic scriptures, the pearl of great price is the image of the soul.

Metals also have their spirits. Smiths and metal-workers have always been regarded as magic-men, capable of transformatory processes. The work of alchemy is the transmutation of matter, specifically metals, through the gamut of lead to gold. Gold has been seen as the revitalizing energy of the sun as well as the blood of Mother Earth, as the final perfection of matter. Greed for the economic value of gold has degraded this ancient belief. Alchemy is truly the art of becoming allied to the full spectrum of life-forms, from mineral to spirit worlds. Classical alchemy was closely related to the unfolding path of the Spirit. Many alchemical texts read like complex shamanic journeys, where the alchemists have become aware of the spirits of the minerals with which they worked. The Egyptian alchemist, Zosimos, experienced a vision of seven stages each guarded by the spirit forms of metals.[12]

Minerals form the basis of our planet's structure. All life draws nourishment from the mineral realm. Although they appear to be inert, dense matter, stones and minerals are capable of imparting essential life; this is evident from studying anyone suffering from mineral deficiencies – when the appropriate salt or mineral traces are supplied, that person becomes revitalized.

Stones, metals and minerals create certain forms of sound. Tibetan singing bowls, used in meditation, are alchemically made out of seven metals (now rarely precious ones) and create a rainbow of sounds which can be powerful bridges between the worlds. The shaman's costume invariably has pieces of metal sewn into it which jingle and vibrate as he dances.

Aldous Huxley wrote: 'Precious stones are precious because they bear a faint resemblance to the glowing marvels seen with the inner eye of the visionary'.[13] The crystalline structure of stones has been used for shamanic vision and healing for centuries. The present preoccupation with crystal therapy may seem a modern invention, but crystals have been used shamanically for centuries. North American medicine bundles contain crystals. In North Asia, crystals were believed to cause rain and were called 'rain stones'. Mongols dried crystals to prevent rain, while the Siberian peoples such as the Altai smoked them in fires and the Yakuts threw them up to the sun. Elsewhere crystals were used to heal, by impregnating the patient with the essential energy of the universe.

Crystals are like radio transmitters: they receive information and pass it on. They store energy and power in the same way that microchips do. They also act as amplifiers of such energy and are therefore very powerful. Stones and crystals have spirits which must be respected. To draw upon their essential qualities without permission is to be spiritually manipulative. Very few crystal-healing teachers or books seem to mention this: they are more interested in the techniques and what they can achieve.[14] The wholesale mining of crystals and their indiscriminate use is an unfortunate feature of the West's spiritual materialism.

The Cherokee teacher, Dhyani Ywahoo, speaks truly when she says:

> . . . misuse of crystal energy can be as destructive to the physical and light bodies as the use of drugs. Many of the so-called 'enlightened crystal teachings' can potentially kill a person. It is

especially dangerous to place crystals upon one's energy centres or to sit within certain configurations of crystals without having established stability of mind and purity of action.[15]

Crystals reflect our actions and thoughts directly on to the cosmic web; they amplify any imbalances within us. If we remember that, we will always use them with respect.

Stones, metals and minerals are attuned to the essential structure of the cosmos; they also permit us to become tuned to the universe. The whole of twentieth-century technology is based upon this premise, as we rely upon the microchip to store and retrieve memory, and to exchange information. Shamanic reality is manifest every day all around us.

Practice 18: Consulting the Stone People

Hold any stone, mineral or gem: study its surfaces and texture, feel the creative power and life within it. Be present to it in spirit. You may wish to sing or rattle to begin a gentle sourcing while holding the stone, with the intention of meeting its spirit and seeing if it is willing to become your ally. Consult this stone ally through journeying to ask what nature of help or qualities it possesses, and whether you may have permission to use these in your work. Give thanks.

Practice 19: Learning from Crystals

If you are drawn to work with crystals, select a clear quartz crystal or other stone that has been unused by anyone else. Cleanse it by leaving it for one complete lunation (twenty-eight days) in a dish of crystal sea-salt out of doors exposed to the elements.

Then, holding it in your hand, make a journey to meet the spirit of the stone and ask if it is willing to be your ally. Ask what it can teach you and how it is to be used.

Keep your crystal wrapped or covered when you are not using it.

Practice 20: Becoming the Earth

Soil is the seed-bed for all growth. We can place dead things into it and the processes of nature will break them down to create new life. All that we eat grows in this soil: we are the earth. Middle Eastern and other myths speak of humans and animals being made out of clay, fashioned by gods who breathed life into us. Indigenous peoples ensure that all animal and plant residues are returned to the earth, where they can decompose into humus and re-enter the life-cycle. We can do so too.

This practice is useful for acclimatizing you to an environment or country, helping put you in touch with the spirits of that region in the quickest possible way. Go outdoors and find a patch of earth which has not been polluted by chemical waste or fertilizers. It doesn't have to be a pretty place, just somewhere where the soil has been left to be itself. Touch the soil and greet it. Pick up a palmful; with closed eyes, smell and feel it. Be present to its spirit. Grind a little earth really finely between your fingers and taste a little before spitting it out. Now sit and be with the earth of that region, gently sourcing through chant or song. Allow impressions from the soil to emerge in your song in sounds or words. Return home and journey to the spirit of that patch of earth and ask it to be your ally in your new place.

This practice will be greatly aided if, in the first few months of your move, you include a majority of locally grown foodstuffs in your diet.

4. FAERIES, GODS AND UNICORNS

No god is without animality, no animal without humanity, no man without a part of divinity.

Shiva and Dionysus
Alain Daniélou

All cultures have called upon or been visited by spirits which are not nor ever have been human: mythic animals, faeries and deities are the most common. These spirits have subtle reality

forms which inhabit the three worlds; they manifest in physical reality in many different ways, seen by children, visionaries, seers and prophets, apprehendable to shamans and those who have attuned themselves to forms of subtle reality.

As you begin to journey through the three worlds, you will encounter a variety of such spirits who may become your allies and teachers. This chapter attempts to introduce you to them and how they operate in a shamanic way. We will explore human spirits, heroes, saints and ancestors in Chapters 4, 5 and 6.

Mythic Animals

The appearance of mythic animals in shamanizing should not be treated as a breakdown of your reason, nor indeed as an occasion to vaunt your prowess. Mythic animals sometimes appear as occasional helpers in certain situations. Unicorns, dragons or phoenixes are beasts who solely inhabit subtle reality and so they teach primarily about otherworldly concepts; they teach us to pass over and through, to transcend or transform. The literature of the unicorn and dragon is worldwide, indicating that unrelated civilizations have envisioned and encountered them in subtle reality. They appear in heraldry or as guardians of national institutions, testifying to the fact that their powers are recognized and their protection sought.

Extinct species of animals also become inhabitants of subtle reality only, although they do not usually join the ranks of mythic beasts. Recently extinct animals do not appear as allies very often: I believe that they are busy coming to terms with their new subtle reality state. Certain forms of extinct animals appear to us to warn us that we are approaching a crossroads or threshold. Although they rarely appear as primary helpers, their wisdom or support is often synchronous.

Certain climactic, seasonal and social changes may bring us into resonance with animals no longer living on the earth. The widespread dinosauraphilia from Michael Crichton's book *Jurassic Park* is a case in point: carnivorous raptors of the Jurassic era may invade our dreams with awe and fear but they also subtly reflect the saurian nature of our ravenous consumer society. Few would want a dinosaur helper, but this extinct

species may be appearing in popular consciousness to teach the lesson of greed to a living species which sometimes seems hell-bent on extinction themselves.

Faeries

When we work in the Middleworld, we frequently encounter faeries. Although they have been reported as very small, they have also appeared as very large: these size variations are due to the unlimited dimensionality of the cosmic web, which cannot be defined by human concepts of space and time. Our ancestors were careful to acknowledge their faery neighbours, to offer them food and goods, to be vigilant about not trespassing or building on faery dancing grounds, assembly points or pathways.

Faery lore is found the world over. The Pakistani *bitan* (shaman), Ibrahim of Altit, describes his experience with the faeries or *peri* thus:

> Ordinary people can't see the fairies. But who sees them? First of all, the *bitan*; and after that, the *pashu*, the seer. Between people and the fairies, there is a veil . . . We pour millet [over the offering] and worship the *peri*. We do *barayo* [calling and requesting]. At this request, the fairies begin to gather during the night.[16]

The alliance between faeries and humans is well attested. Practical methods of contacting and co-operating with faery allies are given in the book *Earth Light* by R. J. Stewart, who has a wide personal experience of the faery world.

Reports of faeries abducting children or coming as lovers to human adults are commonplace. People have even reported living among them, or being taken by them into their dwellings. Nowadays, with the increasing noise and industrialization faeries are less often encountered or talked about, so that these reports have become blamed on UFO abductions.

Faeries and elemental spirits often have close association. If you are near the sea, do not be surprised to see mermaids, mermen or naiads in your journeying. Likewise, gnomes and dwarfs appear near caverns and mountains; sylphs and salamanders in cliffs and in fires; tree-elementals or dryads will be found in forests.

Deities and Teachers

The dance of deities upon the cosmic web causes great disquiet among those who practise spiritual totalitarianism, only allowing the existence and authority of their own gods, and regarding all others as disobedient spirits who do not conform to the rules; yet many primal deities and spirits remain embedded in our regional cultures, retaining their power and connection with our world.

We may understand deities as wavebands of power, with different frequencies and qualities, but all deriving from the universal web of the cosmos. All people worldwide have interfaced with deities and there are often startlingly similar patterns in the experiences. For example, we can appreciate the close links between the Christian Virgin Mary, the Chinese Kwan Yin and the Tibetan Tara, to whom the devout go for last-ditch assistance as well as for daily motherly support. Each figure may have a dissimilar myth, but the common pattern of their frequency is like a waveband signature which cannot be mistaken.

Many critical junctions in the cosmic web are marked by a mixture and meeting of powers. Most often deities take human shape but they may appear as a mixture, like Hanuman and Ganesh, the Hindu gods with monkey and elephant heads, or the Egyptian gods with ibis and cow heads, like Thoth and Hathor, or like Dionysius and Christ with the ability to appear as men and as wine.

It has frequently been pointed out that people create god in their own image: some of these forms have been more helpful than others. It is in our best interests to seek out the spirits which are most beneficial and resonant to our path. Where deities have not been relegated to the scrap-heap, they often prove to be powerful sources of assistance. In Tibet and Nepal, for example, the pre-Buddhist land spirits are not relegated to infernal regions but are actively sought out by Buddhist practitioners as guardians and supporters of the *dharma*. They act as threshold guardians who maintain standards of spiritual behaviour.

You may not end up working with existent god-forms but you will certainly encounter their archetypal frequencies in different ways, usually when you go to find your teachers in the three worlds (see Chapters 5, 6 and 7).

The idea of a spirit teacher is not the same as a mediumistic spirit guide who 'controls' the operator, nor like a discarnate spiritual guru to whom you show unswerving obedience. Walkers between the worlds seek teachers and allies in order to learn how the web is walked. We enter into alliances with spirits, not in order to become passively dependent upon our teachers, but for our mutually beneficial friendship upon the web. There is a great sense of companionship and collegiality in the spirit world.

Spirit teachers and allies are the professionals who know the specifics of subtle reality, which we do not. They will guide, inspire, encourage and teach us; they will also show good discernment, rebuke us and pull our legs when we become pompous. They will not become spiritual dictators who tell us how to run every aspect of our lives, although we may indeed consult them when we have problems which we cannot deal with. They will not take those problems away for us, but they may help offer solutions which we then implement. Spirit teachers will remind us of neglected shamanic duties or promises, but they are not nannies

It is often asked why gods, spirits, mythic animals and faeries should bother themselves with humans at all. The answer is, they all lack something which human beings have: mortality and the continuum of physical reality life. Just as we humans seek to have experience of subtle reality and so increase our knowledge and understanding, so too do the non-human spirits wish to have experience of physical reality. The descent of gods to earth and to mortal forms can be seen as the spiritual progress of the deities: Osiris, Demeter, Rhiannon and Christ all enter into the human condition and take the initiation of mortality.

Truly, humans and spirits are the initiators and gate-keepers of each other's realities. We learn from each other and grow together in understanding. Our own capacity for teaching our allies about physical reality should not be underestimated: this is often an embarrassing experience as the shortcomings of human nature become apparent, but at least we are attempting to connect with our different spiritual kindred in a loving way.

Questions about your Spirit Helpers

As you start to use this book practically, certain questions may arise about allies. These are the most common.

I'm unhappy about trusting my helpers

You may have an innately reserved or distrustful nature, but this problem occurs most frequently with those who are dependent upon a dualistic spirituality, whether they practise its ideas or not. As in life, you just have to trust some people: bus-drivers and doctors may be fallible human beings but we have to trust them with our lives or we wouldn't venture out of the door. However, we always retain our free will. If a piece of advice strikes you as inappropriate, or if your allies suggest something you aren't ready to implement, you don't have to.

My helpers don't come when I call

There may be a good reason for this. You may be unprepared through tiredness or illness. You may have lost power and need to re-source yourself. Ignoring your helpers' advice may lead to a temporary breakdown in communication until you have implemented it. Persistent neglect of your helpers ranks with not calling up your closest friends; they will understand good reasons, but wilful neglect will be taken as lack of respect.

My helpers don't talk to me

This problem arises most often in relation to our animal/s. Just because animals don't utter in physical reality doesn't mean to say that they can't in subtle reality. Most spirits can and do speak, while others are of the school of Marcel Marceau: their body-language speaks volumes. Words may not come out of their mouths: they may speak directly to your heart or mind. Another reason for non-communication may be that *you* are doing all the talking. Conversation is two way, so allow space for response.

I feel that I am answering myself

When we begin to source, it is often not very deeply. It is sometimes hard to distinguish between our allies and our own thoughts. Concentrate on being present to your helpers, don't analyse whence advice comes but be thankful and receive. Some days, communication will seen trite; on others, the secrets of the universe explode through every pore of your being.

How can I be sure that the figure I meet is really my ally or teacher?

This common fear arises from a real disquiet about our potential for self-deception. Use the same common sense and instinct about a spirit which proclaims itself your ally as you would for checking out any human. Your particular allies will usually appear well defined and full of vitality and significance for you. You may well have already encountered an ally in a dream or vision, so that it will be familiar. Animals shine with health and are glad to see you. Spirit teachers are notably matter of fact and down to earth; they do not appear as portentious beings in puffs of smoke, spouting upholstered wisdom. All true allies have the eyes of integrity and trustworthiness. You will know your ally is your ally as you know a best friend is a best friend. Our allies choose us, not we them: the kindred companionship that springs up can only be experienced.

I see figures in cartoon, not in real forms

This experience sometimes happens to people with missing soul-parts, especially those who are living their lives at someone else's behest or vicariously through a partner or children. Such people often see cartoon *worlds* as well. When the soul-part returns, or the life-style is changed then three-dimensional subtle reality is resumed. *Note:* helpers will sometimes assume cartoon-like attributes in order to make a special point; check the context and see if this is the case. (For more about soul-loss, see the beginning of Chapter 8.)

How can I have a teacher who is a spiritual leader?

A sense of outrage, astonishment or unworthiness can often accompany the realization that one of your teachers is a spiritual leader, a saint or god. You may have turned your back on your childhood faith only to find that a venerable rabbi or Moses appears to be your shamanic mentor. Sometimes, after a period of working with such a figure, a less archetypal or more approachable teacher who is easier to relate to will appear. Spirit can appear in any form, and will assume the shape most able to approach us. We often encounter primary spiritual figures of this kind as threshold guardians of our spiritual lineage. See page 157.

Can I have a teacher who is a living person?

No, this is not advisable. We sometimes encounter living people during journeying: this person is usually someone who is an important inspirational figure or a person who is mundanely involved with you. When a living exemplar touches your life, you enter the special alliance of their spiritual lineage. Such a bond is actively part of many spiritual traditions from the Apostolic Succession of the Catholic Church, to the transmission of wisdom from Tibetan lamas to their pupils. Sports personalities, artists, musicians and writers may act as channels to constellate fresh teachings. If people with whom you are having difficulties occur, then this may be relevant to your quest or it may indicate that it is time that you sorted our your differences.

How many helpers can I have?

While we all start with one animal and one teacher, your growing experience in the otherworlds will lead to acquaintance with other helpers. Some will become very close friends, others will drop in when certain issues need dealing with, some will appear when you are ready to receive the teaching they wish to give you with gaps of years or months between. In practice, you will probably find yourself working towards having one very dear animal who accompanies you every-

where, a bunch of animals who have specific alliances with you, and a teacher or helping spirit in each of the worlds, as well as the acquaintance of other spirits. Some of us are affiliated with one species more than another: there is no standard acceptable number or right kind of ally.

My guardian animal has changed

Instead of your usual swan, for example, you may find that a new animal, say a wolf, turns up when you start sourcing. This happens from time to time. It may indicate that your training is entering a new stage, or that the demands of your everyday life require a different kind of companion. There is usually a sense of being handed on to another teacher, and a feeling that the cosmic dance has entered a new rhythm for you. When you consciously sense this change, then you are ready to learn something new. Your old animal may turn up again after a brief period, or else become integrated into a small band of helpers and teachers. Some helpers need you only to ask for help: like friends who see you having difficulty but don't like to intrude, they hover around waiting only to be asked or for the right moment to come.

Sometimes I feel that I become my animal/teacher

In walking between the worlds, we enter into deep states of non-duality where the boundaries and borders of identity become blurred. Many people experience flying or galloping as their animal, or feel that their teacher has become superimposed upon them. Identification grows the longer you work with spirit helpers; you feel part of that animal family, allied to this tree-clan, and close to your spiritual teachers as a daughter or sibling. But when your allies lend you their subtle reality bodies, then rejoice and be thankful, for it is a great honour and deep lesson.

I keep encountering a challenging spirit who won't let me pass

Many allies appear as challengers. We tend to regard challenge as aggressive and threatening, yet we must learn to respond

truthfully to such challenges when we journey. Many such challengers guard thresholds to ensure that you understand just where you are going and what your journeying there will mean. Always check your guardian animal's behaviour; if your animal seems totally calm and unconcerned, then rise to the challenge. If you encounter a giant with a staff at a threshold ask him questions, 'What are you guarding? Why aren't you letting me pass?' If he asks you questions, respond, earn your right to pass by a friendly wrestling match if necessary. If your animal councils swift flight, then flee! We must learn to use the same kind of discrimination in subtle reality as we use in physical reality, employing our native caution and gut-response. You have free will. You do not have to accept everything as right for you if you are not ready.

My ally/teacher won't tell me his/her name/gender

Some animals and spirits just do not identify themselves by names. I have known my fish as 'Fish' for over twenty years, but we have a perfectly intimate relationship. One of my teachers is known simply to me as 'Skeleton Woman', but she knows her stuff. Some allies are more chummy than others, while some reveal their nature more gradually. The gender of your animal can sometimes be unclear or can change: let it be what it wants to be. The appearance and gender of some teachers may also change, especially if they first appear in an archetypal 'wise teacher' form. One client of mine has a teacher who changes gender according to the nature of the issue on which she is journeying. Learn to perceive the identity of your allies in subtle ways.

I have just had a most extraordinary encounter with my ally: I hardly like to share it

The experience of consuming one's animal or having sex with one's teacher is very common in journeys and can be extremely disconcerting. Your sexual fantasies are not taking over your life! When eating and sexual encounter occur in this way, view this experience as an important assimilation of spiritual power.

Your animal or teacher is sharing her power with you in the most intimate way. We have to see the assimilation of ourselves and our helpers in the light of the old mystery traditions, where the cooking and consuming of the deity – be it Osiris, Dionysius or Christ – is ritually shared. The human mind finds it very shocking, but this is what is at the basis of the mystery of spiritual power-sharing. The literature of mysticism reveals that union between worshipper and deity is commonplace. St Teresa of Avila experienced the visitation of an angel:

> In his hands I saw a long golden spear and at the end of the iron tip I seemed to see a point of fire. With this he seemed to pierce my heart repeatedly so that it penetrated to my entrails . . . he left me completely afire with a great love of God. The pain was so great that I screamed aloud, but simultaneously felt such an infinite sweetness that I wished the pain would last eternally.[17]

So might a virgin speak of the first night with her beloved! Whether we look East or West, mystics and shamans everywhere speak of the ecstatic union of themselves with the object of their worship or practice. Tibetan Buddhism has a vast literature relating to the mystical relationship between practitioner and tutelary deity which underscores this. Be assured, you are privileged to have experienced such non-dual kinship.

Practice 21: Inner Companion

When you were a child you probably had a secret, inner companion with whom you conversed. The invisible friend may have inhabited the body of a special toy. Bring that friend to mind now, be spiritually present to him/her. What wisdom did you learn, what kind of kinship was between you? Through gentle sourcing, speak to that friend now and call up that deep intimacy of spirit. Ask your companion to please prepare the way for you to walk between the worlds, to alert your guardian animal, allies and teachers that you will be coming to met them soon.

4.　The Middleworld

One touch of Nature makes the whole world kin.

Twelfth Night
William Shakespeare

1. THE MOTHER PLACE

There is no state or condition more holy than the Earth.

Power within the Land
R. J. Stewart

THE EARTH IS MORE than our physical home: it is the mother place, the matrix of planetary life, the locus from which we enter the Middleworld, the Underworld and the Upperworld. Since 1969, we have all been granted the privilege of seeing the physical reality of our planet as it looks from space: you would think that this would make it an even more precious place, but this has not generally been the case. For many, the earth is all that there is, for they have blocked out any consciousness of otherworlds. And yet they continue to abuse the only home they know. Only crazy people wreck their home – or those who no longer feel safe within it. Only crazy people try to kill their mothers.

Nature

Throughout primal world cultures, the earth has been envisaged as possessed of a female and motherly spirit, whom people

have been taught to honour, whose natural laws they have been taught to uphold. This view is now alien to the West. Technology has given the impression that Nature is now our servant. In the middle ages, nature was often portrayed as a traipsing drudge, Dame Kinde, a simple, willing slave for the use of humankind. This degrading image of Nature was inherited from the late classical view of the anima mundi, the 'world soul', as an impressionable and vacillating woman. This diminishment of the great Mother of Life underpins our whole vision of nature and the natural world in which we live. Such desacralization is tempered by the shamanic, animistic view, which invites us to see the holiness and Spirit in everything that is.

Environmentalists and deep ecologists concur that the old stories and myths of the earth are no longer adequate to the situation. The scientist, James Lovelock, has sought to restore the view of the earth's Spirit, as Gaia, the ancient Greek mother of life. This redefinition has brought about a greater response and environmental concern than any consideration of the earth as a scientific phenomenon, comprised of inert matter and gases, could have done.

The Earthly Paradise

At some deep level, we each have a sense of the perfect earth of the Golden Age, before everything went wrong. Countless myths relate how we lost communion with the earthly paradise, with Eden, the Fortunate Islands, Avalon. Each loss is associated with the apple, fruit of the tree of the earthly paradise. We mourn its loss, as we mourn our disrespect for Nature, not understanding why things went wrong and half-hating ourselves for it. These myths have been conceived of as memories of earlier times when the simple, primitive peoples flourished without benefit of civilization. Yet the Golden Age is nothing less than a memory of the Middleworld, within whose subtle reality, the perfect pristine earth remains. Reconnection with the subtle reality of the Middleworld restores us to the Golden Age: we have never really lost anything.

Our separation from subtle reality has been so complete that we have told ourselves complex myths of how we came to be

orphaned from goodness. We have ceased even to recognize the thresholds between the worlds for what they are and have posted fiery angels or fearsome monsters to bar the ways. Some ways have become so completely covered by superstition and avoidance that no one walks between them save priests. Such blockages have caused massive planetary sickness and have severe consequences on the soul-health of all beings.

The Nature of the Middleworld

In our enthusiasm to start journeying into subtle reality, we have to bypass centuries of rubble made up of fear, hope and thwarted possibilities. In seeking to rediscover the thresholds where we can walk between the worlds, we have to remember that although we have lost most of our sensitivity to Spirit, we have also lost much of our innate caution and spiritual discrimination as well. We need the help of our allies to walk between the worlds, just as our allies need us to implement the healing which centuries of neglect have rendered necessary. No human being can, singly and alone, reconnect and bring healing between the worlds.

The Middleworld is our anchor-point, our starting place, our foundation. The Middleworld has two appearances: the ordinary physical appearance of the material world which we experience with our five senses, and the subtle appearance of spiritual reality which is appreciable to our subtle senses.

We may regard these two meshed realities by comparing a photograph and a painting of the same object. The photograph shows us the physical reality, while a good painting will show us something of the subtle reality as well, the spiritual form which is veiled by the physical form. Seers are born with the ability to see both realities at the same time: most shamans do not have this ability, but consciously access the subtle reality of the Middleworld through sourcing and journeying.

In everyday life, we become aware of the subtle reality of the Middleworld in many different ways through our imagination, spiritual awakening, shock or loss of the familiar. Dante likens the beginning of his cosmological journey *The Divine Comedy* to being lost in a dark wood. Great thinkers, scientists and humanitarians have all entered into and partaken of the

Middleworld's subtle reality: Einstein, Marie Curie, Gandhi and others have journeyed deeply beyond the physical realities of the earth, impelled by compassion for its needs, to find pragmatic and implementable solutions.

But for every one person who makes this journey there are many more who will not or cannot, through ignorance or fear: they remain the prisoners of one reality, their lives become one long avoidance of subtle reality in which imagination is shunned as dangerous, where the emotions become betrayers, where rigid control and strictly linear thought patrol the borders between realities.

Generally, we already skilfully move about within and interact with the energies of the subtle reality of the Middleworld in our daily lives. The unregarded synchronicities of life reveal this: without any conscious prior warning, a mother returns home early to catch her child's overseas phone call, a man takes a sudden detour on a planned route and meets up with the business opportunity he really needs, a family decide not to take a flight which subsequently has an accident. These are all incidents where individuals have received messages from subtle reality. Many non-shamanic people are already skilful Middleworld travellers. We have all 'checked ahead' to intuit whether a garage is open, a friend already arrived at a station, whether there is any milk left in the fridge,where a lost object is located, where a parking space may be found: we automatically do a mini-journey, sending out a soul-part to check.

We journey to the Middleworld in order to deal with the present issues, with life on earth now. We may find ourselves travelling forwards and backwards in time, especially if we are dealing with issues involving sequence and frequency. Middleworld journeys might also include travelling to a sacred site, to a sick friend, to a place far distant

The Middleworld is being exhaustively worked by many people in psychotherapies at present; much of what passes for 'guided fantasy' or 'visualization' accesses this world – by calling upon its clients to visualize their favourite recreation spot, or by calling up situations or helpers which can heal. Many people cannot face or are frightened of the Underworld or Upperworld, so that the Middleworld is often their prime means of healing. Middleworld journeying often liberates immediate potentialities and stirs up stagnant situations.

Inhabitants of the Middleworld

Beings encountered in the Middleworld include the elementals, called, in Western tradition gnomes (earth), sylphs (air), salamanders (fire) and undines (water). These may appear in other forms as dryads, faeries, elves, brownies, house-spirits and so on. The beings encountered here are terrestrial entities, guardians and spirits of place who are concerned with the smooth running of the planet.

The female spirit or *juno* of the Middleworld is the Earth Mother or *anima mundi* who is known by many names. Her champions often manifest as heroes and heroines who do not die, like King Arthur. The male spirit or *genius* of the Middleworld is invariably the Green One, appearing as a god of the fields and woods, as Pan, Shiva, the Green Man. Sometimes the *juno* and *genius* appear in partnership, as a pair of deities or as Faery Queen and King.

Guardian animals may be encountered here, often those which appear on the heraldic shields of countries, like the Lion of Scotland or the Eagle of America.

The Middleworld can be the place where we can increase our facility in something or learn a skill that would be useful to us in our daily lives. A form of this method is often used by sportspeople, dancers and practitioners of martial arts: to rehearse their skill without moving their body, thus creating 'skill-lines'.

Interaction with the Middleworld activates the central pathways of our central cerebral cortex and allows them to collate and bridge the separate hemispheres in resourceful ways.

Work through this part slowly before you go on to the next parts.

Practice 22: Entering into Communion with the Earth

Most of us live surrounded by brick and concrete, glass and steel. The humility to attend to the messages of nature is often lacking in us: we have neither the time nor the patience for any such communication to take place. It is therefore very important that we increase our exposure to the natural world. We tend to accept only the mundane reasons for being outdoors such as sport, gardening, car maintenance. Actively seeking the

natural world begins with placing ourselves in the right relationship with it, by willingly offering our time and attention. Single people in an urban environment may need a good reason for being outdoors: jogging or walking the dog may grant acceptable 'invisibility' or protection from disturbance.

Try and spend at least an hour a day out of doors. If your circumstances make this difficult, ensure that you get at least two connected hours at the weekend. During this time, sit upon the ground and be present to the earth. As you breathe out let your breath enter the ground. As you breathe in, let the earth enter you. Let the earth breathe you.

This basic practice will reconnect you daily, making a circuit between yourself and the earth. Your mind should rest upon being present to the earth. If you grow distracted, then gently recall your concentration to your surroundings and the connection between you and them. You are not taking from the earth, but sharing with it.

Practice 23: Finding a Middleworld Journey-centre

In order to learn about a new country we gradually explore outwards from a central point. It is exactly the same with shamanic travel. Our centre or starting point must be somewhere dear and familiar to us, *a real not an imagined place*. It might be a sacred site that inspires you, a place in a country where you go on holiday, a place of childhood play, somewhere in the country where nature's beauty reigns supreme. The bottom line is: it must be or have been in physical reality (in the case of childhood venues now built over, for example); it must be a place where *you* have physically been and be located somewhere upon the planet Earth.

It is preferable for your journey-centre to be a place where you have been safe and happy, rather than a place reminiscent of stale or unhappy situations. So, if you could return to anywhere in the planet to be inspired, happy and refreshed where would that place be?

Without sourcing, just bring that place to mind now. Do not make subsequent journeys until you know your journey-centre very well. If your journeying flounders due to a poor choice, then find another place, and stick to it.

**Practice 24: Middleworld Journey to Find
your Guardian Animal**

Having decided upon your journey-centre, plan to journey to
it and meet your guardian animal. Exclude light, be comfortable, prepare your sound-source and state your purpose: 'I am
making a Middleworld journey to my journey-centre, to meet
my guardian animal.'

1. Start sourcing with an open heart, without prior expectation. Your quest is to find your primary guardian animal
   who will help you with shamanic work. Listen to your
   sound-source, lightly holding your goal in awareness. If
   distractions or mental noise occur, let them fade, and return
   to your listening and your purpose. You may lie down or
   sit propped up.

2. Enter your primary gateway (your journey-centre) to the
   Middleworld. You may arrive at your centre very quickly,
   or more slowly. When you arrive, be present to it; allow
   your subtle senses to enjoy being there – feel, smell, see
   and hear whatever is around you. Be aware of the differences and similarities between the physical and subtle realities. Appreciate the spiritual form and appearance of your
   journey-centre.

3. Now call out and ask your animal to come and appear. It
   may be waiting for you; if it is not, go looking, don't sit there
   and wait for it to turn up. As you search, keep calling out,
   asking it to please appear.

4. Ask any animal you subsequently meet if it is your guardian
   animal. If it is not, it will either ignore you or indicate, by
   speech or body-language, that it is not. If it is your animal,
   it will indicate this clearly.

5. During the search for your animal many things may happen.
   If you are reluctant to accept an animal which offers itself to
   you, either because it is one of the animals which is unsuit-
   able for a primary helper or because it makes you feel uneasy to be with, then thank it for its kindness but decline to
   take it and keep looking.
   If an animal you have rejected or ignored reappears several

times in significant ways during your journey, then that is probably your animal, even if it is one of the species which doesn't normally offer itself as a primary guardian animal.

If your animal runs away from you, go after it and beg it to stop; ask it why, negotiate with it, do a deal with it. It may be avoiding you because of some perceived imbalance or habit which is inconsistent with shamanism: you may have to promise to work on this.

If your animal appears in a flock or herd, single out which one it is or ask it to appear. Bring back only one animal. Very occasionally, a mother animal with young will appear, in which case check if both animals are intended for you.

If an animal is openly aggressive towards you, avoid it, and keep looking.

6. After identifying your animal and accepting it, embrace it, talk to it, remain with it, communicate with it. Do whatever you would normally do on meeting a stranger who is a kindred soul. Finally, embrace your animal and bring it back with you, when the call-back signal sounds.

7. When the call-back signal sounds, return from the other-world by the same route you journeyed through, bringing your animal with you. This return is normally quite fast. Sometimes, instead of carrying or running with your animal, the animal carries you. Emerge in physical reality and record your experiences, however bizarre or vestigial they may initially appear. Check any problems or difficulties against the lists in Chapters 2 and 7. Dance your animal, as in Practice 25 below.

8. If your first attempt is unsuccessful or inconclusive, don't worry or berate your failure. Try again another day and let your expectations graze peacefully. Before your next attempt, become as relaxed as possible.

Permission to get things wrong and to find solutions is here given.

Practice 25: Dancing with Animals

Immediately on returning with your guardian animal, you will need to dance with it. Just as your animal will introduce and

guide you through the subtle realities of the otherworlds, so it is your turn now to introduce it to your own physical reality world. Dancing your animal expresses your joy at finding such an important friend. It also allows the subtle reality of your animal and the physical reality of your own body to become attuned. For your dance, take up rattle, drum or other instrument and provide your own rhythm. Let your awareness keep embracing your animal as you begin to dance, sing, make music. You will find that your body and even your voice take on the characteristics of your animal, as you allow your animal to explore what a human being is like. Let your veneer of adult self-consciousness drop off and have fun. Dance for five to ten minutes and then resume normal awareness again.

Practice 26: Introducing the Animal to the Everyday World

In the next few days, be aware of your animal near and around you. Let it see through your eyes and experience through your senses what your human life is like. In situations where you feel threatened or frightened, call upon your animal to help you. When you have to deal with difficult people or situations, ask for your animal's wisdom in dealing with these. Thank it for any help given.

You may wish to set up an image of your animal somewhere in your house – a postcard, object or something which you have made, embroidered or painted – which need not proclaim your activities to your household, but which acts as a reminder to yourself. We have images of friends and family in our homes after all and they do not all have to be physical reality ones! It is not necessary for you to tell others about your spirits if you don't want to. If you do, choose your confidant wisely; the early stages of any relationship need gentle encouragement not the full blast of media attention. Your animal will reveal who is a good soul-friend with whom to share your shamanic side.

Practice 27: Exploring the Middleworld

The following suggestions are useful in consolidating your Middleworld practice. Before you set out on any journey,

always have at least one ally with you and focus your intention clearly; for example 'I am journeying to understand the difficulties surrounding my new job'. Some of these suggestions involve physical reality tasks only, but each has its own subtle reality manifestation.

1. In everyday situations, without deep sourcing, practise checking ahead on the way to your destination. You may only receive a few 'bat-signals' (see Glossary) from which to intuit response: check these on arrival. Example: 'Does the village shop have any pineapples today?' Proficiency in checking ahead can prevent wasted time and effort.

2. Find an area in which your walking between the worlds can be put to practical use. Journey to seek help, support and guidance in voluntary social work, environmental guardianship, active and financial support for a charity.

3. Adopt a sacred site of your choice. Visit it, then return home to journey there and meet its guardian spirit. Ask its needs and whether your human interest or help is appropriate. Some sites need healing if they have been misused, recently or in the past: be guided by your allies and the spirit of this site. Obtain or draw a picture of the site and place it on your shrine and try to remain in contact/awareness of the place as regularly as possible. It is not advisable to journey at sacred sites unless they are remote or free from interruption.

4. Communicate or make social contact with an ethnic group other than your own. Study the ways of this group and help bridge the divides between races by journeying to ask 'what gifts do this people bring to our community?'

5. Attune regularly in your daily life the different beings of the earth in both physical and subtle reality: deities, animals, plants, trees and minerals. Slowly gain familiarity by study, observation, journeying, always asking permission and showing respect. Your journeys will increase your knowledge and understanding.

Practice 28: Finding a Middleworld Teacher

Your Middleworld teacher is your primal ally in any middle-world shamanic work, someone of whom you may ask advice and guidance. S/he often appears as the spirit of your journey centre and it is in this form that you will seek and find your Middleworld teacher.

Journey to your centre as in Practice 24. Look for the spirit of the place. You may become quickly aware of this being or you may find you need a few return visits. When you meet any living form ask, 'Are you the spirit of this place?' When you meet a spirit which confirms this, greet and thank it. Ask it further, 'Are you my Middleworld teacher?'

If the spirit of the place affirms this, then greet and acknowl-edge it. Your subsequent journey may unfold variously: you may remain in quiet companionship here; you may learn more about this place; the spirit may ask your help in maintaining the guardianship in some way (for example cleaning debris from a stream, seeking help with others to preserve the sacred integrity of the site); you may ask the spirit to help you in your walking between the worlds, or in your daily life.

If the spirit of your journey-centre is not your Middleworld teacher, ask it where the teacher may be found. Consult your guardian animal also. Call out for your Middleworld teacher to appear and go looking.

Teachers nearly always appear in human-like form, although they may sometimes have a mixture of forms – animal with human, human with plant, for example. Ask any living beings that you meet if they are your Middleworld teacher. If you do not succeed, try again another time.

At the call-back signal, thank any helpers and say farewell to the Middleworld teacher, who remains in subtle reality. Return to your body and record experiences.

On subsequent journeys, you will visit your Middleworld teacher to ask about issues such as those in Practice 27.

2. EARTH-CYCLES

Those who practise know that there is something more in woods than in books. Trees and stones will teach you what cannot be heard from a master.

St Bernard of Clairvaux

All shamanic work is grounded in and illuminated by the patterns of the natural world, and they are our primary middle-world teachers. Whatever we learn or gain from our journeys is manifested in the realm of ordinary reality, where time and space give shape to our lives. Although we are learning how to co-operate with the timelessness and unlimited dimensionality of subtle reality, and how to walk in otherworlds, our aim is not to become subtle reality spirits. We should not cease relating what we learn to our everyday world. Though we journey to the three worlds, we must also return to our own.

Some people are born with an innate sense of fitness and timeliness; others lack all sense of occasion. Such people are not properly grounded in physical reality, but are always partially off somewhere else. If you recognize yourself by the following signs, then you need to work through the practices at the end of this section and stop any walking between the worlds for the present:

Failure to note what is said or done near you
Inability to keep stable relationships
Inability to sustain any activity for more than a short time
Lack of interest in the world around you
Intense self-absorption
Continual day-dreaming
Suspicion that everyone is against you
Feeling of being 'out of synch' with life
Never living in the present moment; always brooding over
the past or worrying about the future.

These are all symptoms of soul-straying or moderate power-loss which society normally defines as being antisocial, selfish or mildly paranoid. All of us go through periods of this in our lives, when we wander about insufficiently grounded. Worries, disruptions and problems all have the ability to unsettle us, unseating one or more soul-fragments.

We are not talking about major soul-loss here, just soul-straying, when one or more soul-parts are dislodged and float off, usually remaining close by and within range, to be consciously recalled. Some people live their whole lives in this slightly out of focus way, never really achieving any strong definition in career, relationships or interests. Just when they feel that they are finally grasping what life is about, some slight worry comes along and off floats that soul-part again like a balloon in the wind.

There is no better way to call the soul home than by focusing on the power-cycles of the earth and steering our lives by their currents. Earth-cycles are the co-ordinates of home. People who experience the kind of soul-straying described above primarily need to define where their home is in physical reality; they need to stress their belonging to the earth, to increase their mundane presence. When they have grasped this definition and have become properly grounded and integrated into daily life, they may wish to start exploring subtle reality, but not before. If you had decided that this world wasn't much use to you and that the otherworlds might be more help, then this advice may sound irritating, but it is a fact that the best shamans – and the best people – are those with their feet firmly on the ground, with well-integrated lives and their roots in a variety of mundane pursuits.

Earth-cycles are the power-circuits of which all life-forms in physical reality partake and share. They govern growth and decay and are intimately associated with the flow of life-energy. Such cycles are based upon time, space and the quality of matter, upon the three dimensions of earthly life in effect. When we consider these cycles we begin to apprehend the immensity of the physical side of the cosmic web.

Grounding in Time

The following time-cycles govern the growth patterns of life:

Day-cycle	SUN	Dawn	Midday	Twilight	Midnight
Moon-cycle	MOON	Waxing	Full	Waning	Dark
Year-cycle	STARS	Spring	Summer	Autumn	Winter
Growth-cycle	EARTH	Flowering	Ripening	Harvesting	Seeding

Figure 3. Time-cycles

The diurnal cycle of the sun is marked by one revolution of the earth, giving us day and night. Our vitality is affected by the active light of the sun; our energies fluctuate considerably through twenty-four hours according to the amount of light we are exposed to. In circumpolar regions the year itself takes on a day and night shape, as several winter months are spent in near-darkness and the summer months in perpetual sunlight. If we attempt to work at night we run counter to this cycle and need to concentrate very hard to maintain wakefulness. The movement of objects or people during sacred ceremonies is normally sunwise.

The monthly cycle of the moon is marked by approximately twenty-eight revolutions of the earth. Our creativity is triggered by the passive light of the moon which brings hidden potentialities and seeds to germination. Gardeners, farmers, seafarers and women all understand that the moon's power is not 'just moonshine'. The moon illuminates the night and influences the subtle tides of our lives.

The yearly cycle of the stars is marked by approximately 365 revolutions of the earth. One earth year is the equivalent of one sun day. Our destiny and vocation are reflected by the ever-changing kaleidoscope of constellations, as astrologers of all eras have testified. The larger patterns of our lives, submerged in dream or intuited through vision, sometimes leap into active focus as the seasons succeed each other.

The growth-cycle applies to all life-forms which undergo conception, birth, life and death: some insects may go through one cycle in a few days, while the cycle of trees and rocks may be years or aeons. Many traditional peoples reckoned the growth-cycles by comparing that of different life-forms, as in this Gaelic saying:

> Three ages of a dog, the age of a horse.
> Three ages of a horse, the age of a man.
> Three ages of a man, the age of a deer.
> Three ages of a deer, the age of an eagle.
> Three ages of an eagle, the age of an oak tree.[1]

The time-divisions of the year have been variously calculated by different cultures, some favouring moon-cycles more prominently than solar cycles. All divisions have been defined by stellar observation. The seasonal tides of the year are governed

by the subtle influence of the sun and bring marked changes to our lives. In the northern hemisphere, the spring tide changes at the Spring Equinox; it cleanses outworn ideas and sweeps away the ills of the winter, bringing new ideas and fresh impulses. The summer tide enters with the Summer Solstice, bringing the confidence to expand and broaden our ideas, encouraging the burgeoning of life. The tide of the Autumn Equinox is a time of assimilation and gathering in, when we assess projects and monitor results. The tide of the Winter Solstice brings the completion of long-term projects; in the deep quietness of winter, we may contemplate the year ahead.

If we live attuned to the tides, currents, influences and energies of earth-cycles, we will come into better alignment with our physical existence and have a deeper appreciation of the subtle networks which connect us to the cosmic web.

The passage of time and the continuity of life was clearly understood by medieval peasants who worked the land; only the rich and privileged were exempt from such work and it was for them that the medieval books of hours, devotionals marking the sevenfold monastic daily prayers, were made. These included a yearly calendar of saints' days, with each month commonly illuminated by a depiction of the monthly tasks such as sowing or wood-gathering.

Recently, in both books and training courses, earth-cycles have been similarly codified and ascribed to various frameworks such as the mandala, medicine wheel, tree of life or horoscope. There is no tradition of such a rigidly tabulated method of learning in native societies. To a person living through the cycle of the year, such matters would be so obvious as to be hardly worth stating. It is only as we have grown further away from the natural world that these teaching models have taken on such significance, far greater than was intended.

The correlation of elements, colours, skills, tasks, qualities and so on with certain directions or times of year are misleading to those who take such wheels at face value without personal input or relation to the part of the earth on which they live. A loose codification of such cycles *can be* of great benefit as reminders to modern urban people who have lost touch with the seasonal lessons that unfold, so long as we realize they are only

other people's definitions. It is far better to arrive at your own correspondences.

For one thing, we need to be sensitive to specific power-cycles when we move from country to country, for they change as we move around the globe. National secular calendars rarely have much to tell us about the subtle life of that country; however, local religious and seasonal festivals highlight different aspects of the year and have much to teach us.

Grounding in Space

Our spatial and dimensional relationship with the earth is very important. Ancient wisdom reveals that all peoples regarded their own tribe, village, location as the centre of the universe. This may strike us as either unscientific or presumptuous, but it is a true understanding of subtle cosmology. Wherever we are upon the earth colours our understanding of the universe; wherever we are when we enter into spiritual practice *is* the primal gateway to subtle reality, to the three worlds and to the cosmic web.

Wherever spiritual practice has evolved in dynamic ways, there we find the shrines, temples and sacred landscapes of the earth. Such sacred sites are the junctions where physical and subtle reality intersect and are recognized as places of great power. Certain sacred sites are in geomantic alignment, connected by ley lines or energy currents.

The manner in which we understand our position on the globe affects how sacred places are identified, how and where houses are constructed, where roads are laid and a myriad other factors. The true architect needs to be a geomancer, one sensitive to the art of placement, able to divine the needs of place, time and purpose, able to create a ground-plan that will be harmonious.

Directions are not merely compass-points which lead off abstractly into infinity. Each direction brings us different information with which we need to be in sensitive relation, whether we are on land or sea. Geomantically sensitive people can predict movements of animals, changes in weather, the prospects for the growth-cycle. Diviners and dowsers are able to trace the network of energy veins through the earth to find water, minerals or other substances.

Directions may only be understood in relation to where we stand at this time. The ascription of the classical elements (see

below) to the cardinal directions is a case in point: in North America the earth element is sometimes assigned to the west, in Northern Europe to the north, in Tibet to the east. Shaman-izing in a different land presents us with opportunities to intuit and co-operate with these power-cycles. The ascription of the elements to the directions is markedly different in the southern hemisphere, as the polar ice-cap is in the south, not the north. The association of directions and elements is frequently deter-mined by the nature of the winds which blow over a particular land-mass.

Grounding in Matter

As the sun, moon and stars define time, and as the directions define space, so the four elements define matter. Nearly every people recognizes the four elements in the winds, sunlight, waters and soil of their land as well as perceiving the elemental spirits of their subtle reality.

The four elements are everywhere used to cleanse: bodies are cleansed with sand in deserts; fire is used to cauterize wounds and disinfect surgical instruments; smoking herbs are used to purify atmospheres; water is used for washing. Saunas and sweat-baths use mixtures of the elements to cleanse.

The elements are also agents of decay and physical disposal: upon the Zoroastrian Towers of Silence, the Tibetan and North American death platforms, bodies are subjected to the swift disintegration of the winds; in India and other places bodies are cremated in fire or given to the waters; many cultures inhume their dead in consecrated burial grounds.

The elements are used in sacred ceremonies: air is used in smoke offerings to the spirits, as incense, or as bundles of sweet-grass, sage and other herbs; fire is used to bless and increase growth; water is used to bless and anoint; earth is used to make sacred mandalas.

The associations of different cultures with the qualities of the elements are diverse: some associate water with vision and creation, others see fire as the regenerative element. The elements of fire and water are often the subject of creation myths. Sacred fire-keeping is a universal tradition, stemming from times when the kindling of fire was an arduous routine; stories of stealing fire from the gods abound.

Our bodies have their own reflection of the elements: in the air which inspirits our lungs, in the heat of the blood which circulates our veins, in the water of which our bodies are composed, in the rock-like framework of our bones and the soft earth of our skins. But it is in the realization of the subtle reality of these associations that we begin to learn about our connection with the earth-cycles. 'In the perennial wisdom traditions, our bodies are the most potent form of spiritual realization', wrote R. J. Stewart in his *Power within the Land*.

The admixture of time, direction and matter results in the weather of both the earth and of us. Medieval medical philosophy understood the human body to be influenced by the qualities of the elements and directions, the combination of which created 'the four humours', which demarked the different kinds of physical and psychic constitutions.

```
                         Cold
                         Earth
                         North
Cold + Moist = Phlegmatic            Cold + Dry = Melancholic
Wet                                                      Dry
Water                                                    Air
West                                                    East
    Wet + Hot = Sanguine         Hot + Dry = Choleric
                         Hot
                         Fire
                         South
```

Figure 4. The four humours

An excess of one or other humour was believed to lead to illness and to antisocial behaviour. Modern Indian Ayurvedic medicine still operates by similar principles.

But we have two sets of senses, physical and subtle, shown in Figure 5.

Physical Senses	*Subtle Senses*
Sight	Inner Vision
Hearing	Resonance
Smell	Instinct
Taste	Discrimination
Touch	Empathy

Figure 5. The physical and subtle senses

Our physical sight is complemented by inner vision; our hearing by resonance or the bat-signals of intuition; our physical senses of smell and taste are strongly inter-related, as are our subtle senses of instinct and discrimination; touch is complemented by our ability to empathize and be moved by our subtle reality experiences.

If our physical senses are well balanced and we listen to their messages responsively, we are accordingly well aligned when we walk between the worlds and utilize our subtle senses. We also use our subtle senses in physical reality.

The power-cycles of the earth are implicit in our living; by reintegrating ourselves with the rhythms of the earth we enter more deeply into the Middleworld of shamanic journeying.

Practice 29: Relating to the Time-cycles

Formulate your own daily and monthly cycle by observing the season, weather and mood of the time. Create your own calendrical cycle of the year, marking seasonal changes, significant days, specific time-related activities such as sacred festivals that you celebrate. Before sacred days, journey to your journey-centre with your animal and ask your Middleworld teacher what opportunities and lessons are available at these times.

Practice 30: Harvesting the Sun; Communing with the Moon; Seeding with the Stars

---

The sun, moon and stars provide us with the three kinds of life essential for our well-being: physical vitality, psychic health and creative potential. In times of low vitality, try and spend as much time out of doors as possible, especially if the sun is visible in the sky, even if it's winter. During the summer and autumn, be aware of the sunlight striking your brow and consciously store it within you. During the winter, call upon that store of vitality. Seasonal affective disorder is a condition suffered by people who live near the poles or too much indoors and is related to insufficient light-stimulus.

In times of low expectation, fluctuating energy and difficult

growth, be aware of the moon. Even if you live somewhere where the horizon is crowded by buildings or if the sky is often overcast or dazzled by street-lights, track the moon's journey across the sky by looking up each night. Commune with the moon, receive the patience to be fallow.

In times of great change, challenge or creative struggle, be aware of the stars above you, present even when it is day. Make an effort to visit a place at least once a month from which the stars can be seen. Watch the seasonal dance of the stars and begin to understand the progress of your own life with greater confidence.

You may sing your thanks to each luminary for help received, and dedicate your activities, plans and projects to all beings on the cosmic web.

Practice 31: The Hearth Shrine

Find the centre of your home's inspiration: this might be an actual hearth, if you have a fireplace, or it might be the gathering point where you and your family or guests assemble when the day's work is done. Consider your home's centre by sitting in it. Now, source its subtle reality and, with the help of your Middleworld helpers, ask to be shown the heart of your home. You may become aware of the land-spirits which inhabit your bit of earth (even if you live several floors up!). You may experience the vitality which animates your home in another guise. Ask how you may best honour and maintain this essential vitality or spirit. Return and record. Create a small but potent hearth shrine at your centre. It need not be ostentatious or obviously shamanic to look at: the very minimum is a candle or lamp which can be lit for at least a few minutes a day to bless your home and honour the hearth.

Practice 32: Purifying the Senses

To experience the proper humility which accompanies shamanic work, we need to undergo a purification of the senses. This may entail fasting from food and drink, fasting from common comforts, fasting from television and wrap-round music, fast-

ing from severe or critical thoughts, fasting from phoney spiritual stimulants. Consider your own imbalances and practise one form of fasting, with moderation, this week.

Practice 33: The Messages of the Senses

Let one of your physical senses take you for a walk – in the country or in the town. Listen to your physical senses; for example, when you go shopping for food, ask 'does my body need this?' This is not an exercise in gross self-gratification but an experiment to discover your body's essential needs. Let your subtle senses assess why you stop in front of certain shelves. This goes beyond reading the labels! Go into fruit and vegetable shops and let your body choose your food for the week.

Practice 34: Dancing the Seasons

Just as the stars perform a yearly stellar dance above our heads, so people have reflected this seasonal progress upon the earth with their feet. The Hopi Indians of the North American south-west perform complex cycles of dances which bring rain, growth and integration to the earth. British morris dancers mark the year with seasonal dances. Such dances usually reflect agricultural and elemental changes and the movement or behaviour of animals, symbolically and shamanically marking the effect that these have upon the round of life.

Dance is most often seen as a social and recreative art-form, yet it is central to shamanism, an ecstatic way between the worlds. Explore the nature of the year and find your own sacred points of reference: these need not be strictly calendrical with festivals on fixed dates, but may reveal themselves to you through the first spring flowers blooming, the first day of a new moon, the day when you feel summer has really arrived. With a simple instrument like a rattle, or with clothes or ornaments which jingle, clash or rustle upon you, stand and enter into the feeling which the season evokes in you. Now begin to move on the spot, rattling or jingling. Your movements need not be balletic or have accepted dance forms. Let your mind be

free of self-consciousness, let it roam widely over the season.
Here is an example:

> Dance report. The day of the Spring Equinox was bright and
> blustery. I danced in the garden with rattle and ankle bells.
> Facing the sun, I sang a little and rattled. Then, closing my eyes,
> I let my body feel the sun. My feet began to lift and stamp. I
> circled on the spot, stamping in each direction. The rattle grew
> busy in my hand and my arm began to arc and circle in the
> opposite direction to the one my body was circulating in. I
> started to source as I danced. It was a dancing of seeds in the
> earth and their effort to be out into the air. The seeds became
> bees pollinating flowers. Birds began to call and I sang their calls.
> I saw the migratory birds return to our shores. Then the sun
> flooded everything and there was only a whirling goldenness in
> which I became still and fell to my knees.

Practice 35: Sacred and Power-centres

Many places are imbued with particular power or holiness.
Some are marked by extraordinary structures like Stonehenge
in England, or the Nazca glyphs of South America. Others are
natural sites of awe-inspiring beauty like Ayers Rock in Northern
Australia, or Ise in Japan where there is a shrine to the sun-
goddess, Amaterasu. Sacred centres are 'burning glasses',
where the physical and subtle worlds meet. Visit one with
respect. Greet and acknowledge guardians, and learn what
there is to know. Rather than taking away a part of that site,
leave a gift instead: a strand of hair or a prayer of beneficial
intention towards the site-guardians. Ensure that your gift is
not detrimental to any living thing and does not deface or
abuse the site.

Some places on the earth are special to us; places where
we feel uplifted and encouraged, places where we renew our
energy. Find a place near where you live that works for you.
This may not be a formally designated sacred site. When you
are unconnected, disoriented or out of true with yourself,
when being with other people causes you anguish, go to sit in
your place. Be in your body, not in your head. Let being
outdoors help to centre you; feel your distress subsiding. Let
the elements ground you: be aware of the winds that blow on
you, the sun that warms you, the rain that cleanses your tears;

feel the support of the earth. Sit and acknowledge the elements and ask their help: make connection, let impurities drain out, draw up fresh energies.

Practice 36: Shrining

If you are working in a regular way, formalize a focus for the spirits with the creation of a shrine, either permanent or temporary. A permanent shrine to honour the spirits might be erected in your garden or on a dresser at home. A temporary shrine might be erected when you go outside to work, or in a hired hall where you meet with others. My temporary shrine equipment is always packed and ready to go with me wherever I go. It consists of a stone, a water-bottle, a bowl, a small candle in a tall glass container, a bowl of earth in which to put charcoal and incense, and a cloth. Thus, I always have representatives of the four elements. I will add whatever is appropriate to my practice that day – whether a fallen branch, a picture or postcard of an animal or being, a pile of nuts or berries – as an offering.

Check periodically to see if your shrine is in need of cleaning or changing. If you experience dissatisfaction with it, take it down and build a new one. All urgings to spring-clean the house should start and finish with the shrine since energy can become stalemated or blocked around it. Incoming seasonal tides and currents can be effectively met in this way. As the seasons change, so do different influences arise. Your shrine is a point of contact between this world and the others, which is why you should be sensitive to what it is telling you.

Practice 37: The Seven Directions

The ascription of elements and qualities to the four cardinal directions can only be made by yourself. Wherever you are living on the planet you can use your physical and subtle senses to source these qualities. Answer these questions to determine which feel best.

1. *From which directions does the greatest cold/heat/wetness/dryness come in your country?* This will help ascribe the different elements of earth, fire, water and air to the directions.

2. *What qualities do you associate with these directions and elements?*
   If that direction could appear as an animal, a tree, a plant, a stone – what kind would it be?

Do not let your intellect dictate any fixed and immovable associations. If you cannot decide about the quality of any direction, then journey into that direction with your animal and ask your Middleworld teacher to reveal it to you.

These four directions, and their physical and subtle properties, relate to the Middleworld. Three further directions need acknowledgement: above, the Upperworld; below, the Underworld; and within, the centre of the known and unknown where the heart of the cosmic web intersects the centre of your own being.

Before you shamanize, it is a good practice to acknowledge the seven directions. This can be simply done by singing or rattling in the directions in turn; in more complex work you might wish to sing specific welcome songs to each direction and make elemental or grain offerings. First, seek alignment with the cardinal directions and their spirits. If you live in the northern hemisphere, start in the east and turn sunwise to south, west and north. If you live in the southern hemisphere, the circuit is reversed: start in the east and turn north, west and south. Then, call upon the spirits of the Upperworld and Underworld. Lastly, turn to the silent centre of your own soul within; visualize your soul and the heart of the cosmic web intersecting each other.

When you conclude your shamanizing, reverse this procedure, this time thanking rather than welcoming. When you reverse the cardinal directions, concentrate upon their physical reality – earth as soil, water as a river or sea, fire as sunlight, air as wind.

Practice 38: Invisibility and Becoming Noticeable

Sometimes we wish to be invisible – for instance in places where we may meet time-wasting acquaintances, and sometimes to be noticed – for instance in restaurants when we want to be served or get our bill and leave. The following practices can be quite useful.

To become invisible: relax, breathe, and source your animal. Ask it to help you become invisible: specify whether to all viewers or to some. Afterwards, don't forget to reverse the procedure and become visible. *Note*: it is difficult to become invisible to psychics or seers who may see you as your animal!

To become noticeable, relax, breathe, and source your animal to help you become noticeable: specify to whom. Be careful not to extend your range beyond the projected area or you may become depleted. Concentrate on the abilities within yourself you want recognized. Ensure you reverse this and ground afterwards.

5.   The Underworld

From you,
ancestral holy land,
history nourishes itself.
And I continue to walk
in the paths
of the ancient pilgrims.

The Olive Tree and the Mountain
Carlos Reyes-Manzo

1. IN THE HOUSE OF MEMORY

News from a forrein Country came,
As if my Treasure and my Wealth lay there:
So much it did my Heart Enflame!
Twas wont to call my Soul into mine Ear.

On News
Thomas Traherne

THE UNDERWORLD IS the power-house of the three worlds. Here we draw upon our deep resources, our traditional inheritance, our memory. If we recall Figure 1, where the three worlds are connected by the great central tree, we may understand the Underworld as the rich loam into which the tree's roots go down. In addition, all trees have a tap-root which searches out the nearest source of water, whose nurture it then channels to the rest of the tree. When we enter the Underworld, we too put down our tap-root and draw up refreshment.

The Underworld has a bad press in the West, since in both classical and Christian cosmology it has been understood as hell. Shamans experience the Underworld as a world of foundations and beginnings, a place where the roots go deep, not as a place of fear and terror but as one of primal joy and creativity.

For many religions, the Underworld has become a kind of toxic-waste dumping ground where the spiritual evils of the world are thought to lie ready to recrudesce. Scenarios of unending hell-fire and terror have been set up to guard the gates of the Underworld from unauthorized intrusion. Our communion with the Underworld has been severed by fearful religious dogmas which would prefer us to imagine a region of demons and seering flame, rather than one of restoration and reconnective joy.

Let us be peaceful and confident in soul before we undertake the Underworld journey or read further.

Permission to disregard the instruction that the Underworld is a kind of spiritual dustbin is here given.

The Underworld is a place of mirror images, reversals and complementarities where the physical reality of our daily lives is thrown into startling subtle-reality relief. Imagine the veil between realities as a gauze hanging from floor to ceiling; if you push your hand into the gauze, you cause it to push *inwards* away from your side; anyone standing on the other side of the gauze will see your hand push *outwards* towards them. When we move between the worlds, we often experience the same effect, especially near the thresholds between them.

If we bear this in mind, we will begin to understand why the Underworld journey has been discouraged by non-shamanic cultures: for here the threshold guardians assume tiny or gigantic size, here we meet the spirits of realities we have neglected or ignored. Without strong and willing allies, such encounters can confuse and terrify, and many genuine mystics have gone thither without preparation or ally, returning to report strange sights. Without the correct cosmological information, without a non-dual framework to travel from, religions have correspondingly barred the doors between the worlds.

Wise traditions draw continually upon the Underworld and

are fed by it, and many people are coming to regret deeply that we have lost communion with the rich indigenous cultures of our planet. Our hearts are gripped by the many myths and stories which relate the Underworld journeys of seekers after the treasures of wisdom. The descent of Inanna to take the initiation of mortality and gain wisdom; the descent of Aeneas to meet and consult his dead father; Orpheus's descent to retrieve Eurydice; the initiatory descent of Christian Rosenkreutz into the vault; the descent of Persephone which triggers the coming of agricultural wisdom to earth; the descent of King Arthur to bring home the Cauldron, prototype of the Grail. These myths speak of initiation into wisdom and the winning of empowering treasures through endurance, perseverance and courage.

These heroic descents can also be ours through the shamanic journey. Reconnection with the Underworld restores communication with the voices of our wise ancestors, with traditions which hallow the earth, with the deep empowering teachings and treasures which remain eternally available.

Many of us already access parts of the Underworld, when we check back to a distant memory and access times, places and people who are no longer present in physical reality, or when we are faced with immense difficulties and find superhuman strength and power. Whenever we instinctively resonate to or react against something, we are assessing its true integrity, its primal Underworldly fitness: situations and people who do not ring true often have no firm foundation. We often experience the Underworld when we begin a project: after arduous research we stop, feeling that we can go no deeper, and pure information bubbles up and interconnections are effortlessly made. Whenever we draw upon deep memory, experience primal power and creative joy, or re-enter the richness of childhood play, we are sending down a soul-part, like a tap-root, into the Underworld.

The Underworld is associated, though not exclusively, with the past and is a good place to review the roots of something, or to heal imbalances which are the result of past cause and effect. It is where we perceive the subtext or mythic resonance of things.

The beings encountered in the Underworld include ancestral teachers, clan totems, deities who initiate and empower,

dwarfs, dragons and other subterranean or watery guardians of power. You may encounter ancestral councils or assemblies here. The *genius* of the Underworld often appears as a Lord or King of the Underworld and is sometimes horned or antlered, like the Celtic Cernunnos or the Hindu Pasupati, and surrounded by many beasts. Such beings have been described by Christians as devils of malign intent, but in fact their function is one of gate-keeping and initiating. The *juno* of the Underworld often appears as an initiatory maiden or elder, or as Queen and Mistress of the Underworld, often in partnership with her Lord, like Persephone and Pluto.

Each land has its own Underworld guardians. Awakening and communicating with these native powers is important work. During the early 1980s, I visited many parts of Britain with other walkers between the worlds, specifically to effect such awakenings, as part of the worldwide reawakening of native traditions. As a result of such operations, certain powers have become more widely available and contactable: they have been set in motion by many people in all parts of the web where such work is an ongoing task of native walkers between worlds. It has been termed 'awakening the Sleepers' by R. J. Stewart.[1]

Not all ancient power and wisdom is appropriate for our time. It is important not to evoke inappropriate energies, but to 'clear the ways' between our own world and the deep power of the Underworld after so many centuries of neglect and misunderstanding, so that the primal wisdom of the ancestral traditions may once more flow as a corrective to our over-urban and increasingly fragmented lives.

The Underworld activates our remembrance. It relates to the brain-stem, where the deep memories are stored and which branches out to feed our central cerebral cortex. As the place of primal beginnings, of the ancestors and deep memories, the Underworld is where we often find our most enduring allies.

Practice 39: Finding an Underworld Entrance

In the last part, you found a centre from which to start middle-world journeying. In order to reach the Underworld, we need to find an opening going down into the earth. This entrance should exist in physical reality and not be an imagined place:

an underground cavern, a spring or well, an animal or tree hole, an ancient chambered burial mound. Natural places are best, although I have clients who readily employ a London Underground tunnel. There is no one right way to the Underworld. If your entrance exists near your Middleworld journey-centre, even better, but it doesn't have to be. For journeying in all three worlds I use the same favourite tree, using the hole in its trunk as a way down, its branches as a way up and its actual locus as a place of Middleworld journey. Find an entrance that works for you. If you chose a hole which in physical reality is too small for you, it will be big enough when you come to journey. If you choose to travel down through water, you will be able to breathe.

Practice 40: The Underworld Journey

Since the Underworld Journey is more complex than the middleworld one, we will proceed in stages, as follows.

1. Your purpose for this first journey is to seek reconnection with the Underworld and your power. Exclude light, be comfortable either sitting or lying down, start to source, recalling your purpose, and bringing to mind your entrance.
2. Before going into your entrance, call your guardian animal to come with you. If it does not come fairly quickly, then proceed downwards without it, intending to meet it when you get down. Allies you have met in one world can appear in and accompany you to other worlds. But if your middleworld animal does not appear here, and you do not encounter it in either the tunnel or in the Underworld, then it may be that you will meet a stronger guardian animal in the Underworld.
3. In the tunnel which leads between entrance and Underworld, be aware of your surroundings and keep going downwards. If you meet difficulties or obstacles ask your allies for assistance, even though you may not have one with you at that moment.
4. When you emerge into the Underworld, you may be surprised to see that you are not underground! The landscape into which you emerge may appear as any known geographical

zone of the earth – desert, snow-covered, temperate, sea-scape. Wherever you emerge, whatever you see, this is how the Underworld looks for you. Remember that the cosmic web is not two or even three dimensional: it interpenetrates all zones simultaneously. All people access the Underworld through their personal tunnel and may arrive in different parts of it.

So, how do you know you've hit the Underworld? There is a kind of 'deepness' to it which cannot be confused with other levels. Some people experience this as feeling of homecoming or ingathering, of belonging or wondrous re-membering. Others do not experience this, but feel the Underworld as a place of awesome power or strength. People with tinges of claustrophobia often feel uncomfortable with Underworld travelling, and feel enclosed. In many senses, going there is like returning to the womb. Within the Underworld, we experience and receive teachings by osmosis, just like a foetus in the womb feeding on the nourishment of the placenta.

5. Meet your animal or go looking for a guardian animal in the Underworld, following the directions on page 101.

6. Having made connection with your guardian animal, make your request for reconnection with the Underworld and with your power.

7. Following your animal's direction: you may be shown things, taken places, given advice, encouraged to dance and sing, or many other things. Whatever happens is the answer to your request.

8. Continue journeying until your sound-source signals the call-back. If you have met a new animal, bring it back with you the way you came, briefly record your journey and then dance the animal. If you have received help from your guardian animal, give it thanks and return alone

---

Practice 41: Exploring the Underworld

The following are suggestions for journeys or work involving the Underworld. We access the subtle reality of the Underworld when we need power, traditional wisdom, memory, when we need to access our authentic creative impulse.

1. Retrieve lost knowledge with the help of your Underworld allies. The more you journey, the more allies you will make. They will make themselves known to you.
2. Gain solidarity with your ancestors.
3. Go to regain power when you feel at a loss or vitally depleted, when you need reconnection with your deep self.
4. Ask Underworld allies for personal healing.
5. Investigate the deep causes of world problems and ask for healing.

2. IN THE HOUSE OF THE ANCESTORS

She sometimes wished she could make the earth and stones speak and tell her all about the dead people who had trodden upon them.

Lark Rise to Candleford
Flora Thompson

The Underworld is the place where we are most likely to meet the ancestors. These include our blood relatives, as well as the peoples of the past who lived before our time. Without the ancestors, we would not exist. They bequeath us life: we inherit life from them. For this reason, all indigenous societies recognize and revere their ancestors, and put their elders first in all matters, rather than last as in our culture. The Western failure to honour or respect ancestors has created great problems.

A society which honours its ancestors also honours its descendants; it makes tribal decisions and social changes cautiously, since these will effect not just one, but many generations; it breeds humility and selflessness in leaders; it recognizes the wisdom or futility of past actions and does not repeat mistakes; it nurtures economy with natural resources and a wise use of land. In contrast, our society leaves its descendants a fearful legacy based on a disregard for either past or future: short-term decisions made by hasty, ignorant and arrogant leaders which poison the earth and waste natural resources.

In our culture, we have tended to fear the ancestors because the dead have been seen as jealous of our life and likely to steal whatever vitality they can from us. Most indigenous peoples recognize that the affairs of the dead and the living are normally kept separate, although this does not stop them from recogniz-

ing and giving thanks for the help, wisdom and guidance of
the ancestors at regular intervals. Respect for our ancestors is
not given in order to appease the dead, but to acknowledge
the gift of life which they have given us. This is often celebrated
by an annual festival where the dead are honoured. In the
West, we remember our dead at Hallow'een, the ancient Celtic
festival of Samhain when the ancestors were believed to be
abroad.[2]

The Ancestral Bequest

We each have romantic visions of what our ancestors might be
like. But human nature tells us that, just because a person is
old, it does not necessarily make her also wise. We are each
programmed to fulfil certain ancestral expectations. We may
have an unspoken dread of repeating ancestral patterns in
our lives, aware that these underscore our own life-pattern.
Modern therapeutic methods often address current family
issues by concentrating on analysis of our upbringing and
family relationships: it has been my experience that distant
family history also has a bearing on current situations, that
significant patterns are laid down for generations. Some of
these can be dealt with in family therapy, but some problems
go beyond counselling.

The work of Dr Kenneth McAll,[3] a consultant psychiatrist,
of 'healing the family tree' is based on the principle of cutting
unhealthy links between a person and their ancestors by prayer
and a celebration of the eucharist. Dr McAll works from a
strong Christian belief and is sternly discouraging of all non-
Christian spiritual practices which he sees as evil, yet he has
correctly diagnosed many family problems and illnesses as
having their roots in ancestral unfinished business.

We all understand how certain physical and mental illnesses
are genetically transmitted from one generation to another:
medical research is now attempting to identify and minimize
the effect of genetic inheritances of this kind. But it is also true
that certain habitual patterns set up in past times also resurface
in families: incest and child abuse invariably recur in generation
after generation of some families, for example. We need to say
'the buck stops here' and enlist the help of wise ancestors and

spiritual teachers, for the longer we leave such situations, the greater the responsibility for finding a circuit-breaking solution.

Carl Jung wrote that 'possession is caused by something that could perhaps most fitly be described as an "ancestral soul" '.[4] The habits, angers and frustrations of human existence all create waves upon the cosmic web. We recognize this frequency in ourselves as 'human nature'. Christians call it 'original sin'. We do not need to use dualistic terms but unless we recognize and clarify the issues which surround us while we are alive, we are likely to unintentionally bequeath these to our relatives at our deaths.

The nature of 'the ancestral bequest' varies from family to family, but it can reach quite staggering proportions if it is not addressed periodically. It can be avoided only by each of us taking responsibility for our own spiritual clarification, so that our unfinished business does not descend to the next generation. The ancestral bequest can be cleared with the help of Underworld and Upperworld teachers working in tandem (see Practice 47). The burden of ancestral business can also be lightened by the family as a whole if they become aware of the nature of their problem and earnestly desire to redress the balance. They need to acknowledge (*not blame*) ancestral failures and their continued influence in the family, pray for the release of ancestral spirits from their unfinished business, seek and offer them forgiveness, and actively address the problem so that it is dealt with.

Vengeance, hatred, fear and guilt are the strongest links in the circuit of the ancestral bequest, which is why forgiveness is an important part of relinquishing ancestral patterns, for it is the supreme circuit-breaker. Forgiveness springs from impartial love, which puts the benefit of the cosmic web before any personal benefit. *Forgiveness restores the broken threads of the web: it rebuilds the pathways which allow the ancestral soul finally to go home.*

The National Bequest

Just as families have their ancestral bequest, so too, do countries. This has been apparent in the failure of global negotiations under the umbrella of the United Nations. The disunity and squabbling between nations is like that of a huge family, what we can call the 'national bequest'.

Our avoidance of or obsession with ancestral issues is often at the root of unhealthy nationalism and racism. Pride in our country and forebears must always be balanced by our awareness of the rest of the cosmic web. Many countries are now harvesting the seeds of colonialism sown in past centuries. Ignoring this legacy will not make it go away; our responsibility is to deal with it now. The present conflicts in the Middle East, in Northern Ireland and former Yugoslavia have their roots in unresolved conflicts and territorial disputes of past ages: religious intolerance is not a cause, just a symptom of a festering ancestral imbalance.

Wars and conflicts are most often rooted in territorial boundary disputes, in the invasion of privilege or custom. Vendettas and mafia-type activity are a manifestation of tribal groups, while terrorism is the result of the unassuaged desires and unfinished business of racial groups and countries who, like the ancestors, are not being acknowledged with respect or justice. But to clear the national bequest of one tribe or country requires a massive collective and co-ordinated effort by all people in the world and all their allies in the otherworlds.

We can each work with the guardians and spirits of our native land and ask their assistance, not seeking to blame or to manipulate any particular outcome that we have envisioned, but to ask for ways of healing. We must become aware of our national bequest and the ways in which its accumulated legacy affects our situation now: we must seek and offer forgiveness, the only possible circuit-breaker for such complex accumulations of anguish.

For true international consensus to be reached, each country and people must deal with the issues resultant from their past.

Although we often feel uneasy when family and national problems are discussed, we must pass beyond personal discomfort and any thought that we are raking over old embers or trying to keep old divisions intact; we must go to the heart of the issue and recognize that *we and the ancestors are one*, that we live one collective and continuous life. With this realization in our hearts, we will be able to sing a song of reconciliation that will call home the national soul from acts of defensive outrage and senseless violence.

Encountering the Ancestors

Our first encounter with the ancestors may cause us to be fearful because some personal and family issues will have to be dealt with; but we should not avoid ancestral work, for by so doing, we also avoid the deep ancestors – those who have clarified their souls and are at home in the ancestral realms. In dealing with the problems resultant from ancestral legacies, we must not ignore nor minimize the gifts and wisdom which we inherit from the ancestors. By releasing memories and knowledge we can reclaim our oral and ancestral tradition and enrich our over-intellectual world. As walkers in ancestral realms, we can help rebalance our unstable world by bringing the corrective of practical, humorous ancestral wisdom.

For every set of difficult ancestors, there is also an ancestral teacher who will assist us, initiating us slowly and surely into our true treasury of wisdom. It has been my experience that, with the help of such a teacher, we can proceed with confidence and enter more completely into our present life tasks. When we find the deep ancestors, our sense of family is restored, however unparented we feel, however dislocated from our roots.

Working with the ancestors seems a waste of time to many people who want to focus on living in the present. We do well to remember that the cosmic web is timeless and runs backwards, as well as forwards, without a break. We are the ancestors of children yet unborn, living links between what we regard as the past and future, but which in subtle reality is eternally now. No part of the cosmic web, no spirit that ever was or will be, is absent from the eternal now.

Practice 42: Finding an Ancestral Teacher

When we seek out ancestral allies in shamanism, we are targeting 'the deep ancestors' who are closest to the heart of the cosmic web: these are usually distant ancestors of whose existence we may have had no previous knowledge; yet recently deceased ancestors may also be in this category, having lived lives of great peace and wisdom. Some ancestors are not suitable allies simply because they have not sufficiently clarified

their souls to be of help: they are still actively part of our world, although dead, still bent on pursuing their unfinished business and have not yet entered into their own realm.

You will recognize your ancestral teacher by his or her practical and impartial demeanour. Manifestations of self-importance, selfishness or disregard for life are signs of un-suitability. A knowledgeable discarnate human being is often a more valuable teacher in some cases than a non-human deity or spirit because she knows what human life is about and is thus a more pragmatic guide in the mazes of life.

An ancestral teacher is someone of your blood line who is a guardian of traditional wisdom. This teacher is one to consult when issues requiring Underworldly help are sourced. This might include family matters, issues involving land and its use, whatever requires protection, traditional precedents for mod-ern situations, for accessing ancestral memory and 'lost' knowl-edge and for most issues which directly affect the lives of your immediate community. Proceed as follows.

1. Exclude light, start sourcing and begin your journey to the Underworld in search of an ancestral teacher from the deep ancestors.
2. Go down your Underworld entrance from the Middleworld with your guardian animal, or meet your animal as you emerge into the Underworld. Ask your animal's help in finding an ancestral teacher.
3. With your animal, set out looking. Ask any figure that you meet on the way if he is your ancestral teacher. Your animal will also help and direct you, so keep asking and looking until you find her or him. Check your animal's reaction to the proposed teacher: if your animal is calm, shows excited recognition or attentive appreciation in his presence, you have found your ancestral teacher. If your animal shows complete indifference or signals you to go onwards, you have not found him.
4. Your ancestral teacher may be a deceased relative known to you, but is most often a distant ancestor who is not in conscious memory. *It will not be a person now living.* You may find your ancestral teacher in a group of ancestors, or at his own abode.
5. Greet and meet your ancestral teacher. Ask what kind of

work you will do together. What follows is the answer to your question.

6. At the call-back, say goodbye and return the way you came. Perform Practice 43 afterwards.

Practice 43: Dancing with the Ancestors

Ancestral and traditional memory is retained in a variety of places: not only in the genes and customs of your family and people, but in songs, stories and dances, in non-verbal communication, in places and symbols. Many societies dance, not for their own enjoyment and recreation, but for the unseen audience of ancestors, spirits and deities. Some of the oldest and most potent memories are stirred by dance, where the body itself becomes a receptacle for memory. The rhythms, cadences and intervals of dance music are as redolent and memory-wakening as odours. Because the whole body is involved, the effect of dance is something very special.

Dance is rarely seen to be revolutionary but the Ghost Dance, spread by the Paiute Indian prophet, Wovoka (c.1856–1932), in the 1880s in North America, was indirectly responsible for the last Indian war. A communal trance dance, it was performed to beg the ancestors to help their descendants in a world increasingly beleaguered by a restrictive US government. Alarmed by the large assembly of Indians, the government descended upon Wounded Knee, South Dakota, and massacred an entire Sioux encampment. Similar forms of ancestral dancing are currently being used in ex-Soviet bloc countries to recover ancestral customs and practices.

Find some dance music which derives from the folk-culture of your ancestors (rather than the land in which you are now living, if you are a naturalized citizen of your country). Feel the music through your body, absorbing its resonance, harmony and rhythms; let the *music*, rather than your mind, dictate the movement of your body, the steps that you make. When you feel wholly at one with the music, stretch out your hands and feel the hands of your ancestors in your own. Dancing together, feel the continuity of life. In joyful celebration, rejoice in the tapestry of lives. Finish with a prayer for the continued help of your ancestors and bless them.

Practice 44: Finding an Ancestral or Clan Totem

Each bloodline and family has ancestral helpers which have aided and strengthened it. Some families, especially those which have maintained genealogical records or which have heraldic grants of arms, have a close working knowledge of these helpers. The mythic and armorial beasts which support the family shield in heraldry are the medieval equivalent of the totemic beasts allied to ancient family lines. We can each discover our own clan totem by making a journey to our ancestral teacher and asking to be introduced to our clan totem. This helper, which is usually animal, but may be a tree, plant or other being, may be consulted in matters requiring crucial family decisions. It is possible, by this method, to reach into family strengths and resources. This practice should not be confused with finding your personal guardian animal. Your totemic ally will often accompany you on Underworld journeys.

Practice 45: The Ancestral Shrine

Set up a shrine to the ancestors. This could be a very simple shelf or just a photograph of your relatives, living or dead, or a symbol which represents 'ancestors' to you. The ancestors are the forerunners of our whole life – where would we be without them? All indigenous traditions honour their ancestors, but it is something we have forgotten to do. Many of our present problems derive from inherited ancestral patterns, so we need to stand in right relationship to our forebears, give them their due and pay them respect. This may be especially true if you do not know your ancestry because you are adopted, for example. A journey to your ancestral teacher could help reconnect you with your blood kindred. In this case, your shrine will not have photographs of your relatives but may include other items which you associate with your family.

Practice 46: Learning from the Master/Mistress

By journeying to an eminent master/mistress of a skill we wish to emulate, we can learn from an expert teacher and increase

our awareness and observation. Journey to the Underworld with the intention of finding an expert among the ancestors. This is a specific skill-teacher who will help us with their personal expertise to practise our craft. Ensure that you ask their permission for this help.

Practice 47: Recognizing and Clearing Ancestral Patterns

You will only be able to undertake the part of this practice concerned with spiritual lineage teachers once you have read the next chapter.

All new parents at some point utter the deathless words, 'I shall never make *my* child do such-and-such', in reaction to their own upbringing. However, this often plays straight into the hands of invidious ancestral patterns and reinforces them.

Review your family and all its members known to you, without judging any of them. Which tendencies are a particular feature of your family? You might want to look at both maternal and paternal sides. In what ways do you reflect these features in your own life?

You may come from a family of impatient people who frequently make unfortunate decisions or relationships; there may be a deep vein of anger or resentment running through your family which also mars your life; or you may be delighted to discover that the ability to handle life situations with a light and humorous touch descends to you. Evaluate the qualities you have discerned in a neutral, not negative, way; also see in which situations these qualities would be useful. Impatience may betoken a frustrated enthusiasm, anger a strong sense of justice.

Make a journey to your ancestral teacher and ask 'How may this family quality be of use to the universe?' or 'How may this family tendency be transformed in my life?' If you are a 'learner parent' with your first child, you might wish to ask, 'What does my child need from me at this time?' If all parents journeyed during their child's development, they would find considerable help. If you are adopted or do not have any information about

your family, journey in company with your ancestral teacher and allies to discover your blood lineage ancestors.

Your journey may reveal that the ancestors require acknowledgement. Proper respect will lay the beginnings of right relationship. If you hit a particularly unregenerate bunch of ancestors in your journeying, call upon your guardian animals or ancestral teacher for help.

If you detect a family pattern which needs to be brought to an end, ask your ancestral teacher how this may be done. You may find that this is not currently possible due to the fact that you need other helpers. We have two lineages: the blood lineage of our ancestors and the spiritual lineage of spiritual teachers. *We often have to find a teacher of our spiritual lineage in order to help deal with the ancestral bequest of our blood lineage.* All gods and spirits who assume mortality and then enter the gates of death have this ability, which is why they are regarded as saviours or deliverers.

This is how esoteric medieval Christian tradition understands Christ's voluntary descent into the ancestral realms, which is called 'the harrowing of hell'. This act of reaching down to the peoples of the past is believed to neutralize unbalanced ancestral influences for all Christians. Other spiritual traditions have their own saviours and deliverers who perform similar functions.

To help clear or transform your ancestral bequest more effectively, meet both your ancestral and spiritual lineage teachers at your Middleworld journey-centre and ask their assistance.

Then, when you have clarified your ancestral bequest, perform Practice 45. The souls of your ancestors are now free to return to their home and you can now extend the hand of love to them and dance in harmony for the first time.

We may feel that our known ancestors are a disgrace and that the less we have to do with them the better. If you feel that you have inherited an ancestral legacy of guilt, shame, anger or whatever, it is still possible to honour your ancestors without repeating their patterns in your life. *Love them for themselves and not their deeds,* which may well, in their turn, be the result of inheritance from their ancestors. We are not obliged to carry our ancestors' burdens, but we owe it to our descendants to ensure that they are not passed on down.

3. IN THE HOUSE OF SOULS

They're not dead . . . they are simply touching earth. All manner
of wonderful things will be happening to them. Old spirits are
flowing through their bodies; new spirits are whispering in their
heads.

Lavondyss
Robert Holdstock

Death raises a dark shadow in our society, but few of us have
participated in the experience of death or seen a dead person,
since death rarely takes place inside the home. Yet the doors
of life and death open and close every second, with souls
moving in either direction. We have acclimatization classes for
trainee parents to learn birth procedures yet no preparations
for the process of dying.

Where once a young person's first experience of death would
have been an elderly relative, it is now more likely to be that
of a friend of their own age, by crime, accident or immune-
system related illness. This is already having the effect of bringing the prospect of death and how to cope with it into much
clearer focus, and creating a climate where the procedures
around death and the prospect of the soul's continuing life are
discussed more openly.

Death holds the greatest fear for people to whom physical
reality is the only reality: they cannot share the sense of continuity or homecoming which accompanies the prospect of
death among people who accept subtle reality. For many
people in our culture, death signals the end of the only life they
know about. Yet a majority of cultures hold that death is not
the end.

What is Death?

The easiest way of understanding it is to see death as a birth
into the fullness of subtle reality; conversely, birth is sometimes
a death to our awareness of subtle reality. Soul-life is a circuit
which runs without ceasing. There are various beliefs about
what happens when we die. The following sequence is offered
as a shamanic rule of thumb:

1. At the point of death, life-signs cease in the body.
2. During the next few hours/days, the soul separates from the body and passes into a solely subtle reality existence.
3. Before the body is buried or cremated, the soul may briefly visit the places and people with whom it was associated in life, before passing on to its appointed place.
4. At burial, the soul passes into the realm of the ancestors, conducted by its allies, and is greeted by dear souls who have most recently entered there. This journey can sometimes take a while, if the soul has made no prior preparation for it.
5. Various possibilities arise following this reception. The soul may join the assembly of the deep ancestors. It may work out any unresolved life-problems within subtle reality or it may choose to reincarnate again. The soul may take on new tasks in some part of the three worlds. It may become a teacher or guide to someone in physical reality.

Beyond Death

How is it possible for a soul to be contactable in some part of the three worlds and yet simultaneously be reincarnated somewhere in physical reality? I can only answer that time and space are different in the three worlds, and that the particular soul-resonance of a person is available throughout the cosmic web. There are many different philosophies about reincarnation; most of these reinforce the subtle relationships of life upon the cosmic web. Some cultures have a closer kinship with other life-forms, such as animals, trees and plants; others perceive the reincarnation of human souls as a purely human affair.

In the Celtic tradition of the West Highlands of Scotland, the body is called the soul-shrine. At death, the soul leaves its shrine and passes into the house of souls, which is called the Land of the Dead or the Realm of the Ancestors in other cultures.

One of the prime shamanic tasks is to act as psychopomp, leading departed souls over from life into death into this realm. Many indigenous cultures ensure that the living have rehearsed their passage. The Egyptian and Tibetan Books of the Dead are afterworld maps and itineraries, to be learned before death, so that the soul's journey is made more easily. Recently

many helpful books have been published to enable modern people to prepare their soul-route.[5]

The Journey through Death

The Realm of the Ancestors most often appears as a separate enclave within the Underworld, although it has been my experience that different ancestral groups can be encountered in *any* of the three worlds. It is not advisable to enter the Realm of the Ancestors without good purpose or strong allies. If you don't believe me, read the myths and folk-tales of any culture to confirm this: taboos against eating, drinking or sharing everyday transactions with the dead are encountered worldwide. If the shaman has to enter the ancestral realm, then it is usually to restore soul-parts of bereaved relatives or to have converse with one of the dead. Normally she will not even pass within its boundaries but merely travels to the gates of that realm from where her Underworld or ancestral allies go within. Just as Aeneas had his golden bough as a passport to the land of the dead, so we too need to discover our own signs and allies who will strengthen our soul on this perilous journey.

Death is viewed differently by those who die and those who are bereaved. In every case, the wishes and needs of the dying one take precedence over the survivors, for it is her journey, not theirs. Many people who die suddenly do not realize that they are dead; they may return to the places they inhabited in life and there remain, causing fright or consternation. Ghosts are usually wandering spirits who are lost; very rarely are they persistent spirits whose unfinished business causes them to remain earth-bound. In such cases, these spirits need to pass into their own place. Ask your allies for help in such cases: they may provide particular strategies for enabling earth-bound spirits to move on.

When death is expected, due to age or sickness, then more preparation is possible. It is helpful to the dying one to create opportunities for talking about this process and finding out their wishes and expectations, and helping her to conclude unfinished business as discreetly and efficiently as possible. If the dying one is open to a shamanic perspective, it is possible to help prepare the soul-route (see Practice 49).

When we have to make decisions about who shall live or die, our first thought should be for the subject in question, whether it is someone on a life-support machine, a severely handicapped person or a foetus when a pregnancy has to be terminated. Even among people who are unconscious, injured or unborn, the soul is functional in subtle reality and may be consulted. We can avoid being manipulative by asking the soul in question what its wishes are: only it can make the choice. Make a journey to your allies and teacher to ask whether your help is appropriate; if it is, ask your helpers to take you to the dying one's helpers and find out what is required. This is especially important for those souls who wish to live but are in deep coma after an accident and do not know how to get back to their bodies again, or who need the reassurance that their relatives, partner or friends will support them in appropriate ways if they do come back. In such cases, the shaman can help bring the stray soul or soul-parts home through soul-restoration. Even if there is no choice over aborting a foetus or terminating life-support, it is still imperative that the soul of the subject is contacted and prepared for this process: if this is impossible, then the soul should still be contacted afterwards to ensure that due honour and respect is paid, and that it has passed on appropriately.

Coping with sudden and accidental death is hard on the survivors who have no time to resolve matters with or say goodbye to the deceased. Dealing with bereavement is easier if you can walk between the worlds at will and gain the help of your allies, but the links of need, love and sorrow are not so easily assuaged for others. Writing a letter to the dead and burning the letter so that it goes to the ancestral realms is another good method of saying our goodbyes. This is also useful for people whose sibling or father died before they were born. A simple and appropriate funeral ritual is essential to announce death, to honour the dead and to aid the mourning process (see Practice 53).

It is always best to disperse the physical remains of the dead by burial or the scattering of ashes not longer than a week after death. Cremation is now common, but the etiquette of what to do with the ashes remains a vexed question for some. Many people fail to disperse the remains through ignorance of what to do, wanting a ceremony, but not a conventional one; mean-

while the ashes of Aunt Grace remain on the mantelpiece. Sometimes it is grief that prevents dispersal.

Some spirits of the dead purposely remain close to their loved ones to watch over them for a period. The daughter of Clara, one of my clients, died in a tragic accident while on the threshold of adulthood; Clara was aware that her daughter, Nickie, had not passed on and, in the depths of her grieving, took comfort that she was still near, both seeing and talking to her. After a period of several months, Nickie began to appear in the company of other spirits about the house, as though her friends had come to collect her. Shortly afterwards, the presence of the dead girl left the house. Clara still grieves, but is better able to cope as a result of Nickie's loving presence during the initial months of bereavement.

In cases where the body is not recovered, or is buried abroad, or where a body is retained by the coroner pending investigation, it is often difficult for the bereaved to comprehend the reality of the death. During the slaughter of the First World War, so many men died and were buried abroad that their relatives consulted mediums in order to be reassured that the dead were at peace, and to reassure the dead that they were still loved and remembered. We can also check that the dead have passed over peacefully, by asking for our allies' assistance.

A proper and recognized period of mourning used to be observed in the West, with the bereaved first wearing deepest black and then changing into purple and violet before assuming ordinary coloured clothing again. This was a helpful practice, signalling to all that the bereaved person needed sensitive treatment over a long period, since the process of mourning usually lasts for a minimum of two years. If we treated the bereaved as though they stood on the borders between life and death looking upon a distant land where their loved ones walked, if we would only speak to them lovingly and with humour about the dead rather than avoiding the issue, if we would weep with them and be available long after the event, we would enable their gradual return to daily life.

Facing our own Death

Only by facing and dealing with our own mortality and our certain journey into subtle reality will we be able to improve

communication about death. By good preparation and resolving unfinished business, we will be able to pass into the house of souls and join the ancestors.

Practice 48: Unfinished Business

A salient feature of death is its untidiness. If you were to die in the next twenty-four hours, what unfinished business in your life would worry you the most? An unreconciled quarrel, unresolved plans for someone's well-being, not having made a will? List the ten most pressing items. Issues like these cause our souls to remain earth-bound, but many can be resolved while we are alive and healthy. Now pick one item from the list and journey on it, asking your ancestral teacher and allies how you may resolve it.

The regular practice of self-clarification is necessary if we are not to burden our descendants with our own unfinished business – both our mental baggage and our behavioural problems. A periodic journey to our ancestral teacher to ask, 'What unnecessary burdens am I carrying and how can they be laid down?' will often clarify unconscious problems, and improve our lives as well.

If you have unfinished business with someone who has died, journey to your ancestral teacher and ask to be taken somewhere to meet this person. This may be somewhere in the Middleworld or elsewhere. Remember that the dead person may also have things to say to you.

Practice 49: Preparing the Soul-route

Do not attempt this practice until you have visited all three worlds and gained allies there. This practice is for those who would like to prepare themselves better for their own death. Just as we rehearse the itinerary of our holidays in a far country, so too we can discover our soul-route. Please follow these instructions exactly.

Journey One

1. Journey first of all to your guardian animal and Middleworld teacher and ask whether discovering your soul-route is appropriate for you at this time. If your allies indicate that it is not, do not go further.
2. If your allies advise this journey, then ask if there are any tasks you must carry out before setting off. Ask your Middleworld teacher for a symbol to act as your anchor. Return from your journey and *draw this symbol* until it is imprinted on your memory.

Journey Two

1. Ensure that your sourcing tape has a good recognizable call-back signal. Go with your guardian animal to your Middleworld teacher and ask him to be your anchor for the following journey. Your Middleworld teacher will tie a cord around your symbol which you will hold as you journey; as you do so your teacher will pay out the cord and so keep in contact with you.
2. Now journey to your ancestral teacher and ask to be shown the soul-route which you will take at death *as a map or diagram. Note:* you are *not* asking how or when you will die.
4. Your teacher will show you – by drawing in the earth, or by showing you a map or in some other way – your destined soul-route. *Do not journey into this map.*
5. At the call-back signal, your Middleworld teacher will pull you back. Return and draw your soul-route as a map or diagram.

This journey helps you to chart the route you will follow. If you are on the threshold of death, you can familiarize yourself with your route, and call upon the help of allies, teachers and ancestors to greet and aid you. When the moment of death comes, your itinerary will be known to you and your soul will not wander without direction.

Practice 50: Scroll of Direction

After the journey above, you may wish to create your own 'scroll of direction'. Several Orphic initiates of southern Italy

and Crete in the fourth to the second centuries BC were buried with precise directions about their death route inscribed on sheets of gold in amulets about their necks. The following is an example of one of them:

> Thou shalt find to the left of the House of Hades a spring,
> And by the side thereof standing a white cypress.
> To this spring approach not near.
> But thou shalt find another, from the Lake of Memory,
> Cold water flowing forth, and there are guardians before it.
> Say, 'I am a child of Earth and starry Heaven;
> But my race is of heaven alone. This ye know yourselves.
> But I am parched with thirst and I perish. Give me quickly
> The cold water flowing forth from the Lake of Memory.[6]

From your own journey, compose your own instructions. You may write down directions, as in the example above, or you may choose to paint yours on paper or cloth as a map or picture. Whatever you choose, roll up your verbal or pictorial map and place it in a suitable container (like a roll of leather, a small box) and inscribe your soul-route symbol on it. This can then be stored in your shamanic bag (see Practice 61) until the time you need to rehearse the route, nearer your death.

Practice 51: Passage of the Soul

This ceremony is not one that you will ever personally facilitate: it is a ceremony to mark your own passing, to be celebrated by your family and friends. The existence of instructions for such a ceremony alongside your legal will will be of great benefit to your loved ones who may be too stunned by your death to make arrangements that you would approve of. It also avoids any family contention about your actual spirituality: 'He was life-long Presbyterian and that's how he's going to be buried'. Your ceremony need only be short; it doesn't have to conform to the funeral service of conventional religion. If you wish to create a full funeral service, you can do so; any person appointed by you can legally act as the 'minister' or facilitator at a crematorium. This ceremony enables you to draw upon your personal spirituality while providing a framework for your family and friends to each say goodbye to you. Your

ceremony may come together through long contemplation as well as by journeying to your allies for advice and guidance.

The New Book of the Dead by Dolores Ashcroft-Nowicki is strongly recommended for information on dealing with death, funeral arrangements and the passage of the soul in sensible and ritual ways.

As a walker between the worlds, you will inevitably use and collect items of power. Drums, rattles, feathers, stones and other objects that you habitually use in your shamanizing become empowered, tuned to the frequency of your work. To ensure that they are bequeathed to other practitioners or decommissioned respectfully, leave clear instructions in your will and appoint an executor who will respect these wishes.

6. The Upperworld

For a fortress to be secret, it must be invisible. It must have no boundaries of exclusiveness – it must be an Internal Fortress of Practice rather than an external institution.

Ngakpa Chögyam

1. THE SONG OF INNER SPACE

Thou shalt be in league with the beings of the future, and the generations to come after shall be at peace with thee.

World as Lover, World as Self
Joanna Macy

THE UPPERWORLD IS the visionary and archetypal realm of the three worlds. Here we access knowledge, information and inspiration; here we gain overviews of things and perceive the blueprints of life. If we recall the image of the great tree, Figure 1, we will see that the branches of the tree pierce the upperworld; it is here that we discover the fruits of that tree and are enabled to bring home the harvest of our lives. The pristine beauty and primal connection we experience here is immediate and moving. Here is no shadow of decay, pollution or spoliation, but a paradisal realm of vision.

This realm has been written about by every major artist, poet and visionary. The Upperworld haunts our imagination in dreams of paradise. Many shamans speak about the upperworld as 'the pure country'. Samuel Coleridge's description of

his opium-induced vision of Kublai Khan's Xanadu attempts to convey the pristine perfection of the Upperworld. Wordsworth wrote that 'heaven lies about us in our infancy' and, truly, children whose fontanelles are not yet closed do experience deep communion with this realm. The bones at the top of the skull remain soft and pliant in childhood to allow for the growth of the head. This area is believed to be a shamanic gateway to other worlds. Adults find contact more difficult, but their need for that childhood communion is often so strong that they may have recourse to drink or drugs in order to reach it, to be catapulted out of the body by substances rather than seek the Upperworld by simple exposure to nature's beauty.

Distortions of the Upperworld

The Upperworld has been promoted as the goal in many religions: here the gods dwell in unchanging bliss, here the blessed souls of departed heroes or saints are to be found, from here angelic beings descend as divine messengers. We are told that only the good and truthful and perfect are admitted, while all others are shut out. Many religions have barred the way to this world, seeking to admit only their own members, 'the chosen', to unending bliss, content in the notion that the remainder of humanity (all other species are naturally not admitted, as not having souls!) to the torments of hell. The hubris and exclusivity of fundamentalist claims to heaven have so tainted our view of the Upperworld that many people have declared they would rather burn merrily in the company of the damned than endure a pious eternity in the company of the chosen.

According to the dualist viewpoint, the Underworld is associated with the evils of the past, with the fall from grace in Genesis, while the Upperworld becomes the focus for the millennial and apocalyptic revisions depicted in Revelations. As the second millennium ends many people are attuned to these unfortunate associations. In the West the Underworld has suffered neglect and we had concentrated too strongly on the Upperworld, vaunting its benefits in an unbalanced way which has led to a great deal of delusion. Just as neglect and avoidance of the Underworld create shadowy and fearful projections, so overdependence on the Upperworld creates gross

stereotypes out of primal archetypes, producing people who are intolerant of shadow and who live only for 'the light'. Such people's view of the Upperworld is as false as any Christian projection of hell upon the Underworld. From a distorted Upperworld vision we derive passivity, and expect heavenly beings to do everything for us, with no effort needed from ourselves.

The Spiritual Quest

Loss of communion with the Upperworld is related in countless myths, involving the withdrawal of the gods and great teachers or the severance of the bridge which links us with wisdom and knowledge. The theft of heaven's fire by Prometheus and the theft of divine substance by Sophia are myths about spiritual quest and our reconnection with the Upperworld.[1] We must view these stories with the eyes of mystics and shamans: they reveal that the gods guard wisdom which they intend humans to eventually find, but that many of us steal knowledge without wisdom: *we want the techniques but not the responsibility*. This is why initiatory threshold guardians are encountered upon the spiritual quest: angels with fiery swords, mythological beasts with riddles and gods who change into a variety of challenging shapes. Only those initiates who are willing to take on the task of gate-keeper to the mysteries in their turn are entitled to use the wisdom that they find. Only by practice and personal implementation can we become initiates of knowledge.

Yet we can journey freely to the Upperworld and find inspiration and vision that will nurture our lives and refresh our world. Just as the power of the cosmic web wells up from the Underworld and cannot be kept from flowing into us, so too the embrace of Spirit rains down from the Upperworld and permeates our whole being. Reconnection with the Upperworld restores to us spiritual understanding, intense ecstasy and vision. When we observe clearly the lines of our creative destiny and the patterns of our soul's questing, we are restored to our authentic spiritual vision, which no one can take from us.

Through reacquaintance with shamanic principles of the cosmic web we realize how some religions have kept us from

our true heritage. Our relationship with power and Spirit is primarily experienced in the Middleworld, but it is nurtured by our connections with both Underworld and Upperworld. When we are denied our natural access to the power of the cosmic web, we are denied entrance to the Underworld; when we are denied our natural access to the Spirit of the cosmic web, we are denied entrance to the Upperworld. Effectively, our souls become trapped in one world, in one reality.

Permission to reclaim our own access to power and Spirit is here given.

Rediscovering our own Spiritual Identity

Humankind's territorial greed has extended to the inner space of the three worlds. Many religions have made strong attempts to colonize inner space for themselves and to dictate who may go there and under what conditions. One of the great joys of working shamanically is the freedom to reclaim inner space. Throughout time, humankind has told stories to explain and understand where inner space is, who inhabits it and what happens within it. Many stories tell how beings came out of inner space, from heaven or a high mountain, to help humankind; there are also many stories of how some humans have travelled into inner space for wisdom, power or a healing gift, like Gilgamesh for the elixir of immortality or like Perceval for the Holy Grail. These are not individual quests for a personal nirvana, but heroic reclamations of the common reservoir of inspiration and healing.

Shamanism today is about the rediscovery of inner space. Although we live in a post-religious culture, ideas of inner space are still rigidly laid down, but the fact remains that no one can impose one story about the purpose of life upon all people. This is beginning to be realized as more and more people seek their authentic spiritual identity by other than orthodox means.

But if we abandon 'the one saving story' will we know whence we came or where we go after death, will we known our life's purpose? *Authentic spiritual identity can only be discovered by accessing all the appropriate co-ordinates of our life: these are unique to each person.* Certain groups of people will find

themselves in accord, and will associate together to broadly follow one story or myth, but all myths and stories should be regarded simply as rules of thumb, working plans and blue-prints which have currency upon the cosmic web.

In all generations and times, Spirit manifests in certain energy frequencies which will be picked up in different ways. We are currently undergoing a springcleaning of many old forms relating to what astrologers call the Piscean age: these forms are typified by abnegation of sexuality, by purgation of the body, and by hierarchical spiritual frameworks. And, just as when we go to throw something away, we are tempted to find another use for it or to discover that something is really most precious to us, so some people are discovering that the old Piscean forms are suddenly most attractive and desirable. Waves of fundamentalism shake our world, as this spring-cleaning current is denied. Fundamentalism arises from fear of change, the threat of the new. People correspondingly seek order, structure and community frameworks which totally dictate their lives rather than swim alone in the seeming chaos of the incoming current.

The incoming Aquarian current is heralded by a striving for more liberal and equal social and spiritual structures, for self-empowerment and personal spiritual identity, all regarded as dangerous by those of the old mind-set. Just as the Piscean world-view distorted our perception of the three worlds and barred access thither, so the Aquarian world-view tends to go to the opposite extreme and burst open all gates in order to access information, power and Spirit as quickly as possible.

The walker between the worlds must heed the milestones, signposts and border checks of the three worlds, without either the Aquarian impatience or the fear and exclusivity of the Piscean. She must always remember that she is responsible for her actions and their effect upon the cosmic web. Responsibility for knowledge that we receive may seem an alien concept but all shamanic knowledge-keepers realize that *knowledge must be applied with wisdom*. We do not teach three-year-old children how the controls of a car work; only when they are sixteen or so are they sufficiently mature. When the physicists who discovered nuclear power realized to what terrible uses their discovery would be put, it was already too late for them to be responsible. Knowledge cannot now be forgotten, only used wisely.

Knowledge and Responsibility

When we journey to the Upperworld we discover many things and must forever live with that knowledge. This is why it is important to have a well-balanced life and a good well-grounded knowledge of the Middleworld and the Underworld before we soar off to the Upperworld. This is especially important if the access to power and Spirit have been barred to us for significant periods of our lives. Indigenous societies rightly fear unscrupulous shamans who exhibit a personal affinity with power or knowledge, who appropriate it for themselves: this is how sorcerers, fanatics and manipulators come into being. They gild their own route on the cosmic web instead of being a part of it. We are familiar with this pattern wherever power and knowledge become the perquisite of one group, whether it be in politics, religion or learning.

Our task as walkers between the worlds is not to manipulate the universe to our vision, but to connect with the cosmic web in a healthy way, allowing the power and knowledge of the universe to flow into and through us for the benefit of all, conscious of the Spirit in all places. As we are brought into closer harmony with the cosmic web, we may become guardians of knowledge and power – not in order to bar the ways of genuine seekers or people in need – but in order to keep the connections wisely. And who guards the guardians? Why, none other than our allies in inner space, at whose behest we are appointed, with whom we keep watch, and who offer correctives when our human weakness or lack of vision threatens the work.

Accessing the Upperworld

Let us return to our consideration of the Upperworld. Many of us already access the Upperworld in our daily lives, as when we seek to gain an archetypal overview of a situation, when we turn to any creative or spiritual source for inspiration or enlightenment, whenever we seek guidance in a difficult situation, whenever we bounce ideas around in our heads and get an overwhelming hunch that something will work, whenever we envision the prototype or blueprint of something we wish to create.

As the Underworld is associated with the ancestors, with beginnings and the past, so the Upperworld is associated, though not exclusively, with the future, with possibility and outcome. It is a good place to divine information that we will need, to find sources of inspiration and knowledge, to seek solutions to incomplete sequences of events.

It is not for nothing that the luminaries of the Upperworld, the star-spirits, are associated with the patterns of our destiny. Modern astrology associates our birth date with a sign of the zodiac, which is comprised of the twelve constellations visible to the classical Mediterranean world. Each constellation has a planetary ruler who is considered to be a salient influence. Although modern systems of astrology have been adopted to cover the whole globe, it is clear that indigenous peoples each have different planetary foci, based upon the constellations visible in *their own* night sky. They regard the stars and constellations as powerful teachers, and many peoples derive their tribal genesis and protection from ancestral star-beings.

The influence of the stars upon the Middleworld and the discovery of possibility was the concern of the Hermetic way, which essentially sought to reveal the divine likeness in humanity and in nature by alchemical transformation and spiritual realization. Each planet in neo-Platonic and medieval hermaneutics corresponded to terrestral substances and qualities. This system perceived the underlying and superimposing similarities by which the worlds mirror each other. This was expressed in the hermetic dictum: 'That which is above, is like that which is below, and that which is below is like that which is above.' Hermes was the tutelary deity of this magical way of perception. The arts of healing, change and transmutation were in the hands of magicians who travelled between these worlds in more sophisticated ways than the primal shamans.[2]

It has been suggested that the symbols painted on the drums of Saami shamans may indicate star-patterns visible from the earth.[3] Across the world are many terrestral patterns, the Nazca lines and images, the chalk hill figures of Britain and the configuration of many sacred landscapes: these can only be truly appreciated from the air, yet they were inscribed upon the land by earth-bound human beings. How did they come to be there? Some of these designs have stellar relationships, like the Egyp-

tian necropolis of the Great Pyramid and its surrounding monuments which are reflections of the Milky Way. Perhaps the designers of these sacred patterns were inspired not only by celestial observation but also through Upperworld journeying.

Our Upperworld journeys restore us to a sense of perspective: when the jigsaw of our lives seems to be coming together but we cannot quite see how, an Upperworld journey will give us the piece that we lack and reveal a clearer picture. Just like the Navajo *hatali*, the sand-painting shaman, we are able to restore the *hozho*, the harmony, balance and beauty of our lives by looking upon the shapes of our earth.[4]

Beings encountered in the Upperworld include great birds, large sea-beasts, starry-spirits or seraphic angels who are definitely non-human, deities of spinning, weaving, fabrication and creation, companies of ancestors who are concerned with teaching certain skills, and schools of spiritual teachers. The *genius* of the Upperworld often appears as a creative and solar god, while the *juno* of the Upperworld frequently appears as a spinning, stellar goddess like Ariadne: these may appear in partnership as the guardians of a celestial court, as Logos and Sophia.

The Upperworld stimulates the frontal lobes of our cerebrum, connecting the two hemispheres and drawing upon the deep memories of the brain stem to create brilliant fruits of revelation. As the place of beauty, harmony and vision, of spiritual help and guidance, the Upperworld is where we find the allies who are able to give us answers and solutions.

Practice 52: Finding an Upperworld Ascent

In order to reach the Upperworld, we need to journey upwards. Find a place to ascend which exists in physical reality, not an imagined place: a tall tree, a high mountain or cliff, a waterfall, a rainbow, the smoke of a fire. This ascent might be near your journey-centre, but it doesn't have to be. Again, a natural place is best, but if you want to climb the Empire State Building or the Eiffel Tower by elevator, then it has been done!

In the northern hemisphere, the Upperworld is often typified by the Milky Way and the circumpolar stars, especially the Great Bear which points to Polaris – the nail of the heavens,

around which the circumpolar stars revolve. The Milky Way is a trail which has become associated with many terrestral pilgrimage routes – including the English way to Our Lady of Walsingham and the Spanish route to St James of Compostela. It still makes a good route to the Upperworld.

The Celtic otherworld, which relates to the Upperworld, has many islands which correspond to the stars of the firmament in classic shamanic cosmology. This otherworld is reached by a shamanic oversea voyage in a boat without oars or rudder, piloted by otherworldly allies.[5] Such a boat is another possibility.

If you use a medium which would not lend itself to climbing in physical reality, such as water or smoke, to make your ascent, it will become amenable to your climbing in subtle reality.

Practice 53: The Upperworld Journey

The Upperworld Journey unfolds in the following way.

1. Your purpose for the first journey is to seek access to the Upperworld and reconnection with the sources of your inspiration. Exclude light, be comfortable, start to source, recalling your purpose and bringing to mind your Upperworld ascent.
2. Call upon your guardian animal to meet you at the foot of your ascent. Do not ascend without it. It is possible that, as you climb or when you emerge into the Upperworld, another animal may appear as an auxiliary helper. Follow the procedures for accepting an animal on page 105.
3. Your initial Upperworld journey will usually be more difficult than either the Underworld or Middleworld ones. Your cliff or tree may acquire a nasty overhang, you may start to tire, it may feel as though it's going on too long, you may feel like giving up. At this point, stiffen your resolve and ask for your animal to encourage you. As you reach the heights of your ascent – the top of the rainbow, tree, mountain – you may experience other difficulties: a mistiness may obscure your way, or you may encounter some kind of physical resistance to your journeying further. This is usually experienced as a kind of skin or membrane, or a zone of

confusion or obscurity, a narrow or guarded place. Some people get to the top of their ascent and feel there is nowhere else to go except to jump off.

To gain the Upperworld, you must pass beyond this critical point. Check that your animal is with you and keep on going through the mist, press forward into the skin as if your whole body were a pin going to prick a balloon, go through the obscure door, jump off your mountain top – you will be able to fly. Note that, though on subsequent journeys your animal will sometimes fly or ride you up with great velocity, *it will not precede you on your first entrance to the Upperworld*. Your own efforts must win a way through.

4. Your successful entrance into the Upperworld may be accompanied by a feeling of being sucked through an hourglass or the kind of inside-out feeling that sometimes accompanies fairground rides. This is not generally repeated on subsequent journeys. Check that your animal is with you and look around. You may have been expecting clouds or featureless space, but on emerging through the difficulty of the doorway, you will find a world with land, sea and sky. Because the Upperworld is associated with the gods and blueprints of life, you may see great cities or edifices of extreme complexity, but it may equally appear as a broad and beautiful landscape of any kind of geographical zone.

What does the Upperworld feel like? Unlike the often womb-like enclosure of the Underworld where we draw upon power by a process of osmosis, in the Upperworld we often feel that all our faculties have been given the clarity of crystal. The archetypal brightness and clarity of this place strikes us nearly always as very beautiful and harmonious. You may also experience a complete sense of blessedness, of being led to the emotionally satisfying edge of things.

5. Now ask your guardian animal, or any new animal you have accepted on the way up or when you emerged here, to lead you to the sources of your inspiration. Your animals may work in tandem. Follow its/their direction.

6. Your journey may unfold in a number of ways here. You may be led to a place or series of places where you may meet inspirers and reconnect with them; you may be shown or may engage in skills, crafts or actions which inspire you. Follow your animal's direction; do not try to appreciate

intellectually what you experience during the journey; there is time for interpretation afterwards.

7. At the call-back, give thanks for any experience or gift, return the way you came, bringing any new animal with you, record your journey and perform Practice 54, simultaneously dancing any new animal you have met.

Note: *people who are not well grounded have a tendency to drift off slightly in the Upperworld*. This tendency can be counteracted by concentrating on what is happening, minute by minute and what it feels like: be aware of your body walking, climbing and acting in the journey. Ask your animal to keep you well focussed.

This is a good point to discuss what lies beyond the Upperworld. Many traditions speak of the area surrounding the three worlds as 'the void' and see it as a trackless and unformulated emptiness. I have visited the void during shamanic healing sessions and indeed found it to be a place of great vastness. However, to allay any fear of 'falling off the edge of the universe', I must say that, even in the void, the filaments of the cosmic web do still run. My experience of the void suggests to me that the threads and intersections of the web are here so widely spaced that it is difficult for us to perceive them: but they *are* present.

We do not generally journey into the void except in order to rescue stray soul-parts or for some other good purpose, and then only at the behest of and accompanied by our strongest allies. In many ways it feels like the space-walk of an astronaut: attached by a slim life-support line and totally dependent upon a vast back-up team. The ability to remain calm and directed when travelling through the void is dependent upon the help of our allies, in whom we must have great trust, but they will not direct us thither unless there is important work to do.

Practice 53: Finding an Upperworld Teacher of your Spiritual Lineage

---

In the last chapter, we found an Underworld teacher of our blood lineage, drawn from near or deep ancestral kindred. But we actually have two kinds of lineage: that of blood and that

of Spirit. Our physical relations are our blood kindred, but our spiritual relations are our spiritual kindred. Our spiritual kindred can include our otherworldly allies and teachers, as well as other living beings with whom we share a particular resonance or kinship of heart, mind and Spirit. We each have several human friendships of this nature of which we are aware, as well as certain unspoken and unacknowledged affinities with other species in physical reality.

Our spiritual lineage often has little to do with formalized religion; it is more subtle and inclusive. We are each attracted to certain kinds of activities, ways of thinking and believing, and will gravitate towards others of our kind and to teachers in whom we discern the authentic current of our life's motivating direction. If we trace these influences and correlations beyond the like-minded people and resonant teachers with whom we associate, we come to the broad strands of the cosmic web which lead through the Upperworld into our own world. Like the spectrum of the rainbow, through the range of academic subjects or practical skills, we will find that we arrive at the strong motivating energies which weave the web: justice, compassion, truth, love, healing, guardianship of the mysteries, creation, recycling, vision – we instinctively seek to enter the stream which sings to us the song of our motivating genius.

Our spiritual lineage imparts inspiration through our upbringing, culture, teachers, education and many other factors. Some people have found spiritual inspiration in many different traditions and teachers. *Shamanism does not ask you to give them up or gainsay their help or guidance.* Our spiritual lineage is forever seeking new river-beds. This is especially true at this time when orthodox spiritualities themselves are under demolition and restructuring.

This time you are going to journey to find an Upperworld teacher of your spiritual lineage: that is, a teacher with whom you are in total sympathy of heart, mind and spirit, *not necessarily a spiritual guru or guide.* Your Upperworld teacher will advise, grant wisdom, knowledge, and give overviews: he will not dictate the order of your life nor give advice on trivial matters. A teacher is a companion not a guru. He or she will usually be humanoid in appearance, though not always a discarnate human; he will never be a person now currently incarnate.

Proceed as follows.

1. Exclude light, be comfortable, begin sourcing and journey by your ascent to the Upperworld in company with your animal, in search of an Upperworld teacher of your spiritual lineage.
2. Emerge into the Upperworld and go looking for your teacher, asking your animal for assistance. Ask any figure you meet if she is your Upperworld teacher.
3. When you have found your teacher and you have each accepted the other, ask how you will work together. Follow directions or listen.
4. At the call-back, conclude your business together, say good-bye and return the way you came, remembering the co-ordinates of your teacher's abode.

Practice 54: Dancing with our Inspirers

The spaciousness of the Upperworld can become our dancing floor where we dance with the stars, with our inspirers and spiritual guardians, where we enter into a non-dual and ecstatic dance of unity. Find some music which inspires and uplifts you. Feel it lifting your spirits and move with the music. As you begin to source, stretch out your hands and reach for the hands of your inspirers and spiritual teachers. Dance in a circuit of blissful elation, feeling your steps and movements rippling out upon the cosmic web in joyful inspiration. Rejoice in the wisdom of your inspirers and feel yourself becoming part of the chain dance. Finish by acknowledging the seven directions in slow, formal motions, so that you and the dance are grounded and reflected in the Middleworld (see Practice 31).

Practice 55: Exploring the Upperworld

The Upperworld is where we find the archetypal patterns of our lives. These journeys are often ecstatically moving, and we often find ourselves dancing, singing or chanting here. Knowledge of the divine mysteries of Spirit is imparted here, and the blueprints of the universe are often found stored in the Upper-

world. In standard Western mystery tradition, the akashic records are discoverable here, although these days you may as easily find a microchip library as a conventional book-filled one. You may see 'viewing screens' or windows which access different parts of the cosmic web. The Upperworld is not only attuned to future possibilities and developments, but is important for discovering the potentialities of our present situation.

The following are suggestions for increasing our proficiency in Upperworld work.

1. Which deities/archetypes/heroes/heroines attract you most? What functions/skills/qualities do they have? How are these present within yourself? Travel to the Upperworld and meet with one figure with whom you feel strong connection.
2. Check out your spiritual lineage by asking yourself, 'Who are my spiritual kindred? Who are my spiritual ancestors?' Poets, philosophers, practitioners, artists, musicians, spiritual teachers alive and dead may be included on your list. Give thanks for their lives, inspiration and teachings by writing them on a scroll. This can live on your shrine or be carried in your shamanic bag. Look at it periodically and burn a candle or some incense to honour and celebrate their influence.
3. Journey to your inspirers when you begin or conceive a creative project, to assist your making.
4. Journey to your spiritual lineage teacher to ask 'What is the purpose of my life?' or 'What is my spiritual vocation?'
5. Journey to your spiritual lineage teacher to ask what needs restoration and renewal in our lives, and how this may be accomplished.
6. Ask your teacher what you may restore to the Upperworld.

Practice 56: Creating Spaciousness

The West has attempted to fill its spiritual vacuum by accumulations of consumer durables. 'To a great extent, our culture emphasizes accumulation, enrichment, storing up; other cultures have elevated emptying to the ultimate goal,' writes Holger Kalweit.[6] This principle encompasses all spiritual work: the greater the space, the greater the capacity. To give away is to make space, to create potential.

Many cultures practise almsgiving, tribal sharing of goods – as in the north-west American *potlatch* ceremony, or the voluntary abnegation of possessions prior to an important initiation. The West's attitude to giving things or resources is rooted within a mistaken application of Christian sacrifice: as a painful rather than a meritorious action. We are all too happy to give away our second-best efforts or our outworn things to benefit someone, but we generally avoid giving of our best. Giving of our possessions, resources, service, time and expertise, space and power, helps unseat the deep-rooted consumer-mindedness of our society, reconnecting pathways, creating spaciousness and better distribution of energy upon the cosmic web.

This week make a journey to one of your Upperworld allies and teacher, asking 'What can I give away to create spaciousness on the cosmic web?' This is often a very difficult journey for Westerners to take and to implement, but it is also a very revealing and helpful one.

2. THE SONG THAT SOUNDS IN THE SILENCE

Silence is the general consecration of the universe.

Herman Melville

The lessons of the Upperworld are discovering peace and harmony, becoming resonant with our destiny. Too often we attempt only the mundane correlatives of this quest in the Middleworld – a quiet life, an orderly regimen and a satisfactory collusion with circumstance. These content most people. But when we travel to the Upperworld we begin to suffer 'divine discontent' with such mundane ambitions, realizing that we need to feed our souls, not just our bodies.

The Song of the Universe

We discover peace, harmony and resonance with our destiny only by entering into the spaciousness of the Upperworld and allowing that space into our lives. It is then that the overlay of the Upperworld can open up new dimensions in our lives. The

first essential is to enter into the silence of space, to still the internal dialogue, to separate our song from its entanglement with other songs, to create an internal fortress from which we can review our lives. This is achieved by simple meditation: closing our eyes, breathing and reviewing things with neutrality in the space of silence. Some people fear that to separate ourselves in meditation, for however short a time, is somehow selfish or exclusive. The priestess, Felicity Wombwell, writes tellingly of this fear, reminding us that:

> . . . freedom is space: boundaries represent love. Boundaries and space need to be properly maintained so they are not constantly infringed by society and others . . . if we have our own space where we can go to find the true self . . . we can remember who and what we are . . . This is why meditation is so useful and powerful.[7]

The quietness in which to be ourselves is extremely rare. It is often only in situations of enforced waiting that we have the leisure to enter that silence, when the circumstances or surroundings are usually inappropriate. For many, the spaciousness of silence is intolerable, to be speedily dissipated by radio, television or music. Unused to the desert wastes of silence, we never enter the boundaries of our souls to find that spacious freedom in which peace dwells. For those who have not ventured into their own internal fortress in love and freedom, this peace is perceived as a blank, static emptiness in which nothing happens.

Yet it is only in the intentioned silence of vigil and meditation, or in the quiet places of nature that we encounter the song of the universe. Like the wind through the telegraph wires, this song echoes along the pathways of the cosmic web: it includes the celestial spinning of the planets, as well as the hum of insects and the dancing song of the grass; it includes the song of all the ancestors and spirits as well as the beating of our own hearts. The song of the universe is the voice of Spirit.

Most primal myths speak of the world coming into being through the utterance of sound. The ineffable power of sound with intention is immeasurable; the use of the sacred word causes divinity to be present, as in the Gospel of St John, where the Word becomes flesh, God incarnate in the person of Christ. When Hindus utter the Sanskrit sacred word *aum*, they recreate

the world, for it is the original creative word representing the Hindu *trimurti*, the threefold deities who bound the universe. 'A' evokes the changelessness of Brahma, 'u' evokes the endurance of Vishnu, 'm' evokes the transmutation of Shiva, so that existence, consciousness and experience are comprehended in the one word. 'The past, present and the future are all included in this one sound, and all that exists beyond the three forms of time is also implied in it.' Similarly, classical tradition speaks of the celestial Song of the Spheres, the harmony of the notes issued by each planet in the solar system.[8]

It is in the silence of inner space that we become aware of the harmony of Spirit, of the song that Spirit is always singing in the silence. This is the secret of meditation: not an empty silence or a hollow peace, but a living pulse, a shapely song which becomes the music of our soul.

Since I was a baby, I've always maintained a 'humming brief', unconsciously tuning into the song of whatever space I was in. This got me into trouble at school where successive teachers hissed or shouted at me 'stop that irritating noise!' I have never stopped singing since. When I began to take up my shamanic work in earnest I found that this practice of singing the song of the universe had an important place in helping people. In most soul-work, I use a combination of shamanic vision diagnosis with song and stringed instruments to bring a healing song to my clients. Since it is very rare in our society to be personally sung to, this experience usually awakens the soul and speaks to the heart, helping that person to hear and sing their own song.

'The voice is an instrument that echoes the soul and it is the soul's energy that makes every sound unique,' writes voice expert, Patsy Rodenburg.[9] We only arrive at harmony when we ourselves are in harmony. If we are out of tune, we cannot be resonant with peace, harmony or destiny.

Finding our True Destiny

We think of destiny as being predetermined, laid down ages ago, unchanging and inflexibly related to time. Time bludgeons us into conformity, dissecting the eternal moment and fragmenting the creative hour until frustration threatens to smother

us. The tyranny of time can only be broken by perceiving eternity. It is not in the stop-gap solution or in the sound-bite that we live but in the spaciousness of eternity. Continuity is timeless upon the cosmic web, where 'then' and 'when' have no currency. The healer, Barbara Ann Brennan, reminds us that:

> . . . what occurs in Great Time has sequence, but it cannot be dated . . . As we live our life *now*, it becomes more likely that we are rewriting our personal history, both past and future.[10]

To be at peace with ourselves, we need to know ourselves. Each person's incarnational cord – the connected linkage of life after life – has its own unique twist: this metaphor derives from the spinning of yarn where the thread is teased out of a hank of wool and spun on a drop spindle. We may imagine our lives as such a thread, the wool teased from our ancestral blood lineage and the colour provided by our spiritual lineage; but the twist of the spinning is something we personally provide.

In seeking our destiny in this life, shamanism works with the present incarnation. Whatever our purpose in life, whatever lessons we may be learning, we can discover these from looking at our own life in relation to the cosmic web. Although many people have found regression to past incarnations helpful, the seeking after past lives can be an escape from committing fully to the present life, as well as a means of abrogating responsibility for dealing with issues now. Whichever lifetime of our incarnational thread we examine, we will find a unique twist and colouration which bespeaks our motive and purpose.

In the eternal now of subtle reality, each walker between the worlds must clarify the ancestral bequest and seek out the spiritual pathways which are most appropriate to her. Our incarnational thread is stretched between these two directions; in between these we can examine the nature of our thread, the ways it behaves when we weave with it, the kinds of patterns and blocks of colour it creates. The call signature of our destiny comes to us from our spiritual lineage, just as our physical appearance derives from our ancestral lineage. The behaviour of our own thread is determined by the way we name and ensoul our desires.

When our desires and motivations are hidden from us because we have lost direction or been lured into inappropriate

lines or because we have just failed to provide ourselves access to good soul-food, our incarnational thread enters a meaningless phase of meandering which it will be necessary to unpick before long. (Also see Practice 7.)

The Upperworld challenges us to seek our spiritual pathway for the benefit of all beings on the cosmic web: this call has caused many to scale the heights of altruistic efforts, but it has been frequently ill applied by those who have not as yet unpicked the muddle of their incarnational thread. Conventional religious sentiment has confounded any such spiritual preparation with selfishness. It is very important that we all understand this principle before we go further on the shamanic path: for without vocational impulse, incarnational clarification, and spiritual preparation any shamanic work that we propose will become entangled with our own muddle. Any tendencies and imbalances within us will be mercilessly illuminated by the light of the Upperworld. (See Chapter 7, Section 2, 'Everyday Mythology'.)

Permission to untangle your incarnational thread is here given.

The Upperworld encourages us to take a whole overview of our lives so that we may know ourselves through self-discovery and be able to release the energy which is seeded within us: just as the Underworld encourages us to dive deeply into our heritage and tradition; to realize our resources, to remember our capabilities and to take up the power that flows through the universe, so that our roots are nourished.

But the Middleworld is our mother place, our home, where we work out what we have learned, to which we mediate the advice and healing which we gain from the otherworlds. It is now time to return to this realm and start putting what we have learned into practice.

Practice 57: Soul-food

The issue of soul-malnutrition rarely enters the agendas of governments, yet people are dying of it all around us and we don't even notice. We need soul-food to the same extent as we

need ordinary food. Our soul feeds on beauty and harmony, needing times of recreation, of creativity and of ecstatic uplift. There are no rules about soul-food: you eat when you are hungry wherever the food is offered. Dancing, painting, reading, walking, contemplating, making things – any of these may be soul-food. Communion with the Upperworld necessitates that we seek out the soul-food that we each need for life as a primal responsibility.

Journey to your inspirers and spiritual lineage teacher and ask, 'What nurtures my soul? What soul-food do I lack? Where can it be found?' The response to these questions may entail pursuing your vision and creative quest with continual commitment, realizing that receptivity and rest must be balanced by practice and activity. For our creative processes must follow their own seasonal or natural growth patterns: we cannot always be creative nor always fallow, there will be the between times when practice brings only meagre results.

Permission to make space for soul-nourishment is here given.

Practice 58: Creating the Inner Fortress of Silence

Sacred space generally has meant one thing in our society: a temple or church which has been blessed for sacred practice. In shamanism, all space is sacred. This space can be as narrow as the amount of room your body displaces in physical reality or as limitless as inner space. We all have our own access to inner space where our creative spirit can have reconnection with the universe, an inner fortress of silent space which comes with you wherever you are.

The tantric shaman, Ngakpa Chögyam, writes:

> For a fortress to be secret, it must be invisible. It must have no boundaries of exclusiveness – it must be an Internal Fortress of Practice rather than an external institution.[11]

Your fortress is a strong place of refuge where you can retreat in order to clarify your daily life, where you still the inner dialogue and find the creative silence. In this silence, your shamanic hearing will develop.

If you are irritated, hassled and fraught, the chances are you've not entered your inner fortress for a long time. Practise

this once a day: sit outside, if possible, or inside in a quiet place where you can see some part of the natural world. Release any tensions and worries that you are holding in your body. Still your breathing and enter the rhythm, laying aside all distracting thoughts. If distractions arise in your mind, don't hold them but let them become like clouds that float away. Feel your own body space around you – this is your own space which cannot be taken from you. Now, become aware of the space surrounding the place where you sit/stand. Feel this as a distinct space at first, then allow your space and this space to merge. Experience how your space is also part of the larger universal space. Now turn your thoughts to the abode of your spiritual lineage teacher in the Upperworld and, without straining to retain this image, allow this abode to descend about you as your own internal fortress of practice. Make no attempt to source or journey, but remain in light meditation. Reverse the procedure until you are aware of your own body space again.

Practise this whenever moments of natural introspection come upon you. Use these precious moments of insight to see into the heart of things. At night, enter your secret fortress of stillness to unprocess the day's events; without self-blame, guilt or anger, but with neutrality, make how your actions, words and thoughts have moved the cosmic web today.

Practice 59: Voice as the Soul's Pathway

As you have begun to source and journey, you will have discovered how many parts of your body become vehicles for power, especially the voice. The songs that come to us when shamanizing are not recreational songs. They may come with yelps, animal cries and syllabic vocalizations that are not words – in spirit language, ignoring the accepted musical structures of our culture. Such songs are sacred songs of great power.

No vocal expertise is required for shamanic singing, but many people are alienated from their own voices and reluctant to use them. Learn to enjoy your voice and not be estranged by it. One way is to allow your animal or teacher to sing through your own vocal cords: then it can't possibly be your problem!

The secret of shamanic voice is to follow the experiences which we are having as we begin the source, to let the song

emerge as the images and feelings unfold. This way, you are using your shamanic voice as a soul-path: a song which goes straight through to the cosmic web and which can provide a strong pathway for straying souls.

Next time you journey, instead of lying still, sit up slightly supported and sing what you experience on to a tape recorder. A particularly good sound-source for this method is the musical bow or Tibetan bowl which gives a central unchanging note around which your voice can weave.

When you next dance with your spirits, lend them your voice, so that the song that is always singing in the silence can be heard and given.

Permission to sing this silent book alive is here given.

Practice 60: The Song of the Star-watchers

Some people find the stars dwarf them or overwhelm them with interspatial agoraphobia, but the next time you have a multitude of small personal worries snapping at you like dogs, go out and look up to the stars to gain a sense of proportion. Study the constellations which are visible, year round, from where you live on the globe. Regularly watch their progress through the heavens, periodically selecting particularly significant ones as places to journey to. Go first to your Upperworld teacher and ask for guidance and permission to journey to particular stars or constellations. Ensure you have at least one ally with you at all times. Ask for a song from each star or constellation that you visit.

Note: star-work is very powerful and should be performed only occasionally; as star-spirits are concerned with the germination of seeds throughout the cosmic web, it is especially important that women scrutinize their own fertility cycle very carefully if they don't want an addition to the family!

Practice 61: Gathering your Powers

As you go deeper into this work, you will gradually draw together your powers. On journeys you will encounter new

teachers and helpers. You may be given objects in subtle reality to use in your work. The interesting thing about these gifts is the way they manifest in physical reality as shamanic objects. Gifts acquired in journeys are often subsequently given to you in the Middleworld by friends who say vaguely, 'Oh, I saw this object and thought you might like it'. These gifts represent the gathering together of your powers and are the basis for a collection of objects that will help you in your work. They should be kept securely in a shamanic bag and not given away, unless your spirits tell you otherwise.

Medicine bundles or shamanic bags do not come custom made. You will find your own ways of making a container for your power-objects. Your objects may need to be individually wrapped so that they do not break or injure each other. Needless to say, your shamanic bag is not for showing to all and sundry. I review the contents of mine seasonally to ensure that objects are still willing to remain in my keeping. If they are not, I return them to nature or else decommission them in a ritual way that returns them appropriately to the universe.

We do not own or command the power of any object; it chooses to co-operate with us as an ally. The power-objects which you use can be dedicated in a short ceremony of consecration.

This may be a good place to discuss shamanic regalia in general. Many firms specialize in making power-objects so that it is possible for the beginner to arrive at a shamanic course professionally equipped with custom-made objects of all kinds from drum to clothing. By all means find your own shamanic style, but let the objects come to you in the course of your life, or make them yourself if you can. They will mean more to you if the spirits who have contacted you in journey are able to help you create an object and imbue it with their power.

Create your own short ceremony for consecrating power-objects in your shamanic work. Different objects may need specific dedication; the use of a crystal for cleansing or healing may need a different dedication from an eye-fringe or a rattle. A simple method is to ask the spirits of the cosmic web to bless your power-object; or you might symbolically pass your object through the four elements or the three worlds.

7. Divination

Everything can serve prophecy. You only have to pay attention. The universe is full of signs. When you learnt to look at things the right way, you will understand what I'm trying to say. The shape of clouds, the way birds fly, the sounds of nature, an unexpected meeting – all these transmit a message that expresses the will of the gods.

Maria-José
Brazilian Macumba priestess

1. MAPPING THE THREE WORLDS

Whoever departs from this world without having realized his own inner world, to him life has been of no service: it remains unlived, like an undone deed.

Brhad-aranyaka Upanishad

DIVINATION IS LITERALLY the art of 'asking the gods or spirits'. It is a prime shamanic task whereby we turn away from our own intellectual processes to unzip the universe and perceive the answer which is often staring us in the face. We turn to divination when we don't have the answers. This process involves recognizing the patterns which are constellated around any issue under scrutiny.

We all remember playing 's/he loves me, s/he loves me not' with a petalled flower. As children we all watched raindrops falling down windows and betting which one would reach the windowsill first. We have all touched posts, jumped cracks in

pavements, played counting out games all in order to determine whether an action shall happen or not. Children know more about divination than most adults.

Divination has been more recently associated with divination systems, but commercial cards or symbols are not needed for you to ask the universe your question. Anything in this universe can and has been used for divination: the flight of birds and the behaviour of animals; the sequence of cards, stones and twigs; lines on hands and bumps on heads; tea-leaves and coffee grounds; and many other bizarre methods. In this book we are using journeying to discern the subtle patterns of the cosmic web.

The Purpose of Divination

To ask Spirit for answers, to question the Creator is regarded as blasphemous in many religions. This is why they have always relegated the practice of divination to experts or forbidden it entirely that blind faith might be safeguarded. Indeed, looking for signs and wonders in every small and insignificant event can become a bad habit, if unchecked. Without interior understanding divination can soon deteriorate into a superstitious and meaningless practice.

Passive fatalism or innate superstition have no part in shamanism. Trust in the spirits of the universe, good oracy and alignment with it are better friends. We divine only for issues that are beyond our human capability to solve; the use of divination, whether by cards, stones, twigs or by journeying to determine everyday affairs, is a misuse of spiritual help. It reveals sloppy alignment to attribute some minor ailment or occurrence to some totally unrelated prior cause, such as 'I must have missed that train because I was meant to/because of Mercury going retrograde'. This may make us feel better about missing a connection, but the real reason is more likely our unpunctuality than any mystical influence.

The fortune-telling element of divination has unfortunately become a dominant feature in all prognostication: a virtual obsession with the outcome or final result. Divination is really a two-way process of alignment which may be likened to stretching a musical string between an issue in physical reality

and its correlative in subtle reality: we stretch our string and then pluck it to see what kind of resonance it has. A resonant note tells us that the issue is well aligned and connected; a buzzing or totally unresonant string tells us that the issue lacks alignment and purpose. This process merely tell us *what adjustments are necessary* not what will come to pass. The implementation of divinatory advice remains in our hands.

All divination turns about the way we frame our question. If we ask our question badly, we will receive evasive answers or none at all. The very basis of our spiritual direction is the questions we ask in life: *if we ask the right question, we will achieve our quest.* (See page 54.)

The Voice of the Spirit

When we question the spirits, the answer comes by way of oracle, which is 'the language of the spirits': an answer which is rarely conveyed in words but rather in arcane correspondences. Sometimes the oracle does come in verbal form, with a person acting as the god's voice. We call such people mediums in our society, though this term is narrowly associated with spiritualist mediums who act solely as oracles for the departed. Many countries have state oracles. Before the Chinese invasion, Tibet's state oracle was the prophetic voice of his people: this is still practised in Ladakh. The oracle of Delphi was the sibyl who acted as the voice of Apollo. Such oracles do not speak in mundane language, but in the heightened speech of seers and poets. Irish shamans used a poetic form of prophecy called *teinm laegda*, where cumulative poetic phrases created a full solution to problems.[1]

The interpretation of this advice is of course the critical feature of divination. We all want to know what things mean and flock to experts or divinatory manuals to be enlightened. Divination is really about discerning the deeper patterns of life from criteria which are only clear to the individual diviner. As walkers between the worlds, we are gradually amassing a series of criteria from our own journeying which will eventually form a divinatory database. Each person's database is different: some areas may be common, others will be personal.

Every time we journey, we are divining. But as we have not

been trained as diviners, making sense of our journeys is an art in which we will become more practised when we have more experience. You will not always understand everything. The authenticity of your own practice will come from trusting your helpers and the experiences you have on journeys. The more you practise, the more journeys you log, the greater your oracy and alignment. This is why it helps to have good records of your journeys. As you accumulate 'flying hours', so will you be navigating and mapping new areas of inner space.

Over the last one hundred and fifty years or so, our society has made great strides with literacy: this has also meant the erosion of our symbolic literacy. We no longer respond to symbols and images in an immediate way. Our oracy has been sacrificed to literacy. More recently, metaphor and symbol have been jettisoned and the descent from literacy to literality has begun. When we journey or divine we have to relearn our own symbolic language.

We need to trust the symbols and images that appear to us in journeys and to break our reliance on encyclopaedias of symbolism. It is true that many symbols are shared by the collective understanding of world culture, but each also has a localized significance to a part of the globe and a core meaning to each person. We each have power-bearing images in our oral-pool, images that bear banners, symbols that are mysterious yet charged with meaning. The gift of a white feather in a journey may signify cowardice to one person or the power of inner flight to another. We cannot seek arbitrary meanings, only personal ones; we must contextualize our own findings and trust our own personal nuances of meaning.

Making sense of our journeys requires us to pay close attention to what we experience and to cross-relate it to all the factors. Beginners often want to pigeon-hole their journeys into a known frame of reference, such as that of conventional psychology, but shamanic experience is too broad to be confined within such a structure. Nor can the stream of information to be synthesized and understood be submitted to analytic or scientific categorization, or be catalogued on file cards. As well catalogue poetry or dance!

Having looked at the symbolism and metaphors of our journey, we have to look at the different scenes or episodes into which it falls: what story is emerging? Finally, we must look at

the whole journey, for we can fail to see the wood for the trees if we concentrate too much upon one or other factor.

Notes for Interpreting your Journey

The following questions will help you crack open your journey if the answer is not clear. Beware of interpreting your experience by means of conventional psychological methodology. Journeys usually have a sequence: some have many scenarios. Break these down and deal with them in turn, as they unfolded, before looking at the whole journey.

1. What was the object of this journey? (Always relate what you experienced to your original issue, quest or motivation.)
2. Which part of the journey held most power for me? (Recall which parts in particular evoked strong emotion.)
3. Which part was most difficult? (Recall any blockage of emotion.)
4. How did my allies help me?
5. What did they tell me, verbally or non-verbally, about my issue?
6. Did they ask/advise me to do anything during the journey? How did I react?
7. What power/gift was I offered on this journey?
8. What did my journey show me? How will I implement this? What next step is suggested by this journey?
9. How was Spirit present on this journey?

With particularly obscure journeys it can also be helpful to write it down as if it were a story. Write in the third person if this helps you unlock it. 'Once upon a time a woman climbed a high cliff and met a jaguar who took her to a far country . . .' Giving ourselves distance from our experience will sometimes help reveal the answer.

Advanced Troubleshooting for your Journey

We all encounter difficulties and problems in our practice. Some of the following are commonly experienced. All of them are about trusting information received shamanically.

Is it all right to move from one world to another during a journey?

Yes. Sometimes your quest cannot be accomplished in just one world; allies normally initiate this movement to another place. Ensure that your guardian animal remains with you when you move swiftly. You will soon recognize the corridors, doors and windows which connect the three worlds for you, apart from your central routes up and down.

How can I trust that what I experience is right?

This worry can still occur in more experienced walkers between worlds. You retain your free will and are under no obligation to accept literally any advice or instructions. Check journey content against your subtle senses – does it feel instinctively beneficial to you? Act 'as if'. (See 'None of it seems real' below.) Interpret the symbolism and metaphor of your journey carefully: some things will reveal both their physical and subtle reality simultaneously and you will instinctively know which these are. If you have a hunch about a possible meaning but can't verify this, wait a few days and see what your daily life and dream life bring up. Some validations follow journeys almost immediately. It is often a matter of understanding the way you and your spirits talk to each other: expect humour, outrageous puns and sudden spotlights as you go through life.

My journeys are very different from my friend's – is one of us doing it wrong?

There is no 'right' way to perceive shamanically. You are a unique person with your own connective pathways to the other-worlds. Your journeying will unfold an inner map *from your own point of departure*. The things you see and experience will appear in your own symbology: only you can interpret them.

Beware of interpreting other people's journeys, dreams and visions for them: only the person who has experienced these can hold the keys. You can help a friend arrive at their own interpretation by asking some of the questions on p. 175, always referring back to the context of their quest.

How can I implement the advice I receive as it involves others?

The advice we receive is resultant from the question or purpose we have journeyed with. We cannot expect to be able to implement journey advice for others if we have journeyed without consulting or asking permission of others in the first place. We cannot give enlightenment to another, nor can we manipulate the cosmic web in order to help someone accept something.

Why did my teacher lop off my head on my journey?

A common and disconcerting experience of journeying to one's teacher for healing, change and initiation into knowledge is that of losing parts of the body. The stripping away of flesh, reorganization of the body, treatment of organs, removal and replacement of body parts may all take place within a journey. The reconstitution of the body is the final experience before returning. What does this all mean?

It is an initiatory and healing experience in which spaciousness and nothingness are critically present. The Dzog Chen school of Tibetan Buddhism actively meditates upon this process, and many Tibetan and South American depictions of the process are extant. To experience it, is to be spread over the universe and reconstituted so that the whole universe is simultaneously re-membered within you.

What do I do if I encounter something frightening or become blocked by some obstacle?

If you encounter something you can't deal with on journeys, don't try. Consult your allies: they will advise you on the appropriate course of action, or take you another way. If they have no strategies, get away.

Is it all right to fly or swim on journeys?

The way in which we travel through the worlds varies tremendously, and is often influenced by the nature of the ally

we travel with. You may fly, crawl, leap, swim, or slither to your destination. Travelling in all the elements is a skill which can be acquired. You might also try shapeshifting into the form of your animal/s and see how that feels when you journey. Always travel with at least one ally.

None of it seems real

When you are learning to perceive subtle reality, it takes a lot of practice for journeying to seem normal. The adage, 'act as if it were real', is a useful one to adopt: when you perceive that the answers and advice do work when you implement them, you can move with more confidence.

Nothing happens when I journey

People who have good mental control find sourcing difficult, because they have to let go. Journeying is about releasing control, not dictating what you experience. Trick the 'watchdog mind' by story, song or monotony. Experiment by spending at least three hours with no possible distractions: you can do this indoors at night by switching off the lights; you can go out into nature and sit perfectly still; you can stare at a brick wall. Record what happens when you do this. Removal of stimulus and mental chatter results in a new kind of perception. Journeying is like learning to float – the universe will hold you up!

I keep seeing irrelevant things when I journey

Ask yourself: 'Is this *really* irrelevant?' Don't automatically dismiss what you experience as irrelevant. I recall a client who realized halfway through his journey that the scenario he was in was identical to a film he had once seen; his disgust was immense, but he pressed on with his animal, complaining heartily. His issue was how to survive in his chosen profession. The film scenario of his journey was about the sole survivor of a plane crash in a deserted region, and his return to civilization. He realized that though this journey was borrowed from a film,

it was indeed relevant to his situation, and it eventually enabled him to cut through immense difficulties to achieve a real breakthrough in his career.

How long should I journey for?

Normally the length of your journey will be determined by the length of the tape you are using: fifteen to thirty minutes is average, but find your own limits. Sometimes you will experience the whole universe in two minutes, at others, twenty-five minutes may pass slowly and uneventfully. You will also have your off days when nothing seems to work. If someone is drumming for you, you can signal when you have concluded by a prearranged gesture. If you are drumming for someone who shows no signs of coming back after a reasonable time, you may need to sound the call-back and go on sounding it. If this does not work, start singing a calling-home song.

I shared my journey with my partner and now he's convinced I'm deranged

Journeys can seldom be shared with non-practitioners because there is no common conceptual vocabulary, no shared cosmology, and an unequal perception of reality. If you want to talk about your practice, seek out a soul-friend on whose support and discretion you can rely (see Practice 72). If you want to share some part of your practice with a relative or partner, if only in order to allay their fears, then choose your words wisely, use non-specialist vocabulary and speak in that person's conceptual framework.

My journey was inconclusive

Sometimes the call-back sounds before you have finished: try to conclude briefly any action or exchange before returning, but do not hang about hoping to continue. Sometimes, the journey itself may require another journey to explain it or to sort out a prior problem. But even enigmatic journeys which conclude

abruptly can still reveal important clues, however episodic they may seem; try applying the interpretation questions above. Aimless journeys often result when we have failed to pose our question to our allies. If your journey was inconclusive as a result of any of these factors, it is often better to journey again the next day. As with all divining, repeated consecutive efforts on the same day often result in non-responsive journeys or a stern instruction from one's allies to leave matters alone for the time being.

My experiences are very different from the ones outlined in this book

Do not be afraid to accept that your route to the worlds may sometimes vary from ones you have been taught or read about. Do not worry if you find different animals come to help you in different worlds. Accept that your inner teachers will assume different guises at different times. No book or teacher can possibly prepare you for the variety of experiences that you have; your own life and background are the most important framework.

Ways of Improving your Journeying

1. Avoid journeying when you are rushed.
2. Deliberately leave your burden of worries behind when you journey, unless you are focusing on one of them as your journey issue.
3. Ensure that more than half of your journeying is on non-personal issues: journey to benefit the cosmic web in some way.
4. Ask allies what you can do for them.
5. Maintain neutral expectation and maximum receptivity.
6. Simplify the way you frame your issue: repeat it to yourself several times before sourcing.
7. Do not analyse your experiences as you journey, but allow them to unfold like a story.
8. Always check with your allies when decisions are required on journeys. They will not think you are stupid.
9. When making a series of journeys about an issue, refer back to records of previous journeys before each new journey. How have things developed since the last journey?

10. Ask allies to explain or repeat things if you don't understand.
11. Record your journeys aloud on tape and play them back. Listen to the quality of your voice at significant moments: does your voice achieve release or become stressed – relate the significance of these moments carefully to your quest.
12. Upgrade your journey record into a real navigator's log and look for connections with your daily life.

Practice 62: Mapping the Worlds

We each have our own maps of the cosmic web which teach us about the otherworlds. Our otherworldly explorations are analogous to the rediscovery of lands once frequently visited. Only you can understand how all the worlds fit together for you.

Start first with the appearance of the three worlds. You may find that the mood of each of the three worlds brings a different colouration to your journeys. Underworld journeys are frequently calm, strong and empowering: many people feel that nothing much has happened, because the Underworld is a place where the body receives deep and moving changes, but these changes are nevertheless profound. Upperworld journeys tend to be ecstatic, moving and enlightening; there is a greater sense of definition, and archetypal perception. The Middleworld journey is generally busy and practical, bringing clarification and order.

Moving between the worlds comes with practice. The unity of the three worlds is much more apparent when you have journeyed over a long period. We must remember that they are not three distinct and separated zones, but worlds which interconnect.

Regions that you visit may become increasingly familiar, but exasperatingly unconnected. You may know only that on your last journey you visited 'the ivy-covered house where the broken piano waits' – a place familiar to you from recurrent dreams. The mapping of your inner landscape can be likened to living in a town with an underground railway which connects everything. If you travel by it regularly, you will theoreti-

cally know which regions link up, but you will seldom know what the ground level looks like and how regions really join on to others.

Try to collate the information gained on your journeys and see if you can work out a map of how it all relates. Do you have specific pathways between the worlds? Check out which scenarios, teachers, animals appear in the three worlds. What kinds of help/information/healing are given in these places by these spirits? What gifts have you obtained in these realms? What uses do they have?

You may find it helpful to draw your journeys; great artistic ability is unimportant – as a glance at any shaman's sketch of the spiritual worlds will show. The important thing is to understand how *you personally* relate to the spiritual worlds.

Take a large sheet of paper and begin to sketch a map of your findings. As you proceed with journeying, this map will change and come into greater clarity. Shamanic work requires spontaneity and creative response. No human being has ever totally mapped the cosmic web; we can only have our own sketch-map where we know help will be found. Keep on exploring and discovering.

Practice 63: Stone Divination

Create your own divination method by bringing together a series of stones. Each can be assigned a particular quality or you may wish to source each stone and discover its own gift. Play with these until you begin to know them by their distinctive features, colours and shapes. Fill a wooden tomato-box with silver sand and practise throwing the stones. See what shapes you come up with. Or you might create a cloth marked with divisions for areas of activity, such as health, relationships, work. You might wish to create a cloth which has the co-ordinates of your own otherworldly map marked upon it in symbolic and oblique fashion. In this way you may be able to help people answer specific questions: they might throw the stones and listen to your interpretation, or else they might be invited to place stones according to their intuition. This form of divination can be helpful for non-practitioners.

2. EVERYDAY MYTHOLOGY

You don't have anything if you don't have the stories.

Ceremony
Leslie Marmion Silko

Shamanic divination has two aspects: the walker between the worlds looks both at the signs of personal life-patterns and dreams, as well as accessing the otherworlds for help in gaining a broader or more precise overview. By reading these in concert, not in separation from each other, we receive a lively oracle. With this broad view, it is possible to live in a more balanced and insightful way, for we will have gained true oracy – the capacity to hear, remember and relate.

Our journeys are important episodes in our own ongoing story, revealing ways in which our life inter-relates with the rest of the cosmic web. In these storylines, we discern patterns, sequences and archetypes which we call myth: stories by which to live, empowering and ensouling pathways which align us with the cosmic web. Our culture frequently misunderstands myth as an untrue, fantastic or imagined story, but we can see myth as a subtle reality story which is mediated to physical reality by shamans, artists and visionaries.

There are four kinds of human myth. They explore:

1. The relationship of people with nature and their environment.
2. The personal quest.
3. The family, tribal or national preoccupation.
4. The relationship of people and the greater universe.

The codification and integration of such stories have frequently provided us with religions, some of which have subsequently been compulsorily enjoined upon our belief. In each case, these mythic schemas have been responsible for the evocation and manifestation of subtle reality spirits whom we call gods, heroes, animal spirits and so on.

Divining our own Myths

We each have a personal myth or 'story to live by'. This may manifest as adherence to a religious belief system and a close

following of a specific spiritual leader's story which is super-imposed upon personal lives as a spiritual template to be imitated. Within this century, fewer people have wished to constrain their lives in such a way, but have sought out other ways of living. Whoever we are or wherever was live, we each abide by some written or unwritten personal myth by which we guide our lives, whether it be a political ideology, an ideal of social commonwealth, a mystical set of values or an identifi-cation with a hero, heroine or other figure who inspires us. Our 'story to live by' can comprise one or many of these aspects in combination: these become the constants and frameworks which dictate our behaviour, direct our attitudes and moral judgements and fuel our lives, the bottom line beyond which we will not willingly pass.

In their original format, these stories have power and Spirit, but myths often lose their currency as time goes on because human beings change. It has been my experience that if a story doesn't move you to tears or laughter, to exaltation or pro-found personal change, then it is not a story you need to worry about. It is certainly not one you should be steering your life by.

Stories lose their power when we are no longer personally walking their pathways. When we begin to question the authenticity of our current myth or discard it as outworn, our soul goes forth in search of a myth which truly aligns us with the cosmic web once again. As the third millennium dawns, more and more people are redefining their spiritual and social myths.

Nothing stays unchanging in the universe; everything has its own rhythm. Re-divining our shared myth or personal story is something we must do periodically if they are not to become powerless and disensouled by habit and familiarity.

The mythic pathways we need to find are those which align us with our spiritual and ancestral lineages but which allow our personal story to be strengthened and encouraged at the same time. In the great collective redefinition of myth which is currently shaking the cosmic web, it is often hard to perceive the pathways which have greatest resonance for us, and many people are thrown into a consideration of their own story with-out regard for the greater mythic resonance. Our own story is part of the universal story: this should be remembered both as

an encouragement to maintain our story with courage and as a humble reminder that our personal story is not the only one.

There are many story-paths transecting the cosmic web: some of these have greater resonance than others, some leave broad tracks into which our personal story-path sometimes merges. The biologist, Rupert Sheldrake, defines his notion of 'morphic resonance', as 'the influence of previous structures of activity on subsequent similar structures of activity' by any unit, whether it be a single cell or culture or galaxy; morphic resonance transects time and space leaving discernible pathways.[2] Myth is nothing less than the morphic resonance of life on the cosmic web: its patterns are held in our memory and, if they are steadfastly followed, will result in increasingly habitual pathways.

Oracy

The morphic resonance of our story becomes apparent if we review our lives and become aware of our oracy. Oracy is the horse's mouth; it is our capacity to hear, remember and relate. Oracy is not dependent upon the written word but gives primacy to the oral traditions that maintain our connections with the ancient wisdom whose lines transect the cosmic web. It has no authority except itself. To write of oracy in a book and to ask you to make written notes of experiences may seem ironic, but your shamanic experience is leading you into the heart of your own oracy.

Oracy has been well respected by shamans of all cultures. The druids did not allow their teachings to be written down, fearing that this would erode the capacity of memory. Certain chants and teachings are transmitted only 'from mouth to ear'. This transmission is often thought of as some fixed transfer of data, but I have not found it so. My experience of teaching many groups of people leads me to suppose that any such group always has certain needs and expectations: they come to learn a particular subject, but within its broad criteria, I will find myself speaking and teaching in such a way as to address their needs in ways I had not intended. As a student, I have noticed that certain seemingly 'off the cuff' remarks or personal anecdotes of a teacher will spark exciting realizations within

me, re-constellating information and experiences. Knowledge-transmission seems to happen at a much more creative and uncodifiable level than we imagine. We maintain the oracy of our lives by allowing power and Spirit to enter them freely and spontaneously, by living without a rigid script.

Oracy gives us the immediacy of understanding we get from being shown a technique rather than working it out alone from an instruction manual. The hand-holds and connections of any practice are always best imparted by a practitioner at first hand. This book allows me to speak to you and has been written to be as helpful as possible, but it is no substitute for first-hand transmission. Oracy has its own spaciousness which allows the unspoken and incommunicable to be transmitted. Written words often constrict and confine, creating passivity among those who read them, preventing the Spirit from flowing.

Our way of life can become our morphic field: a pattern which speaks to others through actions, words, thoughts and intentions. We tend towards stories which nurture the morphic field of our oracy. The stories that we read, the televisual stories that we watch, reflect how we seek nourishment for our own habitual story: we use all kinds of stories to keep us going, from the snack (short story, anecdote, magazine article) to the banquet (myth, novel, biography).

We have been used to thinking of stories as written things, but here I encourage you to contemplate the possibility of your life-journey as myth and story.

The stories which we hear in childhood are remembered more clearly by us because we have *heard* rather than read them. Such stories have power. Sarah Grays, a Cree elder, remembers her uncle Otiokmuskoo telling a story about two hunters lost in the snowy wastes:

> I remember I sat under a quilt because his story was about getting very cold . . . we all got lost with them in his story . . . some other elders who saw that us children were really worried and afraid began to talk about what to do if you get lost. We learned quite a bit . . . Those elders had all been lost themselves at least once . . . After that, Otiokmuskoo's wife sewed me a quilt with a map of our region on it. Lakes, some trees, some birds. Also she sewed on it a lot of paths. It was a good quilt to sleep under.[3]

Sarah Grays had the supreme fortune of being part of a story whose boundaries overlapped with her own. The quilted map

gave her a sense of belonging in her story so that she no longer worried about the blurred edges, of becoming lost. From a Western perspective, her narrative would be regarded as non-fiction, while the story of her uncle was clearly fiction: yet, for Sarah, these distinctions do not arise – she *becomes* story.

This is the truth at the heart of divination: we discover meaning by becoming aware of, by entering, our story. If we remain detached from our story, we lose our oracy along with power and Spirit. Neither shamanism nor any form of divination is an end itself: when we have learned where the cosmic web runs, we must get on with out lives and engage with it.

Preserving the power-bearing and soul-nurturing aspects of our story will help us deal with the areas where our power and soul are under threat. In our story, certain events reoccur, creating a series of seemingly set patterns which then become self-perpetuating or by which subsequent life is judged or restricted. These patterns of disempowerment have great influence upon us and make us susceptible to their recurrence. They become our story. You may have picked up the signatures of these stories in yourself and others: be attentive when you hear the words 'I'm always . . . tired, late, unable to cope with money' or 'I never . . . win, hold down relationships, get to sit in the front seat'. These are unhelpful recurrent patterns which cause our story to get stuck. Going beyond these patterns takes great determination and encouragement.

Recognizing and changing these patterns will help us untangle our incarnational thread. We do not need to repeat the disk of old, repetitive stories. These may stem from patterns established in this life or may be the result of past incarnations. In shamanism we avoid past problems and entanglements by relating them to our present life and time-frame: we only need to review our present incarnation and list the related and recurrent difficulties which we continually encounter.

By finding, living and telling stories which have power and Spirit, we become authentic guardians of oracy, the true currency of the cosmic web: it is an open story which has no ending.

Dreams

But sometimes our story is unclear to us and we are unaware of the patterns which lay down morphic resonance on the

cosmic web. This submerged part of our personal story can be divined through our dreams, revealed to us by the spirits who fly at night. Dreams have been used for divining since the world began: they are everyone's door to subtle reality, practitioners or not. Dreams speak to us at night of things we haven't given time for during the day, they utter direct or encoded messages about our life's direction, they offer us opportunities to experience the otherworlds directly.

I often liken journeying to dreaming for people who lack confidence about their ability to journey. In dreams we follow the story that is spun out of our sleep, observing or interacting with it; there are few people who can manipulate their dreaming sufficiently to change the story and we conclude that dreaming is a largely involuntary function which is engaged in by all people. Journeying, however, requires us to follow the story that is spun out of our sound-source and our issue, observing and interacting with it. Although many worry that they might attempt to change the story, very few are actually able to do so. Although both dreaming and journeying are means of accessing subtle reality, we should remember that while dreaming is involuntary, journeying happens in *voluntary* shamanic awareness.

During dreaming, part of our soul is journeying, which is why it is considered unwise to awaken a sleeper roughly. Many cultures recite protective prayers for the soul before sleeping, so that the soul's helpers accompany it during the night. Such are the common prayers of children, providing soul-protection while they are out of their bodies.

Dreams are food and nourishment for us in our sleep. We leave our bodies and journey to those realms which give us what we need. The dreams of those who are deprived of home, loved ones and food, such as prisoners of war, are usually richly nurturing. The dreams of those who are confused or worried often follow labyrinthine contortions which irritatingly mirror the disturbed mental pattern, yet they will also peak in a dream which grants great clarity and direction, giving effective solutions or cessation of panic. In such cases, we visit the Middleworld to derive comfort or to pace over our problems. The really great and memorable dreams of our lives are those which take us to the Upperworld and the Underworld.

Among some indigenous people, dreaming becomes not

only a personal but a tribal activity, where the dreamer's vision, like the shaman's vision, provides the myth of a whole people. This vision is not fixed, but inter-relates with the dreams of the ancestors and with the dreams of descendants – a group alignment of great importance takes place, allowing power and Spirit to flow into the lives of all beings in that place. In a consideration of the aboriginal dreamtime, the writer and traveller, Bruce Chatwin, wrote about the continuity of myth and story:

> I have a vision of the Songlines stretching across the continents and ages; that wherever men have trodden they have left a trail of song (of which we now and then, catch an echo).[4]

Those song, story and myth lines are everywhere to be found, if we will only look into the oracy of our lives.

Permission to become a nomadic story-finder is here given.

Practice 64: The Oral Pool

It is all too easy to lose touch with our oracy unless we occasionally freshen our oral pool and review its contents. Our oral pool is our living memory of teachings, stories and songs of nurture that we remember without the aid of book or tape. Each people or group also has its own oral pool which draws upon group memories. If you were the only survivor of your planet/country what could you relate from your personal oral pool? If all written and recorded media retrieval were to cease, which items of your collective oral pool would you most wish to save in oral memory? Journey to your Underworld teacher and ask to be shown your own oral pool: you may be shown things you need to remember. We source our ancestral oral pool when we seek for forgotten wisdom: here it is possible to recover rituals and find strategies for our community from the council of the deep ancestors.

Practice 65: Exploring our Myths

Memory shows us the handholds of our life's patterns; it reveals the places that our soul has touched. The signposts,

markers, boundaries, restricted areas of our lives form an inner landscape. Every being living has a different set of handholds, signposts, memories. These memories create patterns, song-lines, subtle pathways that weave us into the universe.

What myths do you inherit from your ancestral, educational and cultural background? Which still work for you and why? Which do you discard and why?

What present story is unfolding in your life? Who are the major actors in your story? Who are the challengers, helpers, lovers, inspirers? What patterns are you laying down for the future? Look for the repetitive images, figures and feelings which crop up. Look over your journeys and dreams, under-lining or highlighting significant features which strike you. Tell your life-story to date as a myth, drawing on these major protagonists and patterns, but going further than you have now lived, bringing it to a satisfactory resolution in the next life-phase.

How does your story relate to the shared myth of your age and people? How does it relate to nature and to the earth? How does it relate to the story of the cosmic web?

Practice 66: Dream Diary

Begin to keep a dream diary. A notebook and pen beneath your pillow or close at hand is essential for this. Dreams often take wing on waking, and even minimal movement can cause them to flee. Write down the sequence of your dream and, most importantly, how it made you feel; for example 'reminiscent of holiday in Holland' or 'sense of foreboding and tension throughout', or 'strong smell of geraniums reminded me of Gran'. At the end of each week, review your dreams and entitle them like stories; for example 'Flying With Pink Birds' or 'The Cliff's Edge', or 'In Glasgow with my Sister'. What gift/quality/focus did each dream give you?

Our dream experiences often seem surreal and strange: impossible things like flying or breathing underwater are com-mon, people, things and events appear in bizarre juxtapos-ition. Some dream sequences are remarkably like journeys and we can interpret them by the same criteria. Among preliterate peoples, symbol and metaphor are rich sources of exchange.

Literacy has the effect of damping our imaginative faculties, of promoting our intellectual comprehension at the expense of our soul's comprehension. Symbol causes reaction in the soul, stimulating physiological, emotional and mental response. You must always interpret the symbols and images you experience *from your own symbology*, not from a dictionary of symbols. 'Metaphor is the foodstuff and substance of dreams, which are, themselves, pictographic metaphors, only of the unconscious dimension.'[5] We do well to remember this when we attempt to understand and interpret dreams or journeys. The language of dreams is symbolic, not literal. If you dream of beheading pigs or of sleeping with your aunt, this may be disturbing but it does not mean you have or will do either of these things.

Compare and correlate your journeys and your dreams.

Practice 67: Calling the Dream-spirits

Dion Fortune called dream 'the door which has no key', regarding it as an initiatory way to deeper knowledge.[6] This may seem a very good definition for those people who find it difficult to remember dreams or have no awareness of ever having dreamt. Make a journey to your Upperworld teacher and ask for directions to find dream-spirit allies who will connect you with your dreams.

Dreams as well as journeys can enable us to find solutions to worrying problems. If journeying is not resolving a situation or decision, proceed as follows. First formulate your dilemma as a question to your dream-allies: for example 'Please help me perceive the hidden aspects of this new job', or 'Please reveal healing pathways towards my reconciliation with X'. Before bed, light a candle, bring the question to the attention of your helpers and spend at least five minutes holding the question without emotion, urgency or analysis in your awareness. During this time, you may wish to hum or sing quietly. Now lie down to sleep, saying your own 'incubation' prayer or song, something like this:

> On my right side I lie here:
> May my dreams be crystal clear.
> In the morning as I wake,
> Let me know which way to take.

Do not repeat this practice more than three times in one week unless you are living a very unstressed life-style. Nights are intended for sleep and refreshment of our being, not for work.

You might also open up your dream-life as a form of community service, to divine by dreaming the problems or dilemmas of your people. Before going to sleep, call upon your dream-spirit allies and make a petition either in your own words or like this:

> I offer my dreams for the life of the people:
> I seek to know all about [the issue].
> May my mind be clear,
> May my heart be pure,
> May my recollection be complete.

Practice 68: Navigational Shrine

One of the easiest ways to keep your directional focus in this work and of acknowledging the allies, influences and concerns of your earth-journey is to make a navigational shrine. This could be in the service part of your home – the kitchen, the study, a niche on the stairs – somewhere you are occupied in daily activity. The shrine contains whatever you wish and is subject to frequent changes as your earth-journey continues. Here your own mythology rules. The shrine might contain the following: photos of family and absent friends; flowers, fruits and items of the season; pleasingly shaped stones; an object, picture or poem which represents your present spiritual direction. If you are out of space in your small home, you might create a mobile to hang from the ceiling. At least once a month spend some time adjusting this shrine to the latest focus in your story.

8.   Healing

Healing is remembering what has been forgotten about connection, and unity and interdependence among all things living and non-living.

Woman as Healer
Jean Achterberg

1. SINGING THE SOUL BACK HOME

Soul loss is regarded as the gravest diagnosis in [shamanism], being seen as a cause of illness and death. Yet it is not referred to at all in modern Western medical books. It is becoming increasingly clear that what the shaman refers to as soul loss – that is injury to the inviolate core that is the essence of the person's being – does manifest in despair, immunological damage, cancer, and a host of other very serious disorders. It seems to follow the demise of relationships with loved ones, career, or other significant attachments.

The Wounded Healer
Jeanne Achterberg

HEALTH IS THE CONTINUUM of alignment we enjoy with power and Spirit: when either are disrupted, illness or imbalance result. Our society has associated illness almost exclusively with physical ailments, but illness and imbalance occur at all levels of life. Shamanism has been preserved down the ages because of its ability to provide healing, reconnection and restoration. Indigenous societies usually have a variety of healers: herbal-

ists and bone-setters who doctor bodily ailments as well as shamans who diagnose imbalances of power and Spirit and interact with the spirits. Sometimes the shaman will effect the healing with the aid of her spirits alone, and sometimes with the help of a herbalist. Minor ailments are generally treated in non-shamanic practical ways among indigenous peoples. A shaman is called in to diagnose the spiritual cause of an illness or imbalance and to suggest appropriate healing reconnections.

With the improvement in health-care throughout the world, the primary function of shamans today generally is to look after the spiritual and subtle reality aspects of healing. But in indigenous societies which do not have Western medical care, they also cure physical ailments, by using 'the most ancient system of marshalling the emotional and visual triggers in the brain to mobilize the body's natural immune system to cure illness'.[1]

We must be clear that, although shamanism may have a therapeutic effect, it is not therapy, nor can it be treated like one. By rectifying one imbalance, shamanism brings healing to the whole cosmic web, so that universal, not personal, healing is accomplished. Therapy does not address subtle reality in this way. In addition, shamanic healing is normally accomplished at one time, or over very few sessions: therapy often takes many sessions over many months. Therapy may sometimes be required after shamanic healing in the case of long-established dysfunctions.

Conventional medicine and psychotherapy have brought many benefits, but they have largely ignored the subtle reality side of healing, which has been presumed to be a superstitious irrelevance. With the massive imbalances resultant from urban life and a growing impatience with the neglect of the health of their soul, people have turned to complementary medicine where the spiritual wisdom of healing is acknowledged. The return of complementary medicine helps us discover more organic and wholesome methods of healing which draw directly on the spiritual qualities of plants, stones and many other beings. The principles of healing include:

1. A shared world-view that makes the diagnosis and naming process possible.
2. Positive personal qualities of the healer that facilitate the client's recovery.

3. Client expectations of recovery that assist the healing process.
4. Specific techniques, material and healing procedures that are appropriate to the illness and conducive to recovery.[2]

Shamanically, it is very important that any person assisting or being present at the healing is at least open to the possibility of the client's recovery by shamanic means. Disbelief may act as a barrier to the help of the spirits. Or, put another way, disbelief and healing cannot exist in the same plane. Since shamans access the cosmic web, it is imperative that client and helpers should not block any help so accessed: a general willingness to allow power and Spirit to flow are all that is needed.

Conventional medicine has reinforced an institutionalized passivity in the patient who is not expected to contribute anything to the healing process: 'take this medicine and see what happens'. Indigenous peoples do not understand this passivity and often ask Western doctors what prayers or rituals should accompany the medicine.

It is not surprising that, with a return of complementary medicine, many people should reject the passivity of the patient and seek to have an active part in the healing process. Self-healing is a misnomer in shamanism, since, while we can provide the intention to be well and to co-operate with healing factors, *we* do not heal ourselves. Those who think that they have healed themselves of a malady, have actually used the help of herbs, minerals, and the inspiration or teachings of those who have themselves received spiritual help. Instead of thanking the spirits who helped them, 'self-healers' take credit for their recovery.

Our part in the healing process is primarily a wish to be well and a willing co-operation with our allies to effect such healing. We should not forget that healing can only take place if the subject wishes it. Surprisingly, some people actively retain illness and energy blockages, usually because it is more convenient or familiar to live this way; illness can be worn as a badge bringing care or recognition, energy blockage can be a way of maintaining a selfish dictatorial regime whereby family and friends are subtly manipulated to provide the easiest lifestyle. Imbalance can be so habitual that any healing would be regarded as a threatening change to be sternly resisted.

How do Shamans Heal?

Many shamans and medicine people will abstain from conjugal relations for some days prior to any healing, and often fast as well, in order to prepare themselves. This is nothing to do with any perceived 'sinfulness' in sexual relations or food, but in order to keep personal needs quite separate: the shaman is thus prepared to mediate whatever healing is required. The first process is diagnosis. Some shamans use their acute shamanic vision to look into the subtle reality ambience of the patient's body. Shoshone medicine men can see right through the body with 'X-ray' vision.[3] It was said of the Ultonian healer, Fingen, that he could tell by the vapours arising from a house just how many were sick and of what illness.[4] Such diagnosis is assisted by the shaman singing his medicine-song; sometimes well-wishers or apprentices surround the bed and sing healing prayer-songs as well. The shaman does not always journey, but enters into strong sourcing to ask assistance of his healing spirits to discern the cause of the trouble.

If the disease is to be dealt with shamanically, without recourse to herbs, then one of many different methods of curing is employed: for example, the laying on of hands, the stroking or blowing away of illness, the restoration of power or soul by shamanic journey, or the extraction of a spiritual intrusion or diseased part.

The extraction of spiritual intrusions is practised worldwide; this ranges from the drawing out of subtle reality spirits to the actual removal of very real tumours by 'psychic surgery' practised by many *curanderos* of Central America. Our history is full of accounts of people receiving elf-shot, magical arrows shot by spirits or sorcerers, which must be removed before health can return. Shamans who extract intrusions by sucking must exercise extreme care not to swallow them: usually a bowl with water, earth or meat is provided for the shaman to dry-vomit these intrusions.[5] One of my clients, Penelope, recently had a ball of glutinous, bloody matter sucked out of her back by a Nepalese shaman as part of a healing ritual. Afterwards, she was instructed to take the bowl of offal on to which the intrusion had been vomited to a cross-roads and leave it there to be dispersed. Such techniques can only be learned first-hand from an experienced teacher and do not appear in this book.

For all its scientific advances, conventional medicine and psychotherapy cannot cure all ills: they tend to treat only the *symptoms* of a disease, rarely its cause. Shamanism is concerned with the discovery and treatment of *the spiritual cause* of illness.

What Causes Illness and Imbalance?

Health is wholeness: whatever is separated, divided or fragmented is unhealthy. The following factors are all considered to be causes of illness in shamanism:

Lack of order or cleanliness
Neglect of proper boundaries
Unethical or manipulative behaviour
Neglect of appropriate nourishment
Loss, theft or relinquishing of vital power.

All these factors concern imbalances of power, our vital life-energy.

We may conceive of power as the scaffolding of the soul, with its own appropriate frameworks and connections: if these are well aligned, we remain in good health, if they are fractured, then power-loss results. Power does not flow if there are blockages: dirt needs purification, disorder requires reorganization; unethical and selfish behaviour create imbalance in our power; if we neglect physical, mental or social nourishment we grow weak; in addition, we may lose or relinquish power due to different factors, or it may be stolen from us. When power is severely under threat in these ways, power-loss takes place: if too much power-loss is experienced, the scaffolding which supports the house of the soul begins to fall, resulting in soul-loss.

The following factors are related to imbalances of Spirit and affect our soul:

Lack of self-respect
Neglect of spiritual duties
Addictive behaviour
Neglect of soul-food
Loss, theft or relinquishing of soul.

As the soul begins to fragment, we experience a growing lack of self-respect and may indulge in addictive behaviour to make

good the power-loss we are experiencing: these are symptoms, not causes of soul-loss. Soul-loss is ultimately caused by disconnection with power and Spirit, chief cause of which is neglect of our spiritual duties and failure to nourish our soul; further to this, we may lose or relinquish soul-parts or they may be stolen.

Power-loss and Retrieval

Power-loss is universally experienced to some degree. The minor power-loss which results from lack of food or sleep is easily made good in normal circumstances, but prolonged starvation leads to malnutrition and swift death just as severe sleep-deprivation has been used as a means of torture, to obtain information and gain power over prisoners. Confrontations, examinations, gruelling sequences of events, illness, family circumstances, manipulative relationships can all cause power-loss. Without our innate vitality, without connection to the power of the cosmic web which is always flowing, we become disempowered, depressed and dispirited.

Unfortunately, our society encourages us to 'give away power' nearly every day; we are programmed not to resist giving up our rights, our boundaries, our integrity and spiritual authenticity in a variety of ways. When we fall into recurrent cycles of unfortunate situations, we need power-retrieval. Solutions to power-loss often involve returning to the sources of our power and reacknowledging them; removing ourselves from situations and people who cause power-loss to occur; finding and listening to our guardian animal and allies. (See Practice 71.)

In cases of serious power-loss, whether through debilitating illness, prolonged erosion of self-esteem or any other cause, the shamanic solution is to restore power by retrieving the client's guardian animal. This is done by the shaman going on a journey, with the client lying beside him. Following his allies' advice, the shaman usually searches the Underworld – the place of power – to find the lost guardian animal. When the animal is found, the shaman brings it back and blows the animal into the client's body – through the fontanelles at the top of the head, or through one of the many shamanic doorways

which exist in the human body, such as the heart, navel and palm.

Following a power-retrieval of this kind, the client's vitality returns, and she is able to take up the reins of daily life with more confidence. This method should be practically learned from a shamanic teacher as there are a number of subtle aspects to be considered.

Those with good power-alignment are perceived as powerful and effective in their lives. Acknowledging our power does not entail throwing it about or manipulating others as a result of it. It means keeping clear boundaries, having clarity of purpose and being responsible in our community. Manipulators of power live by appropriating someone else's power: this causes them mental paranoia and massive personality distortion, while leaving the victim powerless and unable to act. Power-theft can occur to both individuals and countries who suffer from manipulative governments and repressive regimes: solutions may involve exile or revolution.

Soul-loss and Retrieval

When we become isolated, separate and unconnected, we are likely to lose power and become susceptible to illness. If disempowerment becomes overwhelming, some people suffer soul-loss and may eventually give up the will to live. It is becoming increasingly difficult to find anyone who is truly at home in their soul; everywhere we encounter women who feel they have no right even to breathe, men who undervalue their contribution to their families, children crushed by cruel abuse. The soul needs lots of help and encouragement to keep going. We can help restore self-worth and encourage each other when times are difficult; I call this work 'midwifing the soul'. Each person is an individual with a living soul and deserves to be treated as such, but our society marginalizes certain individuals and groups, making it very hard for them to feel they belong. Whatever our circumstances, self-worth and a sense of the indwelling soul are important factors for living.

World shamanism supports the notion of a soul of multiple parts which is why soul-loss, or more strictly, soul-fragmentation, can occur. It can be brought about by a variety

of causes: illness, accident, surgery, being in an abusive relationship, bereavement, redundancy, rape, incest, burglary
and violent assault are but a few.

We each suffer soul-part straying on a regular basis, as sometimes when we are angry ('I was beside myself with rage') or
disoriented ('I just feel lost/spaced out'). Most of these losses
are not serious and the ejected part soon wings home when we
are able to co-ordinate ourselves. We have already spoken
about soul-straying and the ways in which it can be remedied
(Chapter 5). But serious soul-loss is another matter: it can range
in intensity from having a minor accident in which a soul-part
is ejected through shock of impact, right through to having a
major accident which leaves the subject in a coma. Death is
complete soul-loss, since all life-power leaves the body.

One of the problematic aspects of soul-loss is that when
human beings lose a vital part of themselves, they resort to
substitutes to 'fill the gap'. This often leads to addictions. Many
good therapeutic treatments are wasted as the subject doesn't
have the appropriate soul-part to be healed. Serious soul-loss
is seldom curable by therapeutic means, since these nearly
always only access the psychological levels and leave the
spiritual ones to fend for themselves. Soul-retrieval restores the
vital energy or 'will to live' without which therapeutic healing
is useless.

Soul-theft usually occurs unconsciously when the client has
been in a dependent or abusive relationship. It is *very rarely*
consciously malicious. Examples of situations causing soul-loss
might include: when relationships break down and one partner
announces 'I'll never let her/him go!'; when a child's vitality or
spontaneity is sapped by an adult; at death, when the dying
one has unwittingly become dependent upon the survivor and
still clings on. We have all, at some time, perpetrated subtle
forms of manipulation on those with whom we live. Sandra
Ingerman, in her remarkable book, *Soul Retrieval*,[6] urges us to
have compassion for the soul-thief, since he is probably a
victim of soul-theft himself. Such cases require the shaman to
'steal', cajole or entice the soul-part/s back.

A soul-retrieval is effected by the shaman making an initial
diagnostic journey to check the story-lines of the client's soul-
loss. Her allies will indicate whether help is appropriate, which
soul-parts are missing, where they may be located and what-

ever special instructions are important for her to know before attempting the soul-retrieval. With the client lying beside her, the shaman then journeys forth into the three worlds to seek the soul-parts, as instructed, always following her allies' advice. The soul-part or parts may be difficult to locate, there may be dangers resultant from malicious soul-theft to avoid, some parts may not wish to return or indeed understand that they belong elsewhere. Through negotiation and the exact instructions of her allies, the shaman will bring home the soul-part and blow it into the client's body, as in a power-retrieval.

The shaman relates her journey and any messages or information that she has received at this point: these are often validated immediately by the client who recognizes their truth or resonance. This work cannot be learned from a book; it needs hands-on tuition and a great deal of shamanic experience. (See Resources for teachers and qualified soul-restorers.)

When a significant or key soul-part is returned and assimilated, the subject finds that other minor soul-parts come home naturally, since the whole being is fortified and enriched by this return, making soul-loss less likely. It is not usual to have more than one soul-retrieval, although new situations may arise which require it.

Soul-restoration often brings the return of honesty and awareness, of a sense of self-responsibility. Abusive relationships and addictive patterns must subsequently be treated in a radical way: this would be the time for addicts to seek formal therapy and for women suffering domestic violence to seek professional assistance. A distaste for old habits and patterns may be experienced. Soul-restoration enables us to be the person we really are, and that will mean *change*. Soul-integration sometimes takes a few weeks, but its strongest validation is when other people begin to notice how much improved we are.

Collective soul-loss occurs during war, famine, disaster, defeat, foreign occupation, disease or loss of a national figure: shamans call this, injury to the group soul. A group soul and identity arise when any group gathers – family, tribe, club, association or nation. If the self-esteem or integrity of that group is injured, group soul-loss can result. The world community must always remember to treat such peoples and countries as sensitively as we could treat someone who has been bereaved, so as to enable the group soul to mend and reintegrate.

Such countries need not only physical resources but experienced soul-workers.

Abuse and manipulation have existed since time began; it is only now that we are recognizing the signs of power- and soul-loss. Unfortunately we have become over-sensitive and see abuse everywhere. Even some forms of therapy set up to deal with abuse have themselves become forms of abuse, creating 'recovered-memory' syndrome where images and events triggered by therapy have been interpreted as true memories. We have to exercise great discrimination in interpreting our own dreams and journeys, always noting that impressions are revealed by symbol and metaphor, that these do not denote physical reality events, and that our imagery and experience of the same events are often radically different from another's. To interpret others' experiences according to our own personal belief-systems or realizations is to be a manipulator of others' power. The excerpting of subtle reality from our society has resulted in a very literal mentality, which relates everything to a narrow set of correlatives.

We live in a society that is showing gross symptoms of soul-fragmentation: disregard for life, neglect of the old and young, lack of communion with nature, forgetfulness of spiritual sources, disregard of subtle reality. Stories and songs are being forgotten and the wholeness of community is disappearing in many places. But all is not lost: many people are now emerging as midwives of the soul, willing and able to co-operate with their spiritual helpers to lead the soul back to its home.

Note on Shamanizing for Others

Nearly all the practices in this book have been for solitary use. Walking the worlds for the benefit of others takes on a whole different perspective when people ask for your shamanic help. This is advanced and specialist work which cannot be adequately covered by any book. The following notes are offered as guidelines; *they are not instructions qualifying the walker between the worlds to set up in professional practice.* Your allies will indicate when you should seek the help of a teacher in physical reality.

1. Have you been asked by someone to shamanize for them? If you haven't, don't.

2. Always journey first to your spirits to ask if work is possible and necessary, and to receive instructions if your help is appropriate.
3. Follow these instructions carefully or refuse the work.
4. Prepare to provide reasonable follow-up or support to your work.
5. If you don't know what you are doing and the consequences of any action, do not work for others.
6. Ensure that you and your space are purified before work and properly cleansed afterwards. Physically clean your room and prepare yourself by fasting for a short period before helping anyone. After helping a client, cleanse your room and any tools (rattles, drums etc) you have used with incense. Wash your hands in salt water.
7. Do not work for severely unstable people, people who have difficulty in distinguishing realities or children unless you are professionally qualified in one of the caring skills and suitably insured.

Compassion and humility are the basis of all work for others. Just as none of us can heal ourselves, neither do shamans heal people – it happens by co-operation with the spirits.

Practice 69: Checking Power-alignment

The following questions can help you establish your current power-alignment and help you recognize danger signs. Some questions concern not only your own power but the ways in which you may be manipulating that of others.

1. Do you continually push yourself beyond your physical limits into exhaustion or collapse? Are you making similar unreasonable demands upon others?
2. Do you maintain your personal standards of integrity and behaviour in the face of opposition or peer pressure? Do you infringe or cause the infringement of others' standards?
3. Do you maintain your basic rights, needs and desires or abrogate them at the behest or need of others? Are you trespassing on the rights of others?
4. When did you last check on the motivations which fuel your life, work, relationships, hobbies and so on? Are the power-connections between you and these still operative?

5. How does your physical personal presentation (not necess-arily your appearance) and home environment reflect your present power-alignment?
6. Are you allowing others to encroach upon your environ-ment, time or resources without conscious permission? How are you encroaching upon that of others?
7. Do you have recurrent illnesses? Of what nature? How do they relate to your power: what kinds of things do they prevent you doing?

Practice 70: Checking Soul-alignment

The following questions will help you check your current soul-alignment and recognize danger signs. As above, some questions are two-edged in that they impinge upon your own behaviour as well as that of others.

1. Are you always depreciating yourself as a worthless person? Are you always running down others to boost your power?
2. When did you last commune with your spiritual source? What opportunities do you provide for Spirit to come into your life?
3. What patterns of addictive behaviour do you discern in your life? What soul-void do these patterns fill? How does your behaviour affect others?
4. Do you ensure adequate soul-nurture for yourself? Are you preventing others from finding theirs?
5. Have you allowed others to encroach upon your emotional, psychic or spiritual space without conscious permission? Are you encroaching upon that of others?
6. Do you have difficulty in being physically present and atten-tive? What are you unconsciously looking for?
7. Do you feel emotionally muffled, apathetic or indifferent to life? Around which activities are these symptoms most apparent? How do they reflect your lack of soul-alignment?

Practice 71: Power Dance

When you are low in vitality and needing to restore your power, get out your rattle or drum and get on your feet. Call

your allies to help show how power may be restored to you and begin sourcing while you dance. As you source, follow your allies.

Practice 72: Finding a Soul-friend

It is difficult to be a solitary walker between the worlds. Other-worldly allies may be great companions, but we are human beings who need a soul-friend with whom to share our journey. A soul-friend (Irish *anam-chara*) is one who is wise and practical: one who can encourage us when depressed and who can bring us down to earth when we lose touch with everyday life. Your soul-friend can also act as a reality or 'bullshit' detector to ensure that you are well aligned and not getting too full of yourself. If you have no such friend living near you, journey to your Middleworld allies and send out a general call for a soul-friend.

Practice 73: Finding Healing Spirits

Healing is able to enter the house of our soul when we unlock the door and invite it in: this means acknowledging that we need healing. One of the greatest healing powers of the world is the Grail which regenerates whatever it touches or whoever finds it; it can only be activated by the right questions: What is unbalanced? or How may healing come? Consider what is unbalanced, misaligned, in need of healing in your life, whether physical, psychic, mental or spiritual. The quest and question must be worthwhile in order for healing to come. Journey to whichever of your allies or teachers seems best suited to give you healing. You may receive important advice to put you on the healing path, or you may receive healing during the journey.

It may be that we also have a particular healing teacher or spirit, especially if our vocation is rooted in healing or soul-work. Journey to your centre in the Middleworld and ask your guardian animal to bring you to your healing teacher, following its guidance. When you have found the healing teacher, ask 'What healing ways do you have to teach?' Your initiation into

healing methods will proceed via this teacher or through one of your already designated allies.

Practice 74: Prayer-songs to the Spirits

The safest way of dealing with seemingly insuperable problems in others, when your help is inappropriate or unwanted, is to pray to the spirits, which is a method of healing that all people can employ. Prayer is a wider prospect than our religious up-bringing has taught us. Prayer and intercession, pleading with the spirits for help and healing, is a common pursuit of shamans, usually in partnership with healing techniques.

Prayer doesn't involve set, written invocations, although traditional prayers are indeed strong pathways to help. The uttering aloud of our need is something we often avoid; we allow that need to turn within and bore into our being where it becomes a path of sickness. Prayer is thus a primary pathway of health which can not only prevent illness but which can also heal. Prayer is a shamanic ladder of help, extending to the otherworlds.

In the case of people who do not wish for or who have not requested your help, *it is essential that our prayer should be of general benefit and not invoke a particular outcome.* It is not our place to manipulate people's lives. Although the temptation to wish for the speedy demise of a tyrant or the victory of one side in a conflict may be great, we do better if we ask the spirits to bring a given situation to a harmonious conclusion for the good of the whole cosmic web: then we cannot be responsible for warping any of its filaments.

With your rattle or other instrument, begin to source, calling upon your allies for an all-purpose healing song. For specific issues or problems, source your allies for particular people or needs.

Practice 75: Singing the Soul Back Home

We all have some hidden grief, shock or fear which causes parts of our soul to hide away. Some soul-fragmentation is not serious: the soul-part/s linger near and can be coaxed back.

Others are further away and, like crabs under rocks, refuse to show themselves. This method is intended for lone use in cases of minor soul-loss only. If you suffer from major trauma which has disrupted your life so that you are unable to work or relate to others, you need the help of a qualified soul-seeker (see Resources).

We can assist soul-restoration by a sincere desire to be whole again, by an intelligent and loving acceptance of the retrieved soul-parts and by a willingness to retain them. It is important to realize that newly returned soul-parts often evoke difficult memories, feelings and physical sensations for a while, and that integration can sometimes take a little while or may require radical life-changes. You can prepare yourself to receive any missing or stray soul-parts by actively courting them in the following ways.

1. With rattle or other instrument, start sourcing for a soul-song that will encourage your soul-part to come home. Spend ten minutes each day singing for and to any of your missing soul-parts; think of them returning and how this will complete your life, in order to send out a clear signal that you want them back.
2. Journey to your allies and teachers so that they can show you if you have any missing soul-parts, where they might be and how to coax them home.
3. Break all ties between yourself and anyone or anything who has been responsible for curtailing your freedom.
4. Before sleeping, ask your guardian animal to fetch any stray soul-parts and bring them home to you as you sleep.

Spontaneous soul-retrieval is also common. An insightful book, an ecstatic uplifting of spirit, a minor accident, sometimes clear a pathway between ourselves and the missing part and we are able to receive it back with grace and love.

Practice 76: Power and Soul Blessings

Preventive measures may help us avoid power and spirit imbalances. Psychic hygiene is a major precaution of indigenous peoples, and something which we can also practise. Since our society has dualistic notions of good and evil, tending to see

everything in terms of black and white, we should regard these methods as soul-strengthening or empowering blessings rather than 'spiritual protections', in order to stress the positive rather than the negative benefits of these methods.

We all encounter situations in which we feel especially vulnerable to power- or soul-loss: some of these cannot be easily avoided in our daily lives, but we can be better prepared for them. Journey to your allies and ask for a blessing or song that will prevent the kinds of power- or soul-loss to which you are liable. You may also be given talismanic objects, shamanic symbols or rituals as remembrances of inner strengths. A typical power blessing might go as follows, to be sung when feeling especially vulnerable:

> Power of eagle have I – power of air,
> Power of serpent have I – power of fire,
> Power of dolphin have I – power of water,
> Power of mole have I – power of earth,
> Power of lineage have I – power of the ancestors,
> Power of spirits have I – power of the gods,
> Power of truth have I – power of the inmost soul.
> Seven powers about me to veil and support me,
> On my journey without fear go I.

Sensible attitudes about power- and soul-strengthening procedures can be maintained by good intention and trust in our spirits. To fear 'being under psychic attack' reflects an ungrounded attitude to walking the worlds, pointing to sloppy spiritual hygiene, a failure to close doors or observe boundaries, and hazy intentions. Go back and look at Chapter 5.

2. THE CIRCLE OF LIFE

> We can have all the knowledge in the universe, and it comes down to one thing: practice. It comes down to going home and step-by-step implementing what we know.
>
> *Women Who Run With the Wolves*
> Clarissa Pinkola Estés

All our shamanic practice is a means of creating the capacity for reconnection. If walking between the worlds does not re-

connect us with our universe then our shamanic knowledge becomes a defunct currency which we can never spend.

The shamanic vocation is the reverse of what is commonly understood as 'the spiritual quest', whereby a person acquires spiritual merit in order to attain personal salvation or enlightenment. The Japanese actor and director, Yosio Oida, speaks of this:

> When people see that society is difficult and stupid, they think that they should distance themselves and withdraw from the world ... People meditate, it makes them feel good and they think they have seen the light. But what is this light, if it is not connected to action in this world? The most important thing in meditation is to find what the right action for you is.[7]

Finding out what action is appropriate for ourselves is often a long and puzzling business. We may be a little like the French poet, Rimbaud, who ruefully wrote that, 'for a long time I prided myself I would possess every possible country'. At the beginning of our work we want to be and do everything, to immerse ourselves in all knowledge and become experts. But shamanic knowledge is not a commodity to be acquired in this way: it can only flow into the channels which we provide. These may be less broad than we supposed, and we may have to discover what specialist areas are best for us.

When we first encounter shamanism we may want to share this wonder with the rest of the world. Our history is riddled with spiritual chauvinism and the missionizing colonialism resultant from convert fervour: shamanism needs no proselytizers. It has existed since the dawn of time and it will go on being needed because it works.

Currently many people seek to understand their vocation through various forms of self-growth. This is an important corrective to numerous forms of spiritual self-neglect and soul-malnutrition which are the heritage of our post-religious society. But self-growth must include self-clarification, self-nurture and self-assimilation, as well as self-forgetting, if self-respect is to result. If self-growth excludes these factors, then it fosters an introverted self-focus which separates itself from the universe. True self-respect is not selfishness, but our duty to the soul and its soul-shrine: it includes caring for our body, mind, soul and

spirit, enabling us to relate to those who give us love and support, as well as those who challenge and stretch us.

Shamanism is not a one-way street, with all the knowledge flowing from the three worlds into ours, nor are all our efforts solely directed towards the cosmic web. Service to the universe balances self-respect. If we dedicate ourselves to the restoration of power and Spirit in our world, then power and Spirit will come into it by the bridge of our dedication.

In the final analysis, all we have to do is be available for this purpose, not to worry about how and where and with whom we shall eventually implement our work. By virtue of our humanity and our living soul, we are connected with the cosmic web: Spirit and power will support us and bring us into connection in ways of which we may not dream. The stoic philosopher, Epictetus, wrote:

> Whoso seeth the sun and the moon and the stars and rejoiceth in the earth and the sea, he is no more solitary than he is helpless.[8]

And yet, 'rejoicing in the earth' has become one of the hardest tasks of our age. As we look upon the beauty that has been soiled by our species and realize the unkindness of our kind, complex emotions overwhelm us. Self-blame, shame, guilt erupt within us, to be followed by a desire to rectify, heal and restore. But some things can never be restored: species have gone, habitats have been destroyed, ways of life and people have vanished. This is not a new story.

Only a short while ago science generally regarded concern about erosion of world resources and the effects of acid rain and global warming as the paranoia of a minority of ill-informed people: now it takes them seriously. Some peoples have always known that how we live affects the world, others have had to learn it through hard experience. The effects of deforestation and intensive agriculture are not new problems: the people of early Mesopotamian civilizations turned their land into desert, the Neolithic peoples of Europe hacked and burned down forests in order to obtain farming land. Not all ancient peoples were also wise.

The same problems lie at our doorstep today. Stop-gap solutions are promoted by self-serving governments determined to see out their term of office without rocking the boat.

A few international gatherings like the Rio Earth Summit of 1991 attempt to create awareness of the need for long-term measures to be followed up by successive world governments, but such decisions are regarded as optional and are rarely implemented because governments are seldom run by politicians of spiritual vision.

Spiritual leaders and mediators have always had the important task of reminding people when balance is being lost and showing how to return to alignment. Greed and short-sightedness underlie our current ecological predicament. Whatever we sow today, our children will reap tomorrow. The West has complex economic and political frameworks, but it has lost many of the doorways which connect it with the cosmic web. It is time for people to rediscover inner space, not as conquerors but as humble explorers and soul-seekers. Regarding the universe with intention is the work not only of a shaman, but of all people. Maintaining spiritual pathways is critical in a time when many assume that the material world is the only reality. When that is the case, then only a narrow environmental response is possible, one which expresses empathy, but rarely compassion and never love.

The self doesn't end at the skin. Arne Naess, the Norwegian philosopher who coined the term 'deep ecology', wrote of the dichotomy experienced by people who associated ecological responsibility with sacrifice and who found moral exhortations to altruism alienating:

> . . . All of that would flow naturally and easily if the self were widened and deepened so that the protection of nature was felt and perceived as protection of our very selves.[9]

The true collegiality between ourselves and nature must be experienced as self-identification. The seemingly finite and discrete nature of human existence is an illusion. We need a house of representatives drawn from the many species of life to remind us of our true place in the scheme of life (see Practice 78). Instead of excerpting ourselves as a species from the universe, we need to find our sense of self within the continuum of the cosmic web.

'Healing the earth' has become a supreme cliché in the last few years, all too often meaning, 'I want to save/perpetuate

myself/my species'. Our planet has survived many millions of years of changes. As the latest species, humankind has perhaps made significant changes, but we are indeed very much latecomers with no notion of how many more species may supersede ours. The earth will undoubtedly survive and with it the stubbornly entrenched DNA of the life spiral, but *human* life may be just one of many further evolutionary developments. To live shamanically and creatively means to accept this at a deep level, if only as a spur to humility. Only by our dedicated reconnection with the power and Spirit of our earth can we offer adequate restitution and open channels of healing.

And what of those people who do not share our vision? Convert fervour often urges us to share our spiritual realization with everyone we meet, in an attempt to influence what we see as unproductive lives. This is not only tiresome to others but highly manipulative. For some people 'the lost places are in this world and belong to the people in it and are all that they have to call home',[10] and there is nothing we can do about this. We cannot give our revelation to others unless they desire it, and even then we may only be the way-showers, not the revealers of mysteries.

Only by our equanimity and living example, by our impartial compassion to all that is can we become guardians of the ways which restore the harmony and balance of our universal relationship. To invite beauty back to our world, we must allow the world soul to return home in its own way. We can be resourceful in the ways in which we do this, so long as we are not manipulative. If we create pathways of connection ourselves, these will in turn provide channels for beauty to return.

Bringing the fruits of our shamanic perceptions to the world about us does not necessarily entail teaching or preaching to others in a formal way. It is about focusing our hearts upon the return of the deep song, about remembering the subtle pathways, the resonance of memory and the oracy of living our lives from that centre. The effect of each person's individual commitment resounds throughout the universe, creating resonant pathways, sounding reverberant notes, restoring the web of connection in a great song of healing.

Practice 77: Restoring the Balance

Our thoughts and intentions have power. Prayer without intention is a collection of meaningless words; prayer with heart becomes full of *kavannah* or 'intentioned transformation'. We can work with this kind of intentioned transformation on behalf of the universe if we do it in accordance with Spirit. We live complex lives which provide plenty of opportunities to forget. Thoughtless acts can destroy the world: intentioned ones help build it up. We can adjust the balance by living at a slower pace, and resisting the urge to speed up all the time, allowing the spaciousness of the otherworlds to be realized here. Those who live in the fast lane have little leisure to perceive clearly; those who live in the slow lane can both perceive and acknowledge.

To become aware of what ails us, we must ask the Grail question. This is given variously in different texts as, 'Why is the land waste?' or 'Why are things like this?' or 'Whom does the Grail serve?' If we seek the answer with humility, bearing in mind past mistakes and areas of neglect, we will find it through one of the otherworldly doors to the cosmic web. By asking our own Grail question we can rebalance the energy of the cosmic web and make restitution. Journey to your Middleworld allies and ask 'What can I restore to the cosmic web?'

Practice 78: The House of Representatives

Only by entering into identification with other life-forms can we keep true awareness of the variety and wonder of life. You have already experienced the close identification between yourself and your spiritual helpers. If your animal is a blackbird, you will feel warmly about any blackbirds you encounter in physical reality. We can also stretch our skin to encompass other beings. Commune with a species near where you live – animal, plant, tree, stone – and be with it in nature. Our dedication to the earth begins locally, but feeds into a larger understanding of planetary wholeness. Returning home, source one representative of this species and ask its permission to enter briefly into its shape and consciousness, to fuse your

two souls together. Experience what it is to be this species. What do you learn from this practice? Thank your subject and return, recording your experience. Repeat this practice to include a variety of different species. These will form your 'house of representatives', your own council of different species, whose voices will be attuned to yours in your daily life, as well as being advisers in local or ecological issues which require sourcing.

Permission to seek your kinship with all life-forms is here given.

Practice 79: Legacy of Wisdom

Our kinship with all forms of life is very close:

> Every cell in our body is descended in an unbroken chain four billion years old, through fish that learned to walk the land, reptiles whose scales turned to fur and became mammals, evolving through to the present.[11]

The loss of one species in our physical reality, is not just a loss of an animal or plant. It is a tearing of the cosmic web, the destruction of a viable bridge to a form of wisdom which keeps our world harmonious. When species revert to subtle reality through extinction they and the wisdom that they bear are still contactable, but only by shamans and seers.

In the next few decades you will die. Before that, many species may become totally extinct. You at least have the opportunity to have relatives and descendants. Create a record of the wisdom, wonder and beauty of any threatened species which you have experienced, based on your own sourcing, which you can leave to your family after your death. Joanna Macy reminds us that time does not run on the cosmic web, that the eternal now gives us opportunities for change: 'The dimension of simultaneity, where we stand shoulder to shoulder with our ancestors and descendants, is appealing to me, it gives context and momentum to work for social change.'

This practice can be repeated for as many species as you wish, in order to create pathways of connection between your everyday world and that of subtle reality.

Proceed as follows:

1. Choose your species.
2. Meet and experience it in physical reality, if possible.
3. Accompanied by one ally, journey in the Middleworld to meet one representative of that species.
4. Offer it what help and love you can give, ask it what wisdom it represents and whether it is willing to share that with you. If wisdom is offered, remember that you will share the responsibility of that wisdom, that you are obliged to manifest it in your life and must pass it on.
5. Return from sourcing and record your experience.
6. Create a record – verbal, pictorial, written – by which this wisdom can be transferred to another generation of your family or community.

This method often results in the creation of a story, poem or artwork which encapsulates the wisdom in ways that can be easily remembered and shared. Manifest your work by actively supporting campaigns to safeguard the survival and habitat of species under threat.

3. A SACRED TRUST

Tis the gift to be simple, Tis the gift to be free.
Tis the gift to come down where we ought to be.
And when we find ourselves in the place just right,
Twill be in the valley of love and delight.

Shaker song

The practice of shamanism has its own ethics based primarily on the fact that the shaman is accountable, not only to the spirits, but to his clients. Their pain is his pain, their loss is his loss. This is the sacred trust of shamanism: to be part of and empowered by the universe, to be vulnerable to Spirit. Egocentric gratification is not part of this work.

A shamanic vocation is not relegated to far-off times and peoples, but is strongly relevant to today when it is so much needed. My belief is that everywhere the spirits are waking up many people and asking for their co-operation. If we follow their call, whether fully dedicating our life to them and the

service of the universe or whether living shamanically in our own sphere of influence, we are helping to reconnect the world.

Commitment and Initiation

Before we commit ourselves to the shamanic path, let us understand that the spirits *request* our co-operation: we do not have to respond. It is as well to take stock and realize now that this path has to be walked at all times, not just in our 'spare time' or when we feel like it. It is an all-embracing way, into which all that we know and are must be synthesized.

Initiation is often narrowly taken to mean 'entry, by means of a ritual, into an arcane or closed group': shamanic initiation is the complete reverse of this. Instead of acquiring status or knowledge which separates us from others, shamans enter more fully into the widest possible framework of the universe in a way that includes everyone and everything. Traditional shamanism maintains that a candidate is called primarily by the spirits. Initiation may also involve training with a practising shaman. In our times, shamanic initiation now happens more often in the spiritual realm, since we have few teachers to confer 'authorization'. In every case, the candidate must ultimately find acceptance by her community.

We do not undergo the complex and painful ordeals which shamans undergo in traditional societies, such as being coated with red ants, fasting for long periods, or total exclusion from daylight. Instead, life's many trials and ordeals initiate us themselves into new areas. Each challenge and dilemma which we encounter is teaching us a new thing; our shamanic response is to trust our spirits even more and to learn from these. Western civilization is a very complex environment to live within if we have shamanic vocation. If we have a shamanic vocation, our ordeals will definitely include the radical changing of our life-style and the effects that this will have upon our friends and family; it may involve putting up with ridicule and alienation. Less glamorous than a dramatic vision-quest in splendid isolation, less dangerous than being pushed off a cliff with our feet attached to vine-ropes, perhaps, but no less effective in strengthening or weakening our resolve.

Shamanic ordeals come in many guises and may be regarded

as tests which stretch our gifts into alignment. They do not come to those who are not ready and willing. It is very important that we realize the cause and effect of our shamanic alignment. When we work within a concept, we become its mediator. Our exploration of inner space creates new pathways and keeps open old ones for others to walk. All that we have experienced validates the tradition we uphold. Consent comes from deep abiding.

Shamanism of our Native Land

This book has been purposely written in a non-cultural light, so that anyone may work with it wherever they live on earth, although it has been primarily addressed to Westernized, urban readers. As you reach its end, you are invited to consider the cultural tradition in which you were raised and in which you live. Your shamanic work must have its home on the earth. Work undertaken within a primal tradition has a direction and strength that is not found in non-cultural work. You may live in a land that seems divorced or distanced from its primal tradition, but it is nonetheless still available in the spiritual worlds.

In the search for shamanic authenticity, many people have been drawn to other cultural traditions, notably the North American Indian ones. Often in a deeply respectful way, they have tried to become part of that tradition and to learn what they can from it. This has caused a great furore in many circles. Some indigenous people find such adoptions abhorrent and insulting, a form of cultural colonization, whereas others have been more supportive.

The West has been quick to take colour and originality from indigenous and tribal cultures worldwide. A walk down the high street confirms this as we see for sale colourful ethnic clothing from all countries, bath-unguents and soaps made from exotic perfumes of far-off lands, jewellery from South-East Asia and even bubble-gum with fabulous Amazonian rain-forest properties! Each product seems to throw into relief the Western inability to find its own original colour or native power. I sometimes wonder, rather frivolously, whether Amazonian tribes and others buy 'Dull, Grey, Boring Urban Splash Lotion' or wear '9–5 Office Deodorant'! The concept of all races of

humanity coming together as 'the rainbow people' is persuasive, but there are many 'national bequests' to address before we may rejoice in this reality. We must give honour and apology where it is due.

Ethnicity can be an instrument of re-empowerment and cultural self-esteem but it can also become a potent weapon for national possessiveness or a cloak for colonial invasion. It can be manipulated to prove and disprove many things. Shamanism, like everything else, can slide into its own brand of political wrangling: 'My tradition is more venerable/more authentic than thine'.

The appropriateness of adopting a spiritual tradition that is not your own cannot be judged by anyone except yourself. Take a hard look at the way you actually live in the everyday world. If your life-style supports your core spiritual practice, then no one on earth can gainsay your adoption. If, however, your spiritual practice merely apes the cultural tradition of another land, you may find it less workable.

If we seek to take fire from another's hearth without due respect for the hearth-keeper or the fire, then we are thieves. It behoves us as Westerners to approach indigenous traditions with respect, as humble students, to say 'I cannot hear my ancestors, I have mislaid their teachings, but I want to belong once again to the human family: please teach me'.

Another problem crops up here. As a Briton with Irish ancestry, I find no conflict in working with the Celtic traditions of my land. However, if I moved to Australia or America, this might be quite different. I hear from many who are attempting to reconcile their ancestral traditions with their national citizenship: should they follow their native heritage or borrow from the spiritual traditions of the land they now inhabit?

Before you can expect someone from a tribal culture to share their ancestral teachings with you, it is only fair for them to ask you to represent your own tribe first. In the West we have not lived in a tribal culture for many hundreds or thousands of years; a few of us still live from the land in an agricultural way, but most are fully urbanized. This dislocation and fragmentation from tribal life is often at the basis of our shamanic search. Most seekers find their spiritual family among other practitioners whom they can meet up with at weekends and on courses, but shamanic practice can become a ghetto-like existence without a social framework where it can be used.

Without the support of tribe or the motivation of a group or community need, the search for our own ancestral teachings can be long and hard, as I can testify. Such a search leads through diverse territories where we can pick up the rags and tatters of past belief and practice. These may serve as a makeshift cloak while we search, but eventually we must leave off searching and live now, today. This problem is not just a contemporary one: knowledge has been mislaid before and has been rediscovered. Many myths, including that of the Egyptian Goddess, Isis, confirm this. She searches for the scattered remains of her husband's body, which has been cut up by his brother, Set. Having reconstituted all she can, Isis finds that Osiris's phallus is missing; undeterred, she creates a phallus and lies one last time with her husband to engender the child Horus. Plutarch writes of this event in more universal terms:

> Set . . . tears to pieces and scatters to the winds the sacred writings, which the Goddess collects and puts together and gives into the keeping of those that are initiated.

No knowledge is ever totally lost, only mislaid or forgotten. It can be found in the otherworlds. If we journey there with trust and an open heart, we will receive teaching.

Dr Pamela Colorado, an Oneida Indian, speaking of the difficulties of native peoples who have mislaid their traditions in the recent centuries of colonization, suggests ways of recovery:

> As native people, we learn to train our minds from the time we are children, to be centred where we are, grounded in reality, and see all the signs that are around us . . . In addition, you have to have the ability to project yourself out, 'to see what it's not possible to see.' I'm just learning this myself, but I know that it is an ability that our people have known for thousands of years and still practice . . . the wayfinding mindset, the ability to project ourselves out, is the knowledge that is necessary if we are to create a healthy relationship with the earth.'[12]

This 'projecting ourselves out' is achieved both by journeying and by using our shamanic sight, by being sensitive on a daily and pragmatic level to the spirits who alert us to the hidden signs scattered about us. The ancient wisdom which our own ancestors treasured is still contactable and recoverable, if we seek it out with true hearts. The spirits of our ancestors, the

spirits of our land are still here: they will reinspire us if we call upon them to help us now. This does not involve reactivating atavistic and inappropriate behaviour nor stimulating ethnic hatred and conflict: rather we mend the broken filaments of our cultural tradition with love and honour. I believe that, wherever we live upon the earth, however mixed and confused our ancestral and spiritual heritage, we will find spirits and allies who will reconnect us with the inner light which illumines the cosmic web.

Spiritual Illumination

Mystics of many cultures have described spiritual illumination as flashes of lightning in darkest night; in the Western tradition it has been called the 'sun at midnight'. Most people have only the retinal image or memory of their spiritual landscape or direction; for others the lightning flashes are few and far between. Aua, an Iglulik Eskimo interviewed by Knud Rasmussen, relates his solitary shamanic initiation:

> In the midst of such a fit of mysterious and overwhelming delight I became a shaman ... I could see and hear in a totally different way. I had gained by *quamanEq*, my enlightment, the shaman-light of brain and body, and this in such a manner that it was not only I who could see through the darkness of life, but the same bright light also shone out from me, imperceptible to human beings, but visible to all the spirits of earth and sky and sea, and those now came to me and became my helping spirits.[13]

This experience of inner light is common to all initiates of mystical traditions. It cannot be learned as a technique: it comes only when we are truly aligned with the cosmic web. This inner glow spreads a long way: you will know it is beginning to kindle in you when people begin to be drawn to you for help, as ships to a beacon. The further and more extensively you explore the web and gain allies in the three worlds, the more help will become available to you.

The validation of your walking between the worlds is not conferred by ceremony nor academic credentials, but by the combination of your practice and experience. It is then that the sun shines at midnight: and it shines out on all parts of the

web so that your living and journeying illuminate both physical and subtle reality.

The ecstasy that comes from an experience of shamanic non-duality is profoundly moving and humbling. The sense of omniscience that accompanies some journeying is truly beyond words, though these might begin to convey something of the experience:

> It's like looking out into time or space or infinity. It's like seeing everything at once. It's like getting out of a train that's going along and seeing it go along, and being independent and part of it at the same time. It's like looking at everywhere at once from everywhere at once.[14]

Such experiences are often so overwhelming that individuals are profoundly changed; isolated people move nearer to the caring social hub of the world, while those who have lived unthinkingly hedonistic lives are jolted into new awareness that needs a desert solitariness.

Thankfulness is part of our reciprocity to the universe. It is the ultimate honesty in shamanism. If we fail to express thankfulness, we are in danger of claiming the power of the universe as our own. In the non-duality of ecstatic communion with the otherworlds, love of the universe brings thankfulness welling to the surface of our heart.

The lightness and equanimity with which we live our lives is our gift to the universe: that it may not be scarred by our passing, that we may continue to be a part of the ongoing chorus of the cosmic web, whose music becomes our song, whose rhythm becomes our dancing.

In walking between the worlds, we will inevitably learn much wisdom. That wisdom is not our possession, though we may have its guardianship for a short while. If, in our thankful hearts, we acknowledge that it is only lent to us, we will avoid the problem of spiritual rigidity which always indicates that wisdom has become a millstone round our necks and not a liberation of Spirit.

We give thanks for what we have learned by sharing it with others. The way we transmit shamanic teaching matters: it is not 'just a technique'. Unless we can put ourselves in the shoes of any living being in the universe, perhaps we cannot give nor receive such teaching. By our oracy we are measured.

Shamanism is both profoundly mystical and very ordinary. It isn't necessary to live in isolation or dress in feathers to practise it. Living with the shamanic awareness of a walker between the worlds is something we can practise wherever we live. There is no final attainment, no great goal beyond the continuing balance of the inner and outer worlds. Shamanism is the stillness in the dancing: it is the soul within the song.

Practice 80: The Primal Tradition

We owe it to our ancestors and descendants to find out about our culture and traditions and bring them into our lives, to become a bridge for living knowledge.

What primal tradition existed in your land before the coming of orthodox religion? What remains? Which spiritual presences informed it? Which tradition holders and teachers are still accessible?

Read all that you can and make a few well-chosen, motivated journeys to research your native tradition: ask your allies and ancestral teacher to show you what is relevant to your own time. Find folk-songs and stories which contain encoded teachings. Research seasonal customs. Speak and listen to the spirits of the land in which you live.

When you have done this, and with the aid of other like-minded walkers between the worlds, you may perhaps begin to address your national or tribal bequest – the unfinished business of your people or country. Ask your ancestral teacher and allies, as well as the deep ancestors, to help you in a collective effort.

Practice 81: Council of Allies

Our spiritual lineage and native tradition already has many teachers and practitioners: some may be alive and practising, others may have joined the deep ancestors or become traditional teachers in subtle reality. We can meet with these in a council of allies. Go to your journey-centre and call your ancestral and spiritual teachers to meet there you and any other allies or animals who wish to help you. At this gathering, ask

to be put in contact with friends and helpers in both physical and subtle reality who will enable your deeper integration into your own tradition: you may be introduced to new allies and teachers, you may be instructed on where or with whom you will find tuition and companionship in physical reality.

Practice 82: The Gift

Without thankfulness we give no gift. The deep gift is sometimes hard to find within us because we have unconsciously become separate. When situations reach stalemate or breaking point, move energy by giving: the act of giving empowers the giver, and reweaves the broken filaments of the cosmic web.

When love fails in your heart and you are unable to reciprocate or make an appropriate response, this is the time to call upon your companions for help. Sing, call, dance, implore: 'I am losing love, it is slipping from my fingers, the dance is losing momentum, the song is losing its joy – come and fill my heart!' Travel from the heart of the loss to the web of connectedness and make a journey for help, empowerment or inspiration.

Don't let your soul grow dull and unreflective because you have blocked off all spiritual pathways to your heart. This is sometimes hard advice to take, when any action seems worthless to you. However despairing or disconnected you feel, get up and make an offering of thanks in whatever way seems good to you. Even if you feel nothing, act 'as if' this were beneficial. Lift your heart and mind and spirit, attuning them with the universe. Step outside your barricades for a moment and experience the timelessness of the gift of life.

Practice 83: Spirit Offerings

We always conclude all shamanic practice with an act of thanks to the spirits who have assisted us; without this important practice, it is easy to become inflated with self-importance. Thanking the spirits is an essential courtesy which helps us retain humility. Praying is one method of thanking. We do not need to take the stance or language of any faith in order to

pray: we just speak from the heart of need, joy or thankfulness, addressing Spirit or the spirits of the universe.

Make a journey or series of journeys to enquire which offerings your spirits appreciate best. Maybe your bear likes to be offered a plate of berries, while your eagle prefers an aromatic-herb smoke mixture. If you receive the help of a shaman, it is good to take gifts for her spirits. My spirits were recently given some very appropriate gifts by Helen, a client for whom I'd done some soul-work; she journeyed to ask what would be suitable and brought them an empty ant's egg, a bell and a skein of golden thread, all of which were delightfully appreciated by my animals.

Journey to your spirits and ask what you can do for them, to show gratitude for all that they do for you. Create a short personal ceremony of thanks in their honour, using the information they have given you and relating this to the nature of their help.

Practice 84: Shamanic Dedication

When you have read, practised and assimilated the practices in this book, you may well feel that you wish to commit yourself formally in some deeper way to the shamanic path. The only initiators in this business are your spirits. Before making any journey, keep a shamanic vigil of dedication, for 'to learn to take the universe seriously there is no quicker way than to watch'.[15] Spend at least one night awake, pondering the dedication that you are contemplating, in a secluded place. If you choose a remote spot, ensure that your soul-friend knows where and when you are making your vigil, and is ready to offer support. Such a vigil clarifies your intentions remarkably. The next day, journey and call together your allies and teachers and ask them how you may dedicate yourself to this work, if you still feel it's your path.

This book has been made up of many separate chapters and practices which you have come to work with over a period of time. Your own experience will begin to show pathways between the scattered realizations you have gained here. New realizations will merge with old ones, abysses of separated

understanding will be bridged. Treat your notebook as a friend to remind you of experiences and practices, but don't get so 'hung up' on the minutiae of information recorded in it or too proud of your own testimony that you can't accept anyone else's experience. Keep in touch with your soul-friend, compare notes and be adaptable.

Finally, I would like to share a few realizations that I have made over the years. They constitute my personal golden rules about shamanism, but you may substitute your own for these or find others. They are not terminally binding on anyone. Consider them as the eight legs of the spider by which you walk the cosmic web.

1. Everything is connected: we are not alone.
2. Help is always near: trust the power, help and advice offered by your allies.
3. Keep your quest or purpose simple.
4. Only attempt healing with those who believe benefit may come.
5. Respect all ways of being.
6. Behave ethically and teach by example.
7. Be thankful and you will become part of the gift.
8. Be detached from results.

Permission to connect what you have learned from your practice is here given.

May you journey well!

Notes

FOREWORD

1. Ripinsky-Naxon 1993
2. Matthews, C and J 1994
3. Matthews, C 1990

CHAPTER 1

1. Ginzberg 1990
2. Hoppal 1989
3. Skafte 1988
4. Siikala 1987
5. Colorado 1991
6. Hoppal 1989
7. Amado 1993
8. Susuki and Knutdtson 1992
9. Ibid

CHAPTER 2

1. Kaplan 1978
2. Ereira 1990
3. Harner 1980
4. Ripinsky-Naxon 1993
5. Ahlbäck and Bergman 1991
6. Ingerman 1991
7. Ahlbäck and Bergman 1991
8. Funk and Wagnall 1972

9. Ahlbäck and Bergman 1991
10. Rodenburg 1992
11. Backman and Hultkrantz 1984
12. Siikala 1987
13. Ripinsky-Naxon 1993
14. Ereira 1990

CHAPTER 3

1. Suzuki and Knutdtson 1992
2. Ripinsky-Naxon 1993
3. See Sams and Carson 1988; Gray 1994; Matthews, J 1994
4. Tompkins and Bird 1991
5. Tompkins and Bird 1992
6. Ibid
7. Macy 1993
8. Guss 1985
9. Lovelock 1988
10. Nachman nd
11. Gould 1993
12. Lindsay 1970
13. Huxley 1956
14. Gould 1993
15. Ywahoo 1987
16. Kalweit 1992
17. Ripinsky-Naxon 1993

CHAPTER 4

1. Matthews, C 1987

CHAPTER 5

1. Stewart 1992
2. Matthews, C 1989
3. McAll 1984
4. Ibid
5. See Rinpoche 1992; Ashcroft-Nowicki 1992; Matthews, C 1991
6. Fix 1979

CHAPTER 6

1. Matthews, C 1991
2. Matthews, C and J 1985–6
3. Ahlbäck and Bergman 1991
4. Ripinsky-Naxon 1993
5. Matthews, C 1992
6. Kalweit 1992
7. Wombell 1991
8. Daniélou 1985
9. Rodenburg 1992
10. Brennan 1988
11. Chöyam 1988

CHAPTER 7

1. Matthews, C and J 1994
2. Sheldrake 1988
3. Guss 1985
4. Chatwin 1987
5. Ripinsky-Naxon 1993
6. Fortune 1972

CHAPTER 8

1. Harner 1992
2. Villoldo and Krippner 1986
3. Hultkrantz 1992
4. Matthews, C and J 1994
5. Harner 1992
6. Ingerman 1991
7. Oida 1991
8. Powys 1974
9. Naess 1989
10. Mayne 1966
11. Seed and Macy 1988
12. Colorado 1991
13. Rasmussen 1929
14. Mayne 1966
15. Hardy 1974

Glossary of Terms
used in this Book

Certain words are used in this book with specific definitions not locatable in standard dictionaries.

ALIGNMENT The poise and balance which the shaman has with the universe.

ALLIES Spirit helpers who are associated with us.

ANCESTORS Not only our near, personal relatives who are no longer living but the deep ancestors of our common bloodlines and genetic memories who maintain guardianship of skills and wisdom traditions and who teach us still.

ANCESTRAL BEQUEST The accumulation of unfinished business which each human being inherits from ancestors of her blood lineage.

BAT-SIGNALS The almost imperceptible messages which are picked up by your subtle senses.

BLOOD LINEAGE Our physical genetic relationship with certain ancestral teachers provides our blood lineage helpers.

CENTRE In this book, your journey-centre or starting place for middle-world journeying.

CLIENT Any person or being who seeks the aid of a shaman.

CORE-SHAMANISM Term coined by Michael Harner to denote applicable, contemporary, non-cultural usage of shamanic methods by non-traditional peoples.

COSMIC WEB The universal alignment of all that is; the interconnecting network of spirit pathways and power resonances of all beings now alive, dead or only existent in subtle reality.

DEEP ANCESTORS The regenerate ancestors who have entered the ancestral realms and are available as teachers.

GENIUS The *genius loci* or male spirit of place.

GIFT A particular alignment, comprising our unique skills and abilities, enabling us to serve the universe.

HELPER Subtle reality allies or companions who accompany, guide and help us in the otherworlds.

INNER SPACE The totality of the otherworlds. The use of 'inner' here does not imply any psychological quality but refers rather to the subtle realities to which we travel in shamanic journey.

JOURNEY A shamanic journey or spirit-flight during which soul-parts of a shaman leave the body to travel into the otherworlds.

JUNO The female *genius loci* or spirit of place.

ORACY Our capacity to hear, remember and relate orally. Oracy is not dependent upon the written word but gives primacy to the oral traditions that maintain our connections with ancient wisdom. It has no authority except itself.

ORAL POOL The pool of our memory, constituted by whatever can be remembered or recalled without the aid of book or tape.

OTHERWORLDS All levels of subtle reality in the shamanic cosmos.

PERMISSION In the context of this book, an encouragement and self-allowance of liberation of the soul and its faculties.

PERSONAL MYTH The belief system or 'story by which we live'.

PHYSICAL REALITY The material substance of the ordinary world which we inhabit, and perceive through our physical senses.

POWER The energy, vitality and alignment which are our true gift.

REALM OF THE ANCESTORS Sometimes also called 'the land of the dead', this region is usually located as a separate enclave within the Underworld, although it is possible to find it in any of the three worlds.

RE-SOURCING Rediscovering the source of our universal belonging to the cosmic web after shock or distress.

SHAMAN From the Siberian Tungus language, the term is universally accepted to mean a person who is able to journey between this world and the others in order to find healing, information, knowledge or help. Many different lands have their own word for this function.

SHAMANISM The practice of reconnecting, healing or restoring the unity of the cosmic web by means of walking between the worlds.

SHAMANIZE To practise as a shaman, through sourcing, journeying, healing.

SOUL-FLIGHT The shamanic journey when the shaman's soul-part/s travel into the otherworlds.

SOUL-FRIEND A close friend with whom you can share your inner and mystical life, who can give counsel, advice or support; derived from the Irish *anam-chara*.

SOUL-LOSS and RETRIEVAL When soul-parts are accidentally ejected from the being through trauma, illness or assault, then soul-loss is said to have taken place; this requires the services of a shaman to

retrieve the soul-parts by taking a shamanic journey to find them and restore them to the client. (See next entry also.)

SOUL-PARTS Worldwide shamanic traditions recognize that the soul has many parts, some of which may be accidentally ejected through shock, necessitating soul-retrieval.

SOURCING The state of consciousness which a shaman enters when beginning to access the otherworlds, prior to and maintained during journeying.

SPIRIT The indwelling sacredness, pervading all things, animate and inanimate. Spirit is without form, yet can manifest in any form.

SPIRITS The many refractions of Spirit which animate all that is and give each thing or being its distinctive nature.

SPIRITUAL LINEAGE HELPERS Any teachers in subtle reality with whom we are in soul-resonance, providing help and teaching; a spiritual lineage teacher is not a spirit guide or guru who directs aspects of your life.

SUBTLE REALITY The unseen reality which exists and interpenetrates physical reality, appreciable by our subtle senses.

TEACHER A shamanic teacher can be a living person, an ancestor, an animal, tree, plant, stone or a combination of these. Certain situations and events are also teachers.

TRADITION Is always used here in its original sense of a core of wisdom and lore to which new information is continually being added, so that ancient lore is thus refreshed and made applicable to contemporary life.

TRADITIONAL SHAMANISM The practice of shamanism among indigenous peoples who maintain ancient traditions today, as opposed to core-shamanism.

WALKER BETWEEN THE WORLDS In the context of this book, one who can move skilfully between the worlds of physical and subtle reality and back again, with the ability to learn, co-operate and commune, but not necessarily a fully operative shaman; term coined by myself and John Matthews in *The Western Way* (1984) to denote one who travels shamanically between the worlds.

Bibliography

Many books listed below are academically technical. I have indicated the more accessible titles with an asterisk. All books were published in London, unless otherwise stated.

*Achterberg, Jeanne, *Woman as Healer*, Rider, 1990

Achterberg, Jeanne, 'The Wounded Healer' in *The Shaman's Path*, ed G. Doore, Boston, Shambhala, 1988

Ahlback, Tore and Bergman, Jan, eds *The Saami Shaman Drum*, Abö, Finland, the Donner Institute for Research in Religious and Cultural History, 1991

*Amado J., *The War of the Spirits*, New York, Bantam Books, 1993

*Arrien, Angeles, *The Four Fold Way*, San Francisco, Harper Collins, 1993

*Ashcroft-Nowicki, Dolores, *The New Book of the Dead*, Aquarian Press, 1992

Backman, Louise and Hultkrantz, Ake, *Studies in Lapp Shamanism*, Stockholm, Almqvist & Wikseil International, 1984

*Bausch, William J., *Storytelling: Imagination and Faith*, Mystic, Twenty-Three Publications, 1984

*Berry, Thomas, *The Dream of the Earth*, San Francisco, Sierra Club, 1988

*Brennan, Barbara Ann, *Hands of Light*, New York, Bantam, 1988

*Chatwin, Bruce, *The Songlines*, Jonathan Cape, 1987

*Chogyam, Ngakpa, *Journey into Vastness*, Shaftesbury, Element, 1988

Colorado, Dr Pamela in interview with Jane Carroll 'A Meeting Between Brothers, in *Beshara Magazine*, no 13, Summer 1991

Danielou, Alain, *The Gods of India: Hindu Polytheism*, New York, Inner Traditions, 1985

*—*Shiva and Dionysus*, New York, Inner Traditions Inc, 1984

*De Chardin, Teilhard, *Hymn to the Universe*, Collins, 1975

*Deren, Maya, *The Voodoo Gods*, St Albans, Paladin, 1975

*Ereira, Alan, *The Heart of the World*, Jonathan Cape, 1990

*Estes, Clarissa Pinkola, *Women Who Run With the Wolves*, New York, Ballantine Books, 1992

*Fortune, Dion, *The Sea Priestess*, Aquarian Press, 1972

*Fix, Wm R., *Star Maps*, Octopus Books, 1979

Funk and Wagnall's Folklore, Mythology and Legend, ed M. Leach, New English Library 1972

Gallagher, Winifred, *The Power of Place*, New York, Poseidon Press, 1993

*Gardner, Joy, *Color and Crystals*, Freedom CA, The Crossing Press, 1988

*Ginzberg, Carlo, *Ecstasies: Deciphering the Witches' Sabbath*, Hutchinson Radius, 1990

*Goodman, Felicitas, *Where the Spirits Ride the Wind*, Bloomington, Indiana University Press, 1990

*Gould, Stephen Jay, ed *The Book of Life*, Ebury, 1993

*Guss, David M., *The Language of the Birds*, San Francisco, North Point Press, 1985

*Hardy, Thomas, *The Mayor of Casterbridge*, Macmillan, 1974 (first pub 1886)

Harner, Michael, *Twenty Thousand Years of Experimentation with Mid-Body Healing: the Discoveries of the Shamans*, (taped talk) Foundation for Shamanic Studies, 1992

*—*The Way of the Shaman*, New York, Harper & Row, 1980

*Heize, Ruth-Inge, *Shamans of the 20th Century*, New York, Irvington Publishers Inc, 1991

*Holdstock, Robert, *Lavondyss*, Gollancz, 1988

Hoppal, Mihály and Pentikainen, Juha, eds *Uralic Mythology and Folklore*, Budapest, Ethnographic Institute of the Hungarian Academy of Sciences, 1989

Hoppal, Mihály and Von Sadovszky, Otto, eds *Shamanism, Past and Present*, (2 vols), Fullerton, Istor Books, 1989

*Hultkrantz, Ake, *Shamanic Healing and Ritual Drama: Health and Medicine in Native North American Religious Traditions*, New York, Crossroad, 1992

*Hutton, Ronald, *The Shamans of Siberia*, Glastonbury, Isle of Avalon Press, 1993

Huxley, Aldous, *Heaven and Hell*, Flamingo, 1994 (first pub 1956)

*Ingerman, Sandra, *Soul Retrieval: Mending the Fragmented Self*, San Francisco, HarperCollins, 1991

*Jonas, Gerald, *Dancing: The Power of Dance Around the World*, BBC Books, 1993

*Kalweit, Holger, *Shamans, Healers and Medicine Men*, Boston, Shambhala, 1992

Kaplan, Aryeh, *Meditation and the Bible*, New York, Samuel Weiser, 1978

*Kelly, Karen, *I See With Different Eyes*, privately printed, Cambridge, 1993

*Launert, Edmund, *Edible and Medicinal Plants of Britain and Northern Europe*, Country Life Books, 1981

Levett, Carl, *Crossings: A Transpersonal Approach*, Ridgefield, 1974

Lindsay, Jack, *The Origins of Alchemy in Graeco-Roman Egypt*, Frederick Muller, 1970

*Lonsdale, Steven, *Animals and the Origins of Dance*, Thames & Hudson, 1981

*Lovelock, James, *The Ages of Gaia: A Biography of Our Living Earth*, Oxford, Oxford University Press, 1988

McAll, Dr Kenneth, *Healing the Family Tree*, Sheldon Press, 1984

*Macy, Joanna, *World as Lover, World as Self*, Rider, 1993

MacDonald, George, *The Princess and the Goblin*, Penguin, 1964

*Matthews, Caitlín, *The Elements of Celtic Tradition*, Shaftesbury, Element, 1990

*— *The Elements of the Goddess*, Shaftesbury, Element, 1989

*— *Sophia, Goddess of Wisdom*, Mandala, 1991

— *Voices of the Goddess*, Aquarian, 1990

*Matthews, Caitlín and John, *An Encyclopaedia of Celtic Wisdom: A Celtic Shaman's Sourcebook*, Shaftesbury, Element, 1994

*— *The Western Way*, Arkana, 1994 (first pub 1985–6)

*Matthews, John, *The Celtic Shaman*, Shaftesbury, Element, 1992

*— *Taliesin and the Bardic and Shamanic Mysteries of Britain and Ireland*, Aquarian, 1991

*Mayne, William, *Earthfasts*, Hamish Hamilton, 1966

*Meier, C. A., *Healing Dream and Ritual: Ancient Incubation, Modern Psychotherapy*, Einsiedeln, Switzerland, Daimon Verlag, 1989

Merkur, Daniel, *Powers Which We Do Not Know: The Gods and Spirits of the Inuit*, Moscow, Idaho, University of Idaho Press, 1991

*Nachman, Rabbi, *Outpouring of the Soul*, Jerusalem, Breslov Research Institute, nd

*Naess, Arne, *Ecology, Community and Lifestyle*, Cambridge, Cambridge University Press, 1989

*Newham, Paul, *The Singing Cure: An Introduction to Voice Movement Therapy*, Rider, 1993

Oida, Yoshi, 'Means of Expression' article in *Beshara Magazine*, no 13, Summer 1991

*Palmer, Martin, *Genesis or Nemesis: Belief, Meaning and Ecology*, Dryad Press Ltd, 1988

*Powys, John Cowper, *A Philosophy of Solitude*, Village Press, 1974

Rasmussen, Knud, *The Intellectual Culture of the Iglulik Eskimos*, Copenhagen, Glydendalske Boghandel, 1929

*Rinpoche, Sogyal, *The Tibetan Book of Living and Dying*, Rider, 1992
*Ripinsky-Naxon, Michael, *The Nature of Shamanism*, Albany, State University of New York Press, 1993
*Rodenburg, Patsy, *The Right to Speak: Working with the Voice*, Methuen, 1992
Seed, John, editorial of *Creation Spirituality Magazine*, vol IX, 2, March 1993
*Seed, John, Macy, Joanna et al *Thinking Like a Mountain: Towards a Council of All Beings*, New Society Publishers 1988
Sheldrake, Rupert, *The Presence of the Past*, Collins, 1988
Siikala, Anna-Leena, *The Rite Technique of the Siberian Shaman*, Helsinki, Academia Scientiarum Fennica, 1987
*Silko, Leslie Marmion, *Ceremony*, New York, Penguin, 1977
Skafte, R., 'Following the Woman-Faced Deer', in *Shaman's Drum*, Summer 1988
*Stewart, R. J., *Earth Light*, Shaftesbury, Element, 1992
*— *Power within the Land*, Shaftesbury, Element, 1992
*Suzuki, David and Knutdtson, Peter, *Wisdom of the Elders: Honouring Sacred Native Visions of Nature*, New York, Bantam Books, 1992
*Thompson, Flora, *Lark Rise to Candleford*, Harmondsworth, Penguin, 1984 (first pub 1945)
*Tompkins, Peter and Bird, Christopher, *The Secret Life of Plants*, Arkana, 1991
*— *Secrets of the Soil*, Arkana, 1992
Traherne T., *Poetical Works*, P. J. and A. E. Dobell, 1932
The Upanishads trans Juan Mascaró, Harmondsworth, Penguin, 1965
Varro *De Lingua Latina* trans Roland G. Kent, W. Heinemann Ltd, 1978
*Villoldo, A. and Krippner, S., *Healing States* New York, Simon & Schuster, 1986
*Wombwell, Felicity, *The Goddess Changes*, Mandala, 1991
*Ywahoo, Dhyani, *Voices of Our Ancestors*, Boston, Shambhala, 1987

DIVINATORY METHODS AND CARD SYSTEMS

Carr-Gomm, Philip and Stephanie, *The Druid Animal Oracle*, (illus. Bill Worthington) Simon & Schuster 1994
Gray, Miranda, *The Sacred Beasts of Albion*, Aquarian Press, 1994
Matthews, Caitlín, *The Celtic Book of the Dead*, (illus Danuta Meyer) New York, St Martin's Press, 1992
Matthews, Caitlín and John, *The Arthurian Tarot*, (illus Miranda Gray) Aquarian Press, 1990

Matthews, John, *The Celtic Shaman's Pack*, (illus Chesca Potter) Shaftes-
   bury, Element, 1995
Murray, Liz, *The Celtic Tree Oracle*, Rider, 1988
Pollack, Rachel, *Shining Woman Tarot*, Aquarian Press, 1992
Sams, Jamie and Carson, David, *Medicine Cards*, Santa Fé, Bear & Co,
   1988
Stewart, R. J.,   *The Dreampower Tarot*, (illus Stuart Littlejohn),
   Aquarian Press, 1993
Stewart, R. J., *The Merlin Tarot*, (illus Miranda Gray) Aquarian Press,
   1989

Resources

SOURCING TAPES

The following tapes are available from Graal Publications, BCM Hallowquest, London WC1N 3XX: please send stamped addressed envelope or two international reply coupons to enquire for details, prices and full tape list.

Just Drumming Four 20-minute journeys with deer-skin drum sound for sourcing and general use

Soul Flights Two 20-minute journeys of goat-skin bodhran for underworld journeying; two 20-minute journeys of metal gong for upperworld journeying

The following tapes are available from the Foundation for Shamanic Studies, PO Box 1939, Mill Valley, CA 94942, USA (tel 415 380 8282; fax 8416). Each tape has sound-sources for two 15-minute sessions on one side and 30 minutes on the reverse, except for *The Singing Journey*.

Musical Bow for the Shamanic Journey with Jonathan Horwitz and Annette Høst

Shamanic Journey: Multiple Drumming with Bridgewalker Drummers

Shamanic Journey: Solo and Double Drumming with Michael Harner

The Singing Journey for Shamanic Voyaging with women's chorus

Tibetan Bowl Sound for the Shamanic Journey with Sandra Ingerman

SHAMANIC STUDIES

No book is a substitute for learning from a good shamanic teacher, nor can it give you the wider experience of sharing knowledge with

a training group. Readers are strongly recommended to find and study with a reputable teacher or organization. When writing to the groups or individuals below, please enclose a stamped addressed envelope, if writing to the same country, or an envelope and two international reply coupons if writing overseas.

Walkers Between the Worlds, BCM Hallowquest, London WC1N 3XX, Britain. Caitlín and John Matthews teach foundation and advanced courses on Celtic Shamanism. Caitlín has a shamanic counselling practice in Oxford and occasionally has vacancies for new clients: this is an active not passive method of shamanizing whereby *the client* is taught to journey and solve problems. Please enclose a large stamped addressed envelope (within Britain) or a large addressed envelope with two international reply coupons (outside Britain). Letters without return postage will not receive response.

Scandinavian Centre for Shamanic Studies, Artillerivej 63/140, DK-2300, Copenhagen, Denmark. Jonathan Horwitz teaches non-cultural, core-shamanism all over Europe. Annette Høst teaches Scandinavian shamanic methods as well as shamanic applications to women's lives. For details of their courses in Britain, write to Shamanic Workshops in Britain, Eve Cunningham, 61 Eldon Rd, Wood Green, London N22 5ED.

Foundation for Shamanic Studies, PO Box 1939, Mill Valley, CA 94942, USA (tel 415 380 8282; fax 8416). This worldwide organization currently has centres in USA, Europe, Australia and New Zealand. Membership ($30 at time of writing) brings a semi-annual magazine and calendar listings of FSS courses. FSS faculty teaches basic and advanced courses in core- (non-cultural) shamanism. Completion of a basic course is obligatory before attempting advanced work. The teaching quality is generally high, as are the course fees. A register of shamanic counsellors who offer healing and soul-retrieval in USA is available from them.

HELPFUL ORGANIZATIONS

Pagan Hospice and Funeral Trust, BM Box 3337, London WC1N 3XX. This organization was founded by pagans to help inform pagans and non-Christians how to cope with death and bereavement, to facilitate funeral services, and to provide information for nursing staff, carers and patients in hospital. It also produces a newsletter, *Thanaton*. Current subscription and membership £10.

Shamanic Counselling and Soul-Retrieval. For details of shamanic counsellors trained in soul-retrieval and other methods in Britain, contact Shamanic Workshops in Britain, Eve Cunningham, 61 Eldon Rd, Wood Green, London N22 5ED. In Europe, contact Jonathan Horwitz, Artillerivej 63/140, DK–2300, Copenhagen, Denmark.

A register of shamanic counsellors who offer healing and soul-retrieval in USA and throughout the world is available from Foundation for Shamanic Studies, PO Box 1939, Mill Valley, CA 94942, USA (tel 415 380 8282; fax 8416).

MAGAZINES

Hallowquest Newsletter, BCM Hallowquest, London WC1N 3XX. This quarterly newsletter brings information on forthcoming events, courses, books by Caitlín and John Matthews. Current subscription at time of writing: £6 (in Britain and Europe), $20 (USA), or £12 (elsewhere).

Sacred Hoop, 25 Cowl St, Evesham, Worcs, Britain. This British-based journal appears 4 times a year. It is dedicated to the full spectrum of shamanism, but mainly concentrates on indigenous American Indian derived groups and teachers. Current subscription at time of writing: £10 (in Britain), £15 (in Europe), £20 (overseas).

Shaman's Drum, PO Box 430, Willits, CA 95490, USA. This quarterly glossy magazine is devoted to cross-cultural shamanism. It carries interesting, usually academic, articles on contemporary and traditional shamanism; it is highly illustrated and carries many advertisements for shamanic goods. Current subscription at time of writing: $15 (in USA), $19 (elsewhere).

Index

Major references and practical examples are in italic.

Other Books in the *Earth Quest* Series

ANIMALS OF THE SOUL
Sacred Animals of the Oglala Sioux
Joseph E. Brown

BEAUTIFUL PAINTED ARROW
Stories and Teachings from the Native American Tradition
Joseph E. Rael

THE CELTIC SHAMAN
A Handbook
John Matthews

THE DRUID WAY
Philip Carr-Gomm

EARTH LIGHT
The Ancient Path to Transformation
Rediscovering the Wisdom of Celtic and Faery Lore
R.J. Stewart

EARTH MEDICINE
A Shamanic Way to Self Discovery
Kenneth Meadows

LETTERS FROM A WILD STATE
An Aboriginal Perspective
James G. Cowan

THE MEDICINE WAY
A Shamanic Path to Self Mastery
Kenneth Meadows

POWER WITHIN THE LAND
The Roots of Celtic and Underworld Traditions
R.J. Stewart

SHAMANIC EXPERIENCE
A Practical Guide to Contemporary Shamanism
Kenneth Meadows

TRACKS OF DANCING LIGHT
A Native American Approach to Understanding Your Name
Joseph E. Rael and Lindsay Sutton

WHERE EAGLES FLY
A Shamanic Way to Inner Wisdom
Kenneth Meadows

E A R T H ◆ Q U E S T

The aim of the *Earth Quest* series is to examine and explain how shamanic principles can be applied in the journey towards self-discovery – and beyond.

Each person's Earth quest is the search for meaning and purpose in their life – it is the establishment of identity and the realization of inner potentials and individual responsibility.

Each book in the series examines aspects of a life science that is in harmony with the Earth and shows how each person can attune themselves to nature. Each book imparts knowledge of the Craft of Life.